PRESSED
against
DIVINITY

PRESSED

against

DIVINITY

W. B. Yeats's Feminine Masks

JANIS TEDESCO HASWELL

Northern
Illinois
University
Press
DeKalb 1997

Material quoted from *Mythologies,* by W. B. Yeats, is reprinted with the permission
of Simon & Schuster. Copyright ©1959 by Mrs. W. B. Yeats.
Material quoted from *The Variorum Edition of the Plays of W. B. Yeats,*
edited by Russell K. Alspach, is reprinted with the permission of A.P. Watt Ltd
on behalf of Michael Yeats and Simon & Schuster. Copyright ©1966 by
Russell K. Alspach and Bertha Georgie Yeats.
Material quoted from *The Variorum Edition of the Poems of W. B. Yeats,* edited
by Peter Allt and Russell K. Alspach, is reprinted with the permission of A.P. Watt Ltd
on behalf of Michael Yeats and Simon & Schuster. Copyright ©1924, 1928, 1933 by
Macmillan Publishing Company, renewed 1952, 1956, 1961 by Bertha Georgie Yeats.
Material quoted from *A Vision,* by W. B. Yeats, is reprinted with the permis-
sion of A.P. Watt Ltd on behalf of Michael Yeats and Simon & Schuster. Copyright
©1965 by Bertha Georgie Yeats and Anne Butler Yeats.
Material quoted from *Yeats's "Vision" Papers,* vols. 1, 2, and 3, edited by
George Mills Harper, is reprinted with the permission of University of Iowa Press and
Macmillan Press Ltd. Copyright ©1992 by University of Iowa Press.

Library of Congress Cataloging-in-Publication Data
Haswell, Janis Tedesco.
Pressed against divinity: W. B. Yeats's feminine masks /
Janis Tedesco Haswell.
p.   cm.
Includes bibliographical references and index.
ISBN 0-87580-222-2 (alk. paper)
1. Yeats, W. B. (William Butler), 1865–1939—Characters—Women.
2. Femininity (Psychology) in literature. 3. Men authors,
Irish—Pyschology. 4. Ireland—In literature. 5. Persona (Literature)
6. Women in literature. I. Title.
PR5908.W6H37   1997
821'.8—dc20   96-43942
CIP

For Rich,
who in his "daimonic" way reaches the best in me.

CONTENTS

LIST OF ABBREVIATIONS

Works by William Butler Yeats:

AS I   *Yeats's VISION Papers Vol. I. The Automatic Script: 5 November 1917–19 June 1918.* Ed. Steve L. Adams, Barbara J. Frieling, and Sandra L. Sprayberry. Iowa City: U of Iowa P, 1992.

AS II   *Yeats's VISION Papers Vol. II. The Automatic Script: 5 June 1918–20 March 1920.* Ed. Steve L. Adams, Barbara J. Frieling, and Sandra L. Sprayberry. Iowa City: U of Iowa P, 1992.

AS III   *Yeats's VISION Papers Vol. III. Sleep and Dream Notebooks: VISION Notebooks 1 and 2, Card File.* Ed. Robert Anthony Martinich and Margaret Mills Harper. Iowa City: U of Iowa P, 1992.

AU   *Autobiography.* New York: Macmillan, 1965.

Collected VI   *The Collected Works in Verse and Prose of W. B. Yeats.* Vol. 6. Stratford-on-Avon: Shakespeare Head, 1908.

Collected VII   *The Collected Works in Verse and Prose of W. B. Yeats.* Vol. 7. Stratford-on-Avon: Shakespeare Head, 1908.

Collected VIII   *The Collected Works in Verse and Prose of W. B. Yeats.* Vol. 8. Stratford-on-Avon: Shakespeare Head, 1908.

E & I   *Essays and Introductions.* New York: Macmillan, 1961.

Letters   *The Letters of W. B. Yeats.* Ed. Allan Wade. London: Hart-Davis, 1954.

Letters I   *The Collected Letters of W. B. Yeats.* Vol. 1, 1865–1895. Ed. John Kelly. Oxford: Clarendon, 1986.

LDW   *Letters on Poetry from W. B. Yeats to Dorothy Wellesley.* London: Oxford UP, 1964.

Memoirs   *Memoirs.* Ed. Denis Donaghue. New York: Macmillan, 1972.

Myth   *Mythologies.* New York: Macmillan, 1959.

VA   *A Critical Edition of Yeats's A VISION.* Ed. George Mills Harper and W. K. Hood. London: Macmillan, 1978. I refer to this work as either *Vision A* or as the 1925 edition, since it was completed in 1925 and issued on 15 January 1926. It was a limited edition of 600 copies.

VB   *A Vision: A Reissue with the Author's Final Revisions.* New York: Macmillan, 1966. I refer to this work as either *Vision B* or as the 1937 edition; the bulk was drafted in 1934 and issued on 7 October 1937.

VP   *The Variorum Edition of the Poems of W. B. Yeats.*
Ed. Peter Allt and Russell K. Alspach. New York:
Macmilllan, 1968.

VPL   *The Variorum Edition of the Plays of W. B. Yeats.* Ed.
Russell K. Alspach. London: Macmillan, 1966.

PRESSED

against

DIVINITY

INTRODUCTION

In November 1936, William Butler Yeats wrote to his friend and fellow poet, Dorothy Wellesley,

> My dear, my dear—when you crossed the room with that boyish movement, it was no man who looked at you, it was the woman in me. It seems that I can make a woman express herself as never before. I have looked out of her eyes. I have shared her desire. (*LDW* 108)

A disarming claim, until we realize that Yeats meant it literally. He seriously believed that "the woman in me" was a real rather than figurative or imagined part of himself. Nor can we be less serious about his claim that the woman in him—he called her his daimon—has spoken through his poetry with new success. He had recently finished two major sequences of poems—"A Woman Young and Old" in the late 1920s and "Crazy Jane" in the early 1930s—in which the female voice achieves startling breadth and complexity. These are not the typical dramatic lyrics we associate so readily with the earlier Yeats: male voices celebrating beauty or despairing of love, heroic voices charting Ireland's mythic past, philosophic voices exploring the spiritual realm in search of ultimate wisdom. Compared to these types of lyrics, his feminine voices in "A Woman Young and Old" and "Crazy Jane" may seem an uncharacteristic lapse in his poetry. Yet I argue, with

Yeats, that the poems emerge from natural changes in his philosophy and appear anomalous only when we remain ignorant of the history of his beliefs about his gendered self.

Let me state outright the most heretical points of my argument. The sequences enact most fully a gendered theory of the mask that Yeats reconfigured in his marathon experiment in automatic writing with his wife, Georgie Hyde-Lees, in the early years of their marriage (1917–1921). Because the transcripts of these writings, collectively titled the Automatic Script, have been made public only recently, scholars have not understood the development and connection of Yeats's notions about self, sex, spirituality, and poetry. Consequently, they have relied on the second edition of *A Vision* (1937) as their window into his worldview, a work that Yeats systematically degendered from its two antecedents, the 1925 edition of *A Vision* and the Automatic Script material.

The legacy of the Automatic Script is his "mature" verse—verse, I argue, superior to and more compelling than earlier lyrics because of a dimension scholars have disregarded: the female voice as synonymous with the voice of Yeats's daimon. The verse generated after 1917 is not a triumphant achievement of a male poet who represses his own voice to assume the alien voice of a female persona. Instead, his mature verse is "double-voiced" in a way unique to Yeats, "double-voiced" because it enacts a male poet and female daimon vying for momentary dominance within a given text.[1]

Between 1917 and 1919 (the most innovative years of the automatic writing experiment), Yeats's theory of the mask developed from the concept of poet and anti-self locked in conflict (as described in *Per Amica Silentia Lunae*) to its completed stage. The consequences of this development are nothing short of profound, as I hope to show. In the Automatic Script, the mask becomes more than the meeting ground of the daily self and the ideal self, even more than the opposition between man and anti-self or daimon. Now the mask signifies two actions. First, it marks the "knitting together" (Yeats's own terms) of poet and daimon, and second, it signifies the convergence of *male* poet and *female* daimon who is "part of me" (*AS II* 211).

This second action is pivotal, and I will refer to it as Yeats's "gendered daimonology." Before this point, Yeats had alluded to his daimon as a genderless spirit or a masculinized (or perhaps universalized) "he." In naming his daimon "female," Yeats clearly designates the daimon not only as a gendered entity but also as a sexually active being. This "gendering" of the daimon elevates the mask from an aesthetic construct to an explicitly gendered psychodrama. That is, the mask itself becomes gendered. From this point on, each mask for Yeats is an enactment of passionate attraction and antipathy between himself and his female daimon. This action involves a variety of voices expressing his multigendered self. Any discussion of Yeats's poetry written after 1917 must therefore address gender as a pivotal component precisely because his theory of the mask converges with his vision of gender in a new daimonology.

This is more easily said than done. Emphasis on gender places readers within Yeats's idiosyncratic conception of what he calls the "universal masculine & feminine in soul" (*AS I* 109). In truth, Yeats's vision of gender is radical on many levels. First, masculine and feminine are not limited by biology; male daimons inhabit women, female daimons inhabit men; women are not wholly female, men not wholly male. Second, since Yeats's vision of gender is interwoven with his occult interests, readers encounter a type of mystical sex—what I will refer to as Yeats's sexual dynamic—wherein sexual love and mystical reality converge. And finally, Yeats depicts the feminine in progressively complex and contradictory forms. There is Sheba—seductive, regal, and docile queen—but there is also Crazy Jane, outspoken and irascible. Yeats's feminine masks are stunning in their range: for every traditional voice, there is a rebellious one; for every handmaiden, there is an iconoclast. No individual mask marks a fixed manifestation of gender, nor does Yeats repackage static attributes of the feminine from a previous work.

The critical ramifications are formidable: this radical view of gender inspired in Yeats a radical aesthetic—informed by his gendered daimonology and enacted in his double-voiced verse, as I will attempt to show. But this view of gender also demands an innovative reading strategy, a balance of method that neither circumscribes gender nor falsifies Yeats's enactment of it. Such a strategy should allow readers to interpret Yeats's masks in light of the poet's own rationale for what and how he writes. If my first argument is that Yeats's double-voiced verse is a direct result of his gendered daimonology, my second is that any reading strategy that does not or cannot deal with Yeats's vision of gender is seriously limited.

And here the critical plot thickens again. Attempting to deal with Yeats's idiosyncratic vision of gender means butting heads with his occult philosophy. Because the Automatic Script provides new and explicit insight into Yeats's daimonology, the substance of this study revolves around W. B. and Georgie Yeats's intricate and densely packed exploration of temporal and supernatural existence. While this focus may seem too narrowly concentrated on a brief period in Yeats's career and on outlandish experiments in table rappings and conversations with "spooks" (Harold Bloom's term), it brings with it both an affirmation of and a corrective to contemporary critical lenses. By working toward an understanding of Yeats's use of gender—his creation of female personae and his articulation of gendered voices—readers will perforce be interpreting against the grain of existing readings that elide gender, mysticism, or both. But it is my faith that ultimately they will be better able to naturalize (in Jonathan Culler's sense) Yeats's eccentric fixation on automatic writing, daimons, and phases of reincarnation. That is, readers can "recuperate" the communicative value of Yeats's mystical beliefs by understanding his use of gender, with gender thereby functioning as a more familiar convention that brings his mature work "within our ken" (Culler 134). Without a doubt, Yeats's elaborate aesthetic is grounded in an equally distinctive and elaborate vision of gender. But other writers like William Wordsworth, Elizabeth Barrett Browning, and James Joyce (to name only a few) display equally complex enactments of gender. This exercise in reading Yeats's double-voiced verse has an application far beyond Yeats Studies alone.

Precisely how do existing interpretations deal with gender in Yeats's poetry? In general, gender has never been systematically studied.[2] Many approaches neutralize or neuter gender, i.e., they minimize or even efface the gender component of the mask. In this gender-neutral category, I would include studies by critics who automatically translate Yeats's male speakers as the voice of the poet himself, thereby overlooking the possibility that they are masculine masks, or who allow the subject of gender to surface only in terms of Yeats's personal relationships or his lifelong obsession with Maud Gonne. I would also include analyses that interpret the Yeats corpus as unequivocally his own production, thereby diminishing Georgie Yeats's crucial role in the formulation of the solar/lunar system and daimonology in the *Vision* material. The Automatic Script makes all such gender-neutral positions untenable. The question is not to what extent gender should become an element in the interpretation of Yeats's mature verse. Rather, the issue is how readers should deal with poetry in which, by Yeats's own definition, gender is always present on both mundane and spiritual levels.

Not that there aren't other theoretical approaches that offer a promising code by which readers may translate Yeats's eccentric daimonology. Jung's theory of the anima is an obvious choice. Here I will only gloss the primary affinities between Jung's theory of man and anima (what Jung called the "master-piece of psychology") and Yeats's theory of man and daimon (what Yeats saw as the "first portions of being").[3] Jung believed that the anima represented the collective unconscious (*Collected Works* 14:128); Yeats believed that the daimon rises out of the *Anima Mundi* (*Myth* 350). Both anima and daimon operate as contrasexuals. According to Jung, "no man is so entirely masculine that he has nothing feminine in him . . . the feminine belongs to man as his own unconscious femininity, which I have called the anima" (*CW* 7:297; 5:678). In females, this psychological phenomenon is called the animus. For Yeats, the daimon is of the "opposite sex to ego" and inhabits the "dark of the mind" (Yeats, *AS II* 235; *VA* 28). Both the anima and daimon bring conflict. For Jung, the anima "sums up everything that a man can never get the better of and never finishes coping with" (*CW* 9:i, 485). Yeats believed that the daimon "delivers and deceives us," hunting men with a net woven from the stars (*Myth* 336).

Of course the affinity between anima and daimon is rooted in a more fundamental parallel: the concept of androgyny. Jung is clear about man's androgynous nature:

> Either sex is inhabited by the opposite sex up to a point, for, biologically speaking, it is simply the great number of masculine genes that tips the scales in favour of masculinity . . . [every man] carries Eve, his wife, hidden in his body. (*CW* 9:i, 58; 18:429)

Yeats believed that female daimons inhabit men, male daimons inhabit women. But with Yeats's daimon, there is a mystical rather than a biological or genetic imperative at work. Ultimately, his notion of a contrasexual daimonology leads him to bemoan, even berate, the masculine principle in isolation, what he describes as the "embittered sun." His words echo Virginia Woolf's criticism of "unmitigated masculinity" in a single-sexed mind (106). Like Yeats, Woolf bases her theory not on biology but on the genders' "spiritually cooperating": "a woman also must have intercourse with the man in her" (102). Woolf saw such cooperation leading to freedom, peace, and fullness (108). In the same way, Yeats believed the union of masculine and feminine ("the rounded whole") to be the way to completion and freedom. He even uses sexual intercourse as a symbol of the highest good—what he called "Unity of Being" (*VB* 214).

As helpful as these affinities are, the parallels between daimon and anima and between daimon and androgyne cannot finally translate Yeats's system in full. There is a fundamental difference, for instance, in Jung's attitude toward the feminine. True, the anima functions as "the unknown woman" within each man. But Jung speaks of the anima as representing "the 'inferior,' i.e., the undifferentiated function" (*CW* 12:150). Jung himself indicates that the term "inferior" is not simply a synonym for "other" but a value comparison that poisons gender relations:

> Although man and woman unite, they nevertheless represent irreconcilable opposites which, when activated, degenerate into deadly hostility. This primordial pair of opposites symbolizes every conceivable pair of opposites that may occur: hot and cold, light and dark, north and south, dry and damp, good and bad, conscious and unconscious. (*Psychological Reflection* 94)

The consequences of such absolute polarization are grim. As Annis Pratt makes clear, because Jung associates man with logos and woman with eros, mind and body quickly become mortal enemies. In a world where mind is privileged over body, the term "inferior" relegates matter to a derivative of mind, or, in Pratt's words, women become "extensions or even creations of male imagination" (98). James Hillman also objects to the Apollonic edge to Jung's androgynous whole. With the female identified as dark and mysterious—"the abysmal side of bodily man"—feminine inferiority evolves into a metaparadigm in Jungian psychology (*Myth* 215, 217).

The "hostile polarity" that characterizes gender relations in Jung's system cannot approximate the ambiguous, complementary interaction that Yeats describes between masculine and feminine. While he associates the feminine with mystery and the body as does Jung, Yeats refuses to box the feminine into a static position or predictable state of being. Rather, gender is marked by fluid and perpetual action, with masculine and feminine finally defined not by fixed attributes but by their ever-changing and dynamic relationship to each other. Equally important, while Yeats envisions the daimon as antiself and arch foe to her male host, he does not label her as inferior, either by virtue of her sex or her nature. The daimon may be "part of me," but she is also an autonomous spirit, and thus the designation of daimon versus human host is ontological rather than psychological. As spirit, for instance, the daimon wields power over human beings, drawing men and women together in order to unite with another daimon and engineer the conception of a human child.

Similarly, the frame of androgyny is serviceable enough for Yeats's sense of the human person (he speaks of "the woman in me," after all). But again, there are difficulties, as can be seen with a brief review of history that reveals the concept of androgyny falling into disrepute in the last decade. For example, in 1973 Carolyn G. Heilbrun could argue that androgyny was an antidote to sexual polarization, allowing individuals more freedom to express human impulses (*Recognition* x). She saw the androgynous personality as "unlimited" because it does not reduce choices of behavior to stereotypical notions of masculine and feminine. But a decade later, Heilbrun admitted that the potential for freedom had not been realized. Instead, the concept had been used to justify acts of appropriation, with males assuming female aspects but leaving the female with all the "inconvenient female duties" ("Androgyny" 203–4).

Sandra Lipsitz Bem underwent a similar disillusion. In the 1970s, Bem defined androgynous individuals as "non-sex-typed," as people who reject or overcome cultural definitions of masculine and feminine ("Romantic Tradition" 266). She believed such individuals manifest masculine or feminine traits flexibly, adapting to changing circumstances and recognizing an inner capability to be both ("Cognitive" 362, 363). For Bem, androgyny was initially a measure of mental health ("Androgyny" 189). But later she would recant her advocacy of the androgynous individual, in part because androgyny implies an essentialized notion of gender, i.e., masculine and feminine are assumed to be substantive attributes and to have an existence apart from cognition ("Cognitive" 363). Bem also concedes that the disciples of androgyny have dealt with masculine and feminine as "personality structures embedded within the individual" and have been blind to the gender stereotypes that pervade cultural discourse (*Lenses* 125).

The change of heart experienced by Heilbrun and Bem makes clear that even in its heyday, the concept of androgyny described an unrealistic and simplistic mix of masculine and feminine traits. It does not define the nature of gender itself, either within a writer or a text. Androgyny may function as an ideal of flexibility and balance. But it provides little guidance in reading Yeats, who believed himself to be androgynous insofar as he was inhabited by a female daimon, not because he sought to transcend social stereotypes of male behavior. Yeats's expression of "the woman in me" is generated from a compelling need to articulate the complex reality of his own self. This imperative impelled him to create gendered masks (enactments of universal masculine and feminine), not personae of an androgynous nature.

Perhaps one of the most promising interpretive strategies is Elizabeth Butler Cullingford's "lens of a genre-based feminist historicism" (*Gender and History* 3). Cullingford negotiates a fine line between "a positive liberal historicist hermeneutic and a negative feminist one" (164), succeeding in analyzing Yeats's vision of gender in terms of his own cultural context (often defending him as a "liberal" in his own time) while employing keys of feminist critical theory to unlock many of the gender issues latent in Yeats's love poetry.

Certainly one of the strengths of her study is the attention it pays to Yeats's double-voiced verse.[4] There are several feminine masks that Cullingford finds convincing, prompting her to conclude that Yeats could dramatize a female's experience effectively. But she encounters inherent limitations in his efforts to do so. Using "Her Triumph" (from the sequence "A Woman Young and Old"), Cullingford drives home her point: "The limits of this poem lie not in Yeats's writing of the female body, but in his inability to imagine a love without tyrants and slaves, even if those tyrants and slaves frequently exchange positions" (223–24). Under the diction and gestures of a woman, Cullingford discerns the body and mind of a man with masculine drives toward relationships of power—without question a masterful poet and stunning actor, but caught in the act of "cross-gendered composition" (203).

Unfortunately, there is no precedent in feminist theory for Yeats's daimonology. Without the daimon as her interpretive benchmark, Cullingford's feminist reading strategy drifts into what she concedes is the most problematic restriction to her threefold "map" of genre-based feminist historicism: she ends up calibrating in each mask the percentage of "her Yeats" in the poet's artistic performance, trying to define how "the distance between poet and speaker, autobiography and creative fiction, differs from poem to poem" (9). This is difficult and finally misguided—a point I will return to in a moment. Cullingford's attempts reveal her underlying assumptions about male poets who use female voices: "A male poet cannot produce an 'authentic' female voice, but he can adopt a female subject position which contests and in this case [Yeats's poem "The People"] defeats his own prejudices" ("Venus or Mrs. Pankhurst" 21). There is a subtle form of essentialism at work here, an implicit assumption that while imaginative males need not tie gender and sex together absolutely (male poets may assume a female subject position), biological males cannot produce "authentic" feminine voices. Why men attempt to articulate that subject position is another issue, but Cullingford suspects that Yeats's efforts stem, at least in part, from his discomfort with his own sexual identity. "Yeats had considerable trouble becoming a man" (*Gender and History* 5).

What appears as an *a priori* argument, that men cannot speak in an "authentic" female voice, stems from Cullingford's attempt to read the mask as cross-gendered, with the fictional, feminine persona running counter to the real, male voice. Here my reading of the mask follows a different course, for I believe that any attempt to define the "real" Yeats (to uncover the "Man behind the Mask," to use Richard Ellmann's terms) is not only futile but also counterproductive in terms of what the mask attempts and achieves.

My own path of naturalization borrows—eccentrically, I admit—from Derek Owens's discussion of "voice" in the composition classroom.[5] Owens's primary argument is that there is no such thing as an authentic, personal voice, whether the writing be creative narratives or mundane nonfiction. Every act of oral or written communication is a mask: "only one fictive guise in an immense spread of other (also fictive) voices" (160). To support his argument, Owens turns to James Hillman, the maverick Jungian I have already cited, who lays the foundation for a more contemporary understanding of the mask in his discussion of the human personality in his *Re-visioning Psychology*. For me, the thinking of Owens and Hillman rejuvenates the well-worn, nearly trite notion of the mask in the modernist period as a psychological construct, a fiction or "persona."

The self, Hillman argues, is composed of multiple personae, none of which is more or less real than another. If the self is really a spiral of "splintered psyches" and not "a single, autonomous unifying entity," then it is futile for psychologists to translate lives and dreams out of the realm of fiction into the "real"—what actions or fantasies "really mean" or if they approximate the "real self" (Hillman, *Re-visioning* 26, 51; summarized in Owens 164). Rather, attempts to interpret and reinterpret human identity are never-ending. The purpose of communication is to tell, not to solve or resolve, these fictions via the active imagination (Hillman, *Re-visioning* 38).

Thus, the term "persona" does not point to an aesthetic artifact, fictive in nature, as distinct from the real, authentic, unvarying self. The persona straddles that pseudo-dichotomy, being both an imaginative construction and a real projection of the self in its multitudinous forms. While there may be a "favorite mask" of "comfortable familiarity," or a "momentarily fixed version" of the self, that persona is only one image in a myriad of images. It is masked by another persona, and on and on (33). Each time a woman puts pen to paper, each time a man speaks a word, they add yet another mirror to a series of mirrors. But what some might label as a poststructuralist abyss, Owens sees as an imaginative opportunity. To write "is to fashion not so much our identities but bridges that connect various facets of our experience within an incomprehensibly dense and unmapped personal landscape" (Owens 165).

If we apply Hillman's sense of persona and Owens's sense of writing to Yeats's theory of the mask, we indeed see a poet who is a "cartographer" of his own imaginative construction of himself. What makes Yeats appear so eccentric in his notion of the self is not, then, his exuberance in multiplying masks but his insistence on spiritualizing his theory of the mask, i.e., grounding his aesthetic upon the concept of the daimon. In Hillman's terms, Yeats is simply spiritualizing his multiple selves, thereby generating a mystical vision that frames one mask with yet another. If readers look into Yeats's series of "mirrors" to see past the occult and philosophical packaging, they find a vision of the self as an autonomous, unified, and adamant identity that at first seems to defy Hillman's notion of an imaginative fiction. But in fact Yeats's concept of the self as an "entire being" (*AS II* 147) enacts the very multiplicity that Hillman believes typifies human identity.[6]

Yeats describes the self as complicated, even protean in nature. It is composed of soul and body, strung between primary and antithetic elements, anchored by a time-bound ego (what Yeats also calls the "disintegrated identity"), and divided between a daily self (Hillman's "comfortable" fiction) and an anti-self (what Yeats earlier calls the opposite, ideal self or image, and later spiritualizes into the daimon). This "entire being" experiences a series of metamorphoses: in time (twenty-eight incarnations), in gender (alternating male or female form with every temporal return), in corporeal expression (from Husk to Celestial Body), and in moral purification (via six posttemporal stages). Underlying the mystical language is an interpretation of human identity as transcending any static or monolithic state. Yeats insists that a poet never projects a simple self—he "is never the bundle of accident and incoherence that sits down to breakfast"—for the poet "never speaks directly as to someone at the breakfast table" (*E & I* 509). Rather, the poet creates a fiction by which to speak, a mask, and thus becomes "reborn as an idea, something intended, complete" via the imagination (509).

Owens's rhetorical analysis and Hillman's psychological analysis provide readers with a means to naturalize Yeats's daimonology and a reading strategy to avoid the limitations of other approaches. If, as Hillman argues, the self is a cluster of fictional personae, and if, as Owens argues, a writer has no single, authentic voice, then measuring the poet's masks against the "real"

Yeats is only calculating the fit between a particular expression or fiction and a pre-selected set of social conventions and expectations about what that self should sound like. In the case of Yeats's *gendered* voices, readers who accept or reject a particular mask, insofar as it conforms to the authentic voice of the poet, are setting that verse against prefabricated notions about what the "real" masculine and "real" feminine should be, thereby imposing upon the mask either standards of rhetoric or sex-typed codes of behavior.

This book, then, will pursue a reading strategy along the lines of Owens and Hillman. It will try to be faithful to Yeats's use of the mask, which does not express the authentic self but captures part of the poet at a particular moment, even the antithesis of what the daily version of the poet might be. It will assume that Yeats's poetry after 1917 adheres to his notion of the mask as an expression of universal masculine and universal feminine, both part of the poet but neither—once masked—equivalent to the daily self. This notion applies to his male voices as well as to his female ones. Understanding the mask in this way challenges previous scholarship that earmarked Yeats as fundamentally a Romantic poet—a poet out of step with his own time who defended the notion of an inviolable, seamless self. The mask is a complex action because Yeats conceived of himself as a complex being. Yeats's self and his masks are belied by scholarship that reads the masks of Owen Aherne and Michael Robartes (for instance) as the two sides of Yeats's "bifurcated" or "double-decked self," as Ellmann does (*Masks* 76), or interprets Sheba and Crazy Jane merely as fictions (or aberrations) of a male psyche.

In terms of theory, then, I propose to explore the mask as primarily a textual manifestation of human/daimon intercourse, a dialogic fabric woven from Yeats's theosophical and artistic life. In terms of praxis, I propose using Yeats's theory of the mask as a reading strategy to interpret the gendered voices enacted in his verse. Chapter 1 defines the theoretical stakes of the study based on the gendering of Yeats's mask theory. Working from his autobiographical and theosophical essays and the Automatic Script, I define how the gendered mask immediately impacts Yeats's view of oppositional relationships and the human person. The so-called "iron law of contraries" develops from a purely oppositional dynamic to a complementary one. Yeats continues to speak of conflict between himself and his daimon, but he also stresses completion and freedom through union with the daimon. He further defines how gender contraries interact in his exploration of the "Four Faculties," which are shared reciprocally by daimon and human host so that the self, "no matter how habitual, is a constantly renewed choice" (*VA* 18).

Chapter 2 works with the Automatic Script and the first and second editions of *A Vision* as distinct historical stages in Yeats's reading of gender, chronologically evolving from highly personal and sexual to less gendered and more philosophical. This third, degendered phase—the 1937 edition of *A Vision*—is the most familiar to scholars, and consequently they have failed to trace Yeats's mature verse to his vision of the daimon as a sexual being. The third chapter studies the initial impact of the sexual dynamic in *The Only Jealousy of Emer* (1919). The influence of the Automatic Script is clearly evident in Yeats's use of the twenty-eight Phases of human personalities to depict the hero Cuchulain in a new type of gender configuration: complementary and reciprocal relationships with an ensemble of female characters. Yeats's developing daimonology progresses to a psychoanalytic enactment of wholeness founded on the principle of masculine/feminine balance.

In Chapter 4, I trace how Yeats's new daimonology translates into verse. The lyric dialogues "Solomon to Sheba" (1918), "Solomon and the Witch" (1919), and "Michael Robartes and the Dancer" (1918) serve as prototypes of the feminine mask. They document how early on, Yeats's gendered daimonology brought together three critical tenets: his veneration of the feminine as a privileged avenue to the sacred, his association of the act of loving with the act of masking, and his vision of daimonic and human interaction. While these poems of 1918–1919 use sexual relations as a metaphor for converging complements (male and female, physical and intellectual, temporal and spiritual), their deeper purpose is to depict the act of masking itself, an aesthetic innovation that proves both radical and problematic.

Chapter 5 addresses Yeats's greater success in enacting the universal masculine and feminine in coherent, autonomous, and complex voices. In the sequences "A Man Young and Old" and "A Woman Young and Old" (1926–1929), Yeats dramatizes what in the Script he calls Initiatory and Critical Moments, wherein the sexes interact and lives profoundly change. Rather than reading the sequences in counterpoint, I interpret them as a single story—the universal saga of sexual relations—told from two perspectives that together reveal how the daimon uses sex for mystical ends.

In Chapter 6, I read the Crazy Jane sequence as the full emergence of the daimonic voice. Jane speaks from a daimonic world, a feminine world, the masculine world in reverse. She embroils herself in constant conflict and affirms the power of the feminine and the vital importance of intimacy. I will argue that the mask of Jane is the pinnacle of Yeats's aesthetic achievement— the complete enactment of contraries in action and the full expression of his mystical/sexual aesthetic. In the final chapter, I test Yeats's vision of complementarity against recent interpretations of one of his most controversial poems, "Leda and the Swan" (1923). I will offer a new reading of the poem to counter claims that Yeats justifies violence against women for the sake of historical change.

Perhaps more than any other poet of our century, Yeats deliberately and self-consciously works within a sense of the fictional self, generating multiple masks that create for readers a flexible network of selves. In his gendered masks, Yeats imagines and reimagines himself, true, but he also reimagines what masculine and feminine look like at this moment, in this relationship, in this encounter. What some scholars call an "eccentric" and "fictive" treatment of the self, or an "essentialist" and "idiosyncratic" view of gender, I see as representative of our century.

Thus, the implications of this study extend beyond Yeatsian scholarship. While his vision of gender and his aesthetic theory are unique to Yeats, and while his gendered mask appears more complex and self-conscious than works of most other writers, the act of masking and the exercise of gender are hardly his exclusive domain. There are complex motivations behind Yeats's feminine mask, but his are no more complex than those of other authors—Virginia Woolf, D. H. Lawrence, or Toni Morrison. Understood in this light, Yeats is not so outlandish in his attack on monologic, essentialized, and gender-exclusive expressions of the self. What is distinctive is that he not only expresses his multiple selves but also develops a theory to explain his attempts to do so. This analytic, as found in the Automatic Script and *Vision* material, may seem inaccessible or irrelevant to contemporary criticism. But I believe it serves as a pioneer model for writers to find their multiple voices and to express what Yeats, for one, believed to be a dynamic and fluid mystery: gender as it is found within the self, and gender as it is enacted in the mask.

CHAPTER I

GENDER, THE MASK, AND COMPLEMENTARITY

"Yeats was true to his deepest poetic principles, and
the Irish element in his vision is rarely an imaginative impediment, as the occult element often is."
Harold Bloom, *Yeats* (65)

"The mystical life is the centre of all that I do & all
that I think & all that I write."
W. B. Yeats, *Letters I* (303)

In 1917, at the age of fifty-two, W. B. Yeats published his most complete
occult treatise to date, the essay *Per Amica Silentia Lunae*. At the core of
Per Amica Silentia Lunae is a new, even revolutionary understanding of a
spirit Yeats called the daimon, an integral partner—equal to the poet himself—in generating the aesthetic device we call the mask. Had he not married a few months later, Yeats perhaps never would have written what is now
regarded as his greatest metaphysical work, *A Vision* (1925). The daimon
assumes center stage in *A Vision* as well, but the difference is that in the earlier essay, Yeats's daimon is defined as arch foe and spirit, in *A Vision,* as
arch foe, spirit, and female.[1] This reconfiguration of the daimon into a gendered and sexual being not only enlarges Yeats's understanding of temporal and spiritual reality but also radically transforms his interpretation of the

aesthetic process. Without the occult discoveries that inspire *A Vision*, Yeats's "mature" verse never would have been written.

Until the publication of the Automatic Script, scholars have not been privy to the context of that transitional moment wherein the daimon becomes gendered. The Script documents the private occult experiment by Yeats and his wife, Georgie Hyde-Lees, initiated only days after their marriage in October 1917 and continuing into 1921. Buried within literally thousands of questions and answers between husband and wife, ranging in subject from the afterlife to their personal sexual history, is a consistent and determined attempt to define and understand the daimon in gendered terms. In the next chapter, I will identify key passages in the Script and offer explanations for their emergence. The present discussion will concentrate on those critical, bookend points in 1917 and 1925 to explore the significance and ramifications of the gendering of the daimon in Yeats's definitive theory of the mask.

The most complete discussion of pre-Script daimonology is found in *Per Amica Silentia Lunae (PASL)* drafted in the early half of 1917, only months before his marriage to Georgie Hyde-Lees and the initiation of the Automatic Script. While most critics speak of *PASL* as one of his pre-*Vision* occult treatises, the essay is more accurately the fullest discussion of aesthetics Yeats had published to date. His thoughts are introduced by the poem "Ego Dominus Tuus," in which he debates the source of genius in Dante and Keats. This debate continues on in prose, and here Yeats offers his most detailed description of how a poet generates verse: a poetic image materializes from the collective memory (the *Anima Mundi*) via the subconscious. The rhythm and pattern of the verse emerges from the conflict between the poet and the second self, also designated as the anti-self. In an explicit denial of his earlier style, Yeats asserts that as a poet, he neither expresses his emotions nor speaks out of personal experience: "those elaborate, brightly lighted buildings and sceneries appearing in a moment . . . must come from above me and beyond me" (*Myth* 326).[2] This process is true for all great poets: they do not write out of the "lineaments" of their own lives; rather, they write to combat their destiny in a "blind struggle in the network of the stars" (328).[3] As examples, Yeats cites William Morris, "a happy, busy, most irascible man," who creates verse of "dim colour and pensive emotion"; Walter Savage Landor, who from the "daily violence of his passion" writes with calm nobility; and John Keats, a man imprisoned by poverty, ignorance, and poor health, but whose thirst for luxury generated "imaginary delights" (328–29).

Thus, poetry is a misleading and seemingly contradictory arena for readers who expect sincere and honest depictions of emotions and personal experience. Happy poets speak of misery, hungry poets of satiation, violent poets of harmony. And why? Because poets (Yeats qualifies them to mean poets "who are no longer deceived") quarrel with themselves; their verse is the stage of that quarrel (331). Their internal conflict pits the daily, conscious self against "the other self, the anti-self or the antithetical self" (331). Yeats calls the anti-self both "the second self" and "something not one's self" (334), a presence within the poet yet separate from him, accessible through the act of imagining that we are "different from what we are" and through the action of assuming "that second self."

At this point in *PASL*, Yeats begins speaking of the anti-self in terms new to him. The conflict between self and anti-self becomes not an instance of psychological fragmentation but of ontological confrontation. The anti-self is not a psychic projection but a psychic phenomenon, another being, a spirit (here also called ghost) who comes to a man "seeking its own opposite" (335). The daimon was not a new concept to Yeats; he was familiar with daimons through his reading of Greek philosophy. But in *PASL* he now rewrites these classical sources. If we examine them, Yeats's innovative use of daimon becomes readily apparent.[4]

The most familiar source is Plato, who conceived the universe divided into spheres. Between the inner and outer spheres roam the spirits or daimons, who serve a unitive function by preventing the universe "from falling into two separate halves" (*Symposium* 81). Each person has a daimon, "that kind of soul which is housed in the top of our body and which raises us— seeing that we are not as an earthly but a heavenly planet—up from earth towards our kindred in heaven" (*Timaeus* 245). While Plato's daimon marks a meeting point between temporal and spiritual spheres, Plotinus' "Guiding Spirit" establishes a more personal, even intimate relationship between human beings and daimons. Before the birth of the soul into the temporal order, a daimon is appointed to aid the soul in its efforts to accomplish its destiny. Although the guiding spirit is superior in nature to the soul because spirits feel no attraction to the sensible realm, it "presides inoperative" while the soul, once materially embodied, freely chooses its course of action (Ritvo 45). In Plutarch, the third major classical source, the daimon is described again as a kind of guardian angel, a spirit that dwells in the higher dimension of the mind. Joining the human being in the cradle, the daimon "guides him in all the actions of his life . . . presiding over and by divine instinct directing his intentions" (Plutarch 388). This daimon is more active for Plutarch than for Plotinus in the human life it protects, speaking to the soul in sleep when the passions and turmoil of the body are minimized (404):

> but if a soul hath gone through the trials of a thousand generations, and now, when her course is almost finished, strives bravely, and with a great deal of labor endeavors to ascend, the Deity permits her proper Genius to aid her, and even gives leave to any other that is willing to assist. The Daemon, thus permitted, presently sets about the work; and upon his approach, if the soul obeys and hearkens to

his directions, she is saved; if not, the Daemon leaves her, and she
lies in a miserable condition. (414)

Once a soul no longer is incarnated into a body, it becomes a "guardian"
daimon in turn, and presides over others (413).

Yeats's new use of daimon in *PASL* reflects the influence of Plato (daimon
as bridge between spiritual and temporal realms), of Plotinus (daimon as
destiny) and of Plutarch (daimon as guardian). Like Plotinus and Plutarch,
Yeats regarded the daimon as a spirit-inhabitant of the human psyche. He
believed it to be a discarnate soul engaged in its own posttemporal purging
but present in its human host, who in turn can recognize the daimon's activity through psychic connections. But these classical influences extend only
so far in Yeats. His daimon, more active even than Plotinus' guiding spirit,
is a temporal, confrontational, and problematic link to spiritual reality. It can
directly interfere in human action and use its host as a vehicle to fulfill its
own designs.

Yeats's preliminary discussion of daimon as anti-self in *PASL* projects the
daimon as choosing to reside within a particular person because human and
daimon feed on the complementary hungers in each other's hearts (*Myth*
335).[5] It is the quintessential love/hate relationship. For Yeats, the daimon
stands for destiny because life is fundamentally a struggle with the daimon.
The daimon "delivers and deceives us," hunting men with a net woven from
the stars. "There is a deep enmity between man and his destiny," but Yeats
adds, "a man loves nothing but his destiny" (336). Once enmeshed, there is
no escape. "We meet always in the deep of the mind, whatever our work,
wherever our reverie carries us, that other Will" (337).

Opposition evokes and welds together conflicted emotions—love and
hate—and they in turn create passion. And passion, rather than sincerity or
originality, is the supreme value for Yeats: "the passions, when we know that
they cannot find fulfillment, become vision; and a vision, whether we wake
or sleep, prolongs its power by rhythm and pattern" (341). This all marks
another critical departure from Greek prototypes: a poet's struggle with his
anti-self is more than a date with destiny—it evokes poetry. The passionate
interaction of poet and daimon generates verse and is sustained by it. It is
the aesthetic process.

In explaining precisely how this occurs, Yeats unravels a poetics based on
his metaphysical vision of the world, both within and outside the human
psyche. In order to select images ("image" is used here in the ordinary, poetic sense), a poet must suspend the critical faculties. This ability may come
naturally or can be learned. If the poet can also suspend desire as well as intellect, images will not only "pass rapidly before" him or her but also "form
at their own will" (344). They come from the subconscious, "anything [the
poet] already possess[es] a fragment of" (344).[6] But these images are not

simply memories from one's past experience or knowledge. They transcend the personal because the subconscious is connected to the Great Memory or *Anima Mundi;* indeed, Yeats envisions the subconscious vastly enlarged by this connection, so much so that conscious, daily thoughts are "but the line of foam at the shallow edge of a vast luminous sea" (346).

His explanation involves no less than the explication of a Platonic universe. Each person consists of a body and soul, the soul defined as "'a substance incorporeal but without sense'" (351). The personality is not constrained either in time or place by the body ("personality outlives the body"); in fact, the body is merely the vehicle of the soul in the temporal order. Each human body is a miniversion, a microcosm or "condensation" of the *Anima Mundi,* itself a vehicle in turn (350). Poetic images "come out of the dark" of the subconscious, which serves as a mirror of the images within the primary vehicle, the *Anima Mundi.* Personal Memory—"that memory is for a time our external world" (354)—is, in turn, carried to the Great Memory "without loss of identity" (356) so that the subconscious works as a two-way mirror, receiving and contributing images that transcend and enlarge an individual's experience. But the human, incarnated being is not the only participant. Images from the Great Memory are given substance "in the faint materialisation of our common thought"—"common" meaning shared between the human self and "a ghost [who] is our visitor" (350). The subconscious, then, isn't the personal property of the poet but shared ground between man and daimon.

Thus the *Anima Mundi* becomes an arena of action linking human and daimon, action that involves a complex sequence of exchanges between them. First, the daimon brings memories from its past life. Yeats believed that the dead reexperience their passionate moments, but once they understand themselves dead, they "may awake or half awake to be our visitors" (360). At that point, daimons and living men keep in touch through the Great Memory, since the dead live in their memories, arranging them like pieces on a chessboard. Such a visit occurs when the living tap into the memories of the dead—Yeats calls this connection "inflow" (361).

During inflow, the daimon leads a person to a moment of choice. Precisely through the daimon's presence and manipulations, the poet now selects from alternatives broader and more diverse than simply his own inclinations. This moment is repeated "again and again." Here Yeats moves from the merely theatrical (selecting a role or pose) to the dramatic, as poet and daimon confront one another. Whose image shall win out? The poet becomes victim as the daimon leads him into situations or makes demands that are most difficult but not impossible (361). But turnabout is fair play; the daimon suffers the presence of the human host as "some firm-souled man suffers with the woman he but loves the better because she is extravagant and fickle" (360). The conflict produces severe tensions, which Yeats calls "evil": "the strain one upon another of opposites" (357).

But the term "evil" is misleading, for this tension generates moments of ecstasy as the poet acts as if a choice has been made for him. There are occasions when Yeats finds himself in a state of excitement, of passionate intensity: "I have no longer any fears or any needs; I do not even remember that this happy mood must come to an end" (365). During such an experience, all petty emotions dissolve away (his anger with a servant, a quarrel with the tradesmen).

> It seems as if the vehicle had suddenly grown pure and far extended and so luminous that the images from *Anima Mundi,* embodied there and drunk with that sweetness, would, like a country drunkard who has thrown a wisp into his own thatch, burn up time. (365)

It is not simply that the *images* are new, different from the prison of his own memories. The poet has set fire to the confines of himself; the intrusion of the daimon allows him to assume a new, alien personality.

Such rare moments of temporal ecstasy are duplicated in "brief intense visions of sleep" much like a state of innocence. And there Yeats is "in the place where the Daimon is." That is, he comes face-to-face with his adversary in the psychodrama. But he does not fully encounter the daimon "until I begin to make a new personality, selecting among those images, seeking always to satisfy a hunger grown out of conceit with daily diet." Perhaps he would go so far as to imply his own freedom and power by the words "I select" in forming a new personality, "not knowing when I am the finger, when the clay" (365–66).

While Yeats appears to emphasize their opposition, their "struggle" and "passion," he is in fact focusing on how and when poet and daimon are "knitted together." Moments of ecstasy are quasi-orgasmic as they mark a union of opposites. When a poet chooses not to write out of his real self or his personal experience but to assume a mask "whose lineaments permit the expression of all the man most lacks, and it may be dreads, and of that only" (335), then he enters into momentary union with the daimon. The poet is thus capable of working on a different plane, a multidimensional level where the golden rule of art—striking a boundary line between this figure and the next—cannot distinguish between man and daimon, locked in opposition yet knitted together within the mask. But Yeats adds that if he could "see our handiwork the Daimon would fling himself out, being our enemy" (339).

The conflict between man and daimon can be resolved only in the mask; whether it *is* resolved is problematic, because the ultimate felicity of spirits extends far beyond temporal existence and into a series of stages that take place in the supernatural order. Human/daimonic encounters may serve both participants, but those participants act at cross-purposes. The daimon is working through a sequence of posttemporal stages and uses its encounter with a human to further its *own* development. The poet also follows his own spiritual journey through temporal existence. Each aids the other as they move "side by side in the same cycle" (*VA* 221), but their final destinations are not aligned—hence the true drama of the encounter. The relation between man and daimon is not simply a state of being (i.e., poet and daimon contacting each other via the *Anima Mundi*). It is more properly an act of being: occasions of conflict and ecstasy that are shaped by converging but not harmonious designs. In this sense, the mask is both a noun (a poetic artifact) and a verb (a way of being)—a series of perpetual and volatile flashes of dramatic and psychic convergence.

Clearly, *PASL* marks Yeats's most complete discussion during this "middle" period of the aesthetic process in terms of the daimon. Although the topic of the mask itself is notably underdeveloped, Yeats succeeds in tracing the inflow between spiritual daimon and human poet—moments when poetic images flow up from the subconscious or down from the *Anima Mundi* and surrender themselves to rhythm and pattern, forming a mask that reflects the daimon (as the man's opposite or anti-self) yet remains the poet.

There is of course ancillary discussion in *PASL,* but I would like to note one critical section that is more than an interesting aside. It is section 8, where Yeats attempts to describe through deep imagery the nature of opposition between man and daimon, specifically, the Janus-faced response of attraction and enmity that characterizes their relationship. An analogy "of the warfare of man and Daimon" suggests itself from an arena of conflict very familiar to Yeats—sexual love. "Then my imagination runs from Daimon to sweetheart, and I divine an analogy that evades the intellect" (*Myth* 336). He cites astrology from "Greek antiquity" in his association of sexual love with spiritual hate. Just as the poet's woman fuels and satisfies a man's passion, his daimon feeds the hunger in his heart. And just as the daimon weaves man's destiny out of the stars like a net, the sweetheart gathers up "an entire web of influences" (*AU* 326). Yeats ends section 8 with an equivalent image of conflict and sexual love: "I sometimes fence for a half an hour at the day's end, and when I close my eyes upon the pillow I see a foil playing before me, the button to my face" (*Myth* 337). The analogy of man in conflict with daimon and man in conflict with woman is so exact that Yeats suspects daimon and sweetheart might secretly plot their man's demise: "I even wonder if there may not be some secret communion, some whispering in the dark between Daimon and sweetheart" (336).[7]

PASL stands as a clear statement of Yeats's theory of the mask as conceived just before the Automatic Script experiment. These critical facets of the mask theory formulated in *PASL* do not change for the rest of Yeats's artistic and mystical life—that the poet is divided into a daily self and an anti-self, that this anti-self is another being called daimon, that the mask signifies a knitting together of poet and daimon in a passionate love/hate relationship. Yet in 1917, Yeats is poised on the threshold of a new conceptualization of the daimon, beginning in October of that year. The difference between his understanding of the daimon as analogous to the sweetheart versus the daimon as a gendered being is captured in two key passages, the first from *PASL* (1917), the second from *A Vision* (1925):

> I am persuaded that the Daimon delivers and deceives us, and that *he* wove that netting from the stars and threw the net from *his* shoulder. Then my imagination runs from Daimon to sweetheart, and I divine an analogy that evades the intellect . . . and I even wonder if there may not be some secret communion, some whispering in the dark between Daimon and sweetheart. (*Myth* 336; emphasis added)

> But there is another mind, or another part of our mind in this darkness, that is yet to its own perceptions in the light; and we in our turn are dark to that mind. These two minds (one always light and one always dark, when considered by one mind alone), make up man and *Daimon,* the *Will* of the man being the *Mask* of the *Daimon,* the *Creative Mind* of the man being the *Body of Fate* of the *Daimon* and so on . . . . Man's *Daimon* has therefore her energy and bias, in man's *Mask,* and her constructive power in man's fate, and man and *Daimon* face each other in a perpetual conflict or embrace. This relation (the *Daimon* being of the opposite sex to that of man) may create a passion like that of sexual love. (*VA* 27; emphasis original)

What is notable is the shift in pronouns. While the daimon is referred to as "he" in the first instance, I would argue that Yeats has no sense of the daimon as gendered being, whether male or female. Instead, he uses the male pronoun as a universal, much in the same way he generally refers to the poet as "he." The use of the female pronoun in the second instance is clearly deliberate. This method of gendering, or more precisely, regendering from male to female, has no precedent in Greek daimonology, where it was commonplace to refer to the soul as "she" (as Plutarch does) and to any foreign influence as "he." Yeats explicitly reverses this pattern in *A Vision.*

Subsequent chapters will explore this reconfiguration of the daimon as it occurs in the Automatic Script and then in terms of the mask in specific poems and plays. Here by way of initial groundwork I would like to elaborate and perhaps complicate established notions of two Yeatsian doctrines tied to his theory of the mask. The first doctrine is his conception of the individual. The second is his conception of oppositional relationships, or what scholars have called his law of contraries. I will begin with the latter—it shapes his vi-

sion of the former—by focusing on three interpretations of Yeats as an oppositional thinker. These interpretations serve as examples of how Yeats is li-
able to misreading when a key feature is overlooked—how the gendering of
Yeats's daimonology radically changes not only his vision of oppositional relations but also his rationale for using them. In all three cases, critics have
set out to explain Yeats's oppositional thinking in terms that minimize or
even deny the actual parameters that Yeats himself defines.

The earliest of the three interpretations is the most formative. In his reading of Yeats as a poet of power, Denis Donoghue argues that "Yeats values
above all the energy of conflict" (5) and so sees reality as a series of oppositional pairs. Conflict delights Yeats because it is the prerequisite to power.
Donoghue is not referring to power in a crass sense, but "moral power, self-
mastery, self-definition . . . to transform his own experience" (18). Yeats's
"consciousness as conflict" stems primarily from Nietzsche, who advanced a
hero as "an antithetical fiction; his idiom is power, will; his sense of life dynamic, theatrical" (57). Subsequently, Yeats speaks a new language, the "idiom of combat, theatre, unity of opposites" (61).

Harold Bloom regards Yeats's aesthetic as "antithetical" in the tradition
of Shelley, Blake, Nietzsche, and Pater, but believes Yeats's antithetical vision
is "gnostic," applying the word generically to Yeats's unflagging appetite to
unearth a mother lode of secrets about the world. In analyzing "Second
Coming," "Byzantium," and "Cuchulain Comforted" as gnostic poems,
Bloom sees a "repressive defense" against the anxiety of influence (*William
Butler Yeats* 9). In "Second Coming," for example, Yeats represses Shelley's
influence by depicting experience of the sublime as "uncanny" or "dae-
monic" (13). Here Bloom reduces Yeats's daimonology (a "less rational"
dualism between self and anti-self) to a "more rational" notion: Freud's theory of negation. He concludes that the basis of Yeats's daimonic system is
first his "fixation upon precursors," and then his resistance against "the almost irresistible force of a primal repression" (22).

Joseph Hassett generates a description of Yeats that might be called the
emotive antithesis. The basic premise of Hassett's analysis is simple: because
he believed that poetic images come from the spirits of the dead through the
subconscious, Yeats's art is a "poetics of hate" wherein ancestral hatred and
pride are vented through verse (150–51). But in addition to the passionate
rage of the dead, Hassett argues that Yeats himself is victim to hatred, which
centered around his father. The poet agonized between two desires: to reject John Butler Yeats's scientism and patriarchal influence, and to unite
"with a powerful other." This divided self produces "the familiar Yeats who
would recreate himself as his own opposite [his father], and as the opposite
of his father" (35). Thus, the battle between human and daimon, self and
anti-self, is merely a metaphor for psychological conflict generated by hatred
for the other variously defined: John Locke's materialism, contemporary

theories of progress and human perfection, intellectual abstraction, the English and their language, sexual differences (among others). For Hassett, the mask is a near-pathological response to an adversarial world.

I have described these three interpretations in order of publication to underscore the clear progression—from discussions of "consciousness as conflict" to "antithetical theorist" to "a poetics of hate"—that registers an increasingly negative view of Yeats's oppositional thinking. Only Bloom is explicitly antagonistic to Yeats's mysticism, yet all three psychologize and despiritualize the mask, which therefore appears rooted in a restrictive, even suppressed psyche that struggles to free itself.

To the negative review in recent years of oppositional thinking may be added feminist criticism, which has labeled such thinking "male." Yeats himself was versed in thinkers, such as Porphyry, who construct the world as a series of dualities in order to draw nature "into harmony" (37). Such systems are criticized by feminists as setting out to "hold the world still" and fabricate order where there is none (Ronald and Roskelly 178) or to defeat and destroy the weaker/female component (Cixous). This feminist argument, which associates oppositional thinking with a patriarchal agenda, has called attention to issues beyond dualistic thinking to the rationale behind it. But such discussions often lump all instances of oppositional thinking into the same camp wherein the male psyche engages in power plays to dominate and oppress.[8]

Like the feminists' reductive approach, Donoghue, Bloom, and Hassett also seek a rationale. But just as they eliminate the occult, their interpretations do not take gender into account—we might call their discussions "gender-neutral." My argument flows between their gender-neutral interpretation and the gender-reductive interpretation of some feminists. I argue that Yeats's conception of daimonology and his vision of gender make such oversimplified interpretations untenable. That is to say, the three interpretations by Donoghue, Bloom, and Hassett are correct, but only up to a point.[9] True, Yeats celebrated passion from the time he read Blake: "Passions, because most living, are most holy" (*E & I* 113). True, difference is critical, first as "lineament" or "boundary"—a means of defining and establishing identity:

> "How do we distinguish one face or countenance from another, but
> by the bounding outline and its infinite inflections and movements
> ... Leave out this line and you leave out life itself; all is chaos again,
> and the line of the Almighty must be drawn out upon it before man
> or beast can exist." (120)

After reading Nietzsche (1902), Yeats put the two together—passion and difference. True again, as Donoghue and Hassett note, Yeats adopts Nietzsche's "idiom of combat," and develops a vision of the world that is adversarial, tragic, and antagonistic, or in Nietzsche's terms, saturated with the energy of conflict.[10] Yeats speaks of his youth as a "continual discovery of difference" (*AU* 31) and observes, at the end of his life, that "discord separates the elements and so makes the world we inhabit" (*VB* 67). He cites Nicholas of Cusa as demonstrating that "ultimate reality" falls in our minds "into a series of antinomies" (*VB* 187). He dwells on the incompatibility of love and friendship, describing sexual love as "a battlefield where shadows war beside the combatants" (*Collected VII* 201) and as one of the two great antitheses of human experience (*VB* 268). But this is not the full picture, which will be complete only when we take into account the developments in Yeats's thinking that occur with the Automatic Script experiments.

We have noted the antithesis between poet and daimon (as anti-self) at the core of the mask, an antithesis defined by Yeats in *PASL* as "complete" (*Myth* 356). If Yeats's theory of the mask had remained at this stage, then we could accurately speak of "consciousness as conflict," of an "antithetical theorist," of a "poetics of hate." Or we might find other terms useful, such as "positional superiority" (Edward Said describing Orientalism [7]), "hostile polarity" (James Hillman describing Jung's take on gender [*Myth* 217, 250]), or "abysmal antagonism" (Nietzsche's vision of gender relations [*Beyond Good and Evil* 166]). But after 1919, the idiom of combat that Donoghue refers to is transformed by the metaphysical dynamic of the mask: "The world is made up of a number [of] beings," Yeats believed, "which circle round one another. Man & daimon were the first—they made the first orbits" (*AS III* 187). Yeats internalizes these orbits. Within the human psyche, self and daimon are the "two first portions of being" (*VA* 132). Further, their relationship is more than intellectual, marked as it is by passionate and spiritual conflict. Indeed, the passionate energy generated in their love/hate relationship acts as a stabilizing force wherein attraction and repulsion are held in constant tension.

Understandably, Yeats found difficulty in expressing the paradoxical and complex relationship between human and daimon. He notes that the daimon could not be found "if he were not in some sense of our being," yet "he is of all things not impossible the most difficult" (*Myth* 332). All people serve as hosts to daimons, but most "natural men" are oblivious to their oppositional presence. According to Yeats, the individual ego and its daimon cannot exist apart, but can function without communication (*AS II* 252). That is, the ego can function as if it were autonomous and isolated. Whether "the objective world is then the battle ground of Daimons" (500), internal daimonic activity remains hidden and eludes detection. In 1915–1917, as Yeats grappled with this problem, he turned to a more familiar interaction: relations between men and women that are marked by sexual love and spiritual hate. This love/hate paradox is analogous to the strife and attachment between man and daimon.

This brings us again to the critical shift in the Automatic Script. As long as the connection between daimon and woman is only analogical, it is fundamentally arbitrary. That is, the analogy suggests itself because the relationship between man and daimon is characterized by love and hate, just as (in Yeats's view) the relationship between man and woman. Yet daimon and woman have no essential relation to each other. Once Yeats defines the daimon as female (April 1919), the function of opposition shifts dramatically. The conflict between self and daimon is significant not only because it generates passion but also because it typifies something fundamental to the human condition: "It is the purely instinctive & cosmic quality in man which seeks completion in its opposite" (*AS I* 65). Here "opposite" refers not only to the daily self (man) and the ideal self (daimon) but also to the sexual natures of man and daimon. While antithesis provokes passion, gendered difference promises union: "two complete opposites never unite except in man & woman" (68). The sexual union promises temporary unity in this life: "Love making all things One" (*VB* 247). Sexual union also foreshadows permanent harmony in the next life, what Yeats reveres as "Unity of Being," when contraries are united and antinomies are resolved: "I see in [the natural union of man and woman] a symbol of that eternal instant where the antinomy is resolved. It is not the resolution itself" (214).

Even so, conflict promises completion (*AS I* 65) and unity (68), albeit of earthly guise. Thus, Yeats no longer speaks of evil as the strain of opposites (as he did in *PASL*) but as the cessation of conflict, since conflict is a prerequisite to Unity of Being. Evil is permanent symmetry, a state of calcifying imbalance wherein reason turns upon emotion, logic upon intuition, knowledge upon belief, male upon female—until one member of the duality is threatened with repression. In such a case, the subject rises up against the master and dominates the pair: "If man seeks to live wholly in the light, the *Daimon* will seek to quench that light in what is to man wholly darkness" (*VA* 28). Evil is the cessation of opposition; it is a world devoid of difference.

So while Yeats uses terms like "antithesis" and "opposition," his meaning is more precisely captured by Blake's notion of "contrary," the word I will use throughout this study.[11] "Life is the contact of contraries," Yeats contends (*AS I* 406), adapting Blake's insistence that there is no progression without contraries. "'Contraries are positive,'" he quotes from Blake. The concept does not simply imply difference or contrast ("'a negation is not a contrary'") (*VB* 72). Neither does it denote a kind of mental grid imposed on randomly arranged pairs. Contraries designate an interconnection, a "correspondence" (*AS II* 292) wherein "the existence of the one depends upon the existence of the other" (*VA* 134). Contraries generate action, vitality, and change; they never exclude or deny the other.

The impact of gendered daimonology upon Yeats's oppositional thinking is direct and decisive. Contrary to what many feminists might predict—that adding gender would only instigate a symmetrical, dualistic power imbalance—gender in fact transforms a straightforward oppositional configuration into a complementary one. The reason stems from Yeats's conception of gender itself, a vision that precludes systematization but can be described by four characteristics.

First, in Yeats gendered differences are substantive. The masculine/feminine relational opposition is not simply one in a series; it is the foundation out of which all other oppositions, both real and symbolic, are generated. According to both Platonic and Hermetic myths, the first human being was an hermaphrodite, a "rounded whole," forming a complete circle (Plato, *Symposium* 59). That whole was cut into two parts, male and female, both weaker than the original being and yearning for reunion. "It is as though the first act of being, after creating limit, was to divide itself into male and female, each dying the other's life living the other's death" (*VA* 130). Temporal and spiritual reality embodies the great paradox advanced thousands of years ago by Heraclitus. The mysterious, complex interchange between man and woman provides the pattern Yeats recognized not only as the basis for all opposition but also for the relation between the living and dead, incarnate and discarnate souls.

> I see the Lunar and Solar cones first, before they start their whirling movement, as two worlds lying one within another—nothing exterior, nothing interior, Sun in Moon and Moon in Sun—a single being like man and woman in Plato's myth, and then a separation and a whirling for countless ages, and I see man and woman as reflecting the greater movement. (*VA* 149)

Yeats insists that gender is not simply part of philosophical or occult mythologies, nor is it merely a metaphor for other dualities (sun/moon, objective/subjective, primary/antithetical). Gender is real and imminent, present most immediately as "universal masculine & feminine in soul" (*AS I* 109).

Second, gendered opposition is relational rather than absolute. Here Yeats rejects the path chosen by Blake, whom he interprets as depicting man (symbolizing wisdom) and woman (symbolizing beauty) as "two competing gyres growing at one another's expense . . . which compels each to be slave and tyrant by turn" (*VA* 134). Yeats further clarifies his own position: "In our system also it is a cardinal principle that anything separated from its opposite—the victory is separation—'consumes itself away.' The existence of the one depends upon the existence of the other" (134). In current gender theory, the closest approximation of Yeats's vision of gendered interdependence is Ivan Illich's concept of "ambiguous complementarity." According to Illich, complementarity is an old notion from precapitalistic, subsistence societies wherein men and women work together as right and left hands (72). In this view, masculine and feminine "fit" each other, depend upon each other to survive, see through different eyes, and think, speak, and love in disparate ways. This configuration is neither symmetrical nor asymmetrical but bilaterally asymmetrical, with one gender establishing temporary power over the other. Such reciprocal asymmetry is counterbalanced by ambiguity, which guarantees inherent incongruities and protects masculine and feminine from hierarchy and dependence (76). Complementarity ensures their ongoing need for and connection to each other. As Yeats asserts, "the existence of one depends upon the existence of the other" (*VA* 134).

To illustrate complementarity in general and the interaction of masculine and feminine in particular, Yeats envisions corresponding and intersecting cones or gyres, which he alternately labels as time and space, primary and antithetical, objective and subjective, solar and lunar:

> As these contraries become sharper in their contrast, as they pull farther apart, consciousness grows more intense, for consciousness is choice. The energy of the one tendency being in exact mathematical proportion to that of the other. . . . When each gyre has reached the widest expansion, the contradiction in the being will have reached its height. . . . As man's intellect, say, expands, the emotional nature contracts in equal degree and vice versa; when, however, a narrowing and a widening gyre reach their limit, the one the utmost contraction the other the utmost expansion, they change places, point to circle, circle to point, for this system conceives the world as catastrophic, and continue as before, one always narrowing, one always expanding, and yet bound for ever to one another. (131–32)

I quote extensively from *A Vision A* not to set forth Yeats's symbol system, but to appreciate the complexity of the configuration between contraries. Clearly, terms like "bipolarity" and "antithesis" cannot capture the reciprocal and interactive relationship between them. For one, there seems to be a constant, almost mathematical equation: $x + y = 1$, or masculine and feminine equals a single whole. But there is also this sense of proportion: as masculine (or sun) waxes, feminine (or moon) wanes—as Yeats puts it, there are "a narrowing and a widening"—making the critical feature the presence and interchange between the two rather than the constant state of either one. Masculine and feminine can therefore shift in appearance; they are not inflexible or monolithic states of being. Rather, they are continually in action, ultimately identifiable only in terms of their relational opposition—or complementarity—to the other in a relationship that remains (using Illich's term) "ambiguous." Thus it becomes difficult to ascribe constant features as to what is clearly feminine or masculine. Our inability to formulate Yeats's vision of gender hinges not on a fundamental inconsistency within Yeats's worldview but on a fundamental dynamic and complexity of his view.

Third, gendered opposition is internal as well as external. Yeats speaks of "universal masculine & feminine" in a variety of archetypal manifestations: primary and antithetical, objective and subjective, solar and lunar. Their relative mix explains everything in the temporal order, from cultures to personality types. But "universal masculine & feminine" are first and foremost found in the human psyche, where the male or female host wars with its female or male daimon, who is the archenemy and yet "part of me" (*AS II* 211).

In Yeats's own case, this is nothing less than a bold reconceptualization of sexual identity. If with males the daimon is female and is "that being united to man which knows neither good nor evil, and shapes the body in the womb, and impresses upon the mind its form" (*VA* 220), then men are more integrated and complex beings and closer to that androgynous whole than the Platonic and Hermetic traditions recall. United to his daimon, Yeats is never solely male, for she engages him in passionate and ceaseless contact with the feminine embedded within his own being. For the sake of his destiny in this life and moral purification in the next, the poet must allow the feminine free and formative play in his life and psyche.

Finally, gendered opposition symbolizes Unity of Being. This state signifies the ultimate point of existence for Yeats, the end of the incarnational cycle and the ultimate purpose of the wandering soul. More specifically, Yeats conceives of Unity of Being as "complete harmony between physical body intellect & spiritual desire" (*AS II* 41). It is not merely proportion or even balance, since balance signifies "equal power equally used" (43). Rather, unity is harmony: "All the being vibrates to the note, it is like striking a chord" (*AS III* 27).

Note that harmony does not eliminate any single attribute, body, mind, or spirit, just as the Platonic whole assumes the simultaneous existence of male and female. Here, however, Yeats breaks from the Platonic duality of body and soul that privileges spirit and denigrates matter. Yeats insists that Unity of Being (the highest human state) "cannot exist in separation from the body" (*AS II* 41). While he still speaks of the body as the vehicle of the soul (*AS I* 459), he does not relegate the body to an inferior position, as this dialogue in the Automatic Script reveals:

> [Question]: What is the vehicle of the soul?
> [Answer]: The body & the world.
> [Q]: Meaning that so poor a thing should be the flower of so many ages?
> [A]: That the soul should be so unworthy of its vehicle. (459)

It is a paradox: Yeats emphasizes opposition but values unity. The introduction of gender elevates the level of oppositional configuration; now Yeats's system of sexual complements becomes a prerequisite to unity.

This brings us to the second doctrine of Yeats's worldview mentioned earlier—his conception of the psyche, which is intimately linked with his daimonology. It is no coincidence that as Yeats explored the gendered nature of the daimon and her sexual involvement in his own life, he simultaneously expanded his conception of "Faculties" within the human being and how those Faculties interconnect with the daimon. In *PASL,* before Yeats genders the daimon, he describes the antithesis between self and daimon as the spirits of the dead becoming engaged in temporal events. But he is constrained by his own terms, speaking generally of the terrestrial condition as opposed to the condition of fire, but unable to capture in words the complex action of self and daimon intertwined in the same psyche.

The problem is evident: if the relationship between self and daimon were purely antithetical, then what Donoghue calls the "idiom of combat" would suffice. But self and daimon converge not simply as deadly foes but also as lovers. To make matters even more complex, as Yeats conceives of the daimon as anti-self, he radically redraws the "lineaments" of the human psyche, designing new boundaries that on the outside appear static (the self and daimon remain distinct) but in actuality work in a new, three-dimensional field where simple boundary lines cannot distinguish the two beings engaged in intense attraction and revulsion within the individual.

Over the course of the automatic writing experiment, W. B. and Georgie Yeats gradually flesh out a definition of the person as a complex reality, a being who transcends experiences and memories during any one of its twenty-eight separate Phases. The person is defined as an individual, a term signifying the "entire being" (*AS II* 147). This "entire being" maintains its own unified, adamant identity through "The Way of the Soul between the Sun and the Moon"—as Yeats originally conceived the incarnate phases (*AS I* 13). No matter what, "I am still I" (*AS II* 330). The soul is the cornerstone of a person's unique identity: "no human soul is like any other human soul" (*Myth* 68). But it is not the only essential feature of that identity. The soul needs a means of expression, and that is the body (*AS I* 88). In addition to the soul and body, there is the ego, also called the "disintegrated identity." The ego is composed of such "discordant elements" (154) as the antithetical principle (dreamy, elusive, imaginative, philosophic, artistic) and the primary principle (instinctive, willful, practical) (*AS III* 159), both of which produce the subconscious (*AS I* 95).

Each incarnation marks the death of the ego; the moment of death is that instant when the soul is freed from the daily and anti-self (75). Thus, death is not the end of the individual nor of the identity that is shaped both during and apart from temporal existence. The person as incarnated in time is just the tip of a complex iceberg, the scope and substance of which are only marginally accessible to him or her. Consciousness is one source of knowledge, but so also are the unconscious, the personal *Anima Mundi,* the collective *Anima Mundi,* and the Four Memories. The sequence and phases of human existence are preordained, but within each phase we are free agents. "Man is free in each individual incarnation—that is his chance" (121).

As the soul begins its journey through the twenty-eight Phases of temporal existence, it assumes the form of either a man or woman, depending on what "type of soul" it is, i.e., whether it originates from phase 1 (the solar principle) or phase 15 (the lunar principle) (339). After the initial whole cycle, the soul's gender will switch with every phase, "alternating from man to woman then man then woman & so on" (338). The last incarnational form is always a woman (338; repeated in *AS III* 146–47; *VA* 170).

As W. B. and Georgie Yeats begin to explore the twenty-eight Phases of the moon—a subject that arises in the closing weeks of 1917—they also define the Four Faculties that compose the human being: Will, Mask, Creative Mind, and Body of Fate.[12] The fledgling discussions incorporate definitions of each phase based on proportions of oppositional pairs: solar and lunar elements, primary and antithetical cones. But within only a few days, the Yeatses moved beyond this level of simple antithesis to designing a more complex frame of reference, or stage directions, if you will, for the process asserted but never described in *PASL* wherein the daimon commands and executes a person's destiny.

In polished form, the Faculties are described in the following way: Will is the ability to feel or choose before actual energy is released or a decision made, for there is as yet no object to desire. Mask is "the image of what we wish to become, or of that to which we give our reverence." Creative Mind is equivalent to the pre-Lockean notion of intellect, "all the mind that is consciously constructive," and Body of Fate is outside elements forced upon us (*VA* 15). These Four Faculties work as actors in a play, in which the daimon uses bodies of men and women to work out its own process of purification. Will functions as the actor, while Body of Fate provides the scenario. Creative Mind offers the dialogue of the plot, and Mask is the role the actor assumes, a role "as unlike to natural character as possible" (18). The action is played out through a series of phases or incarnations wherein the ratio of Faculties differs. In each phase, one of the Four Faculties assumes ascendancy and determines the incarnated type.[13]

During each incarnation, the Four Faculties align themselves into two complementary pairs: Will/Mask and Creative Mind/Body of Fate. Each single Faculty within the pairs is commanded either by self or daimon, but it is not a case of one Faculty belonging to the human, the other to the daimon. Rather, self and daimon are interlaced in the pairs so that each Faculty works as its own contrary, depending upon whether we are speaking of the self or daimon. Note again that critical passage from *A Vision A:*

> the *Will* of the man being the *Mask* of the *Daimon,* the *Creative Mind* of the man being the *Body of Fate* of the *Daimon* and so on.
> . . . Man's *Daimon* has therefore her energy and bias, in man's *Mask,* and her constructive power in man's fate, and man and *Daimon* face each other in a perpetual conflict or embrace. (27)

This discussion, as convoluted and mysterious as it seems, reveals Yeats's vision of the complementarity of self and daimon in action. Man and daimon line up against each other as mortal enemies—then again, as lovers—taking command of individual Faculties, themselves configured into oppositional pairs but shared in reciprocal fashion, with the man's Will being the daimon's Mask, the daimon's Will being the man's Mask, etc.

Perhaps more than any other component in his occult system as defined in *A Vision,* the Four Faculties provide a revealing pathway into Yeats's worldview. For one, the interaction of the Faculties reflects the basic dynamic of complementarity between contraries as I have described it, with their perpetually shifting ratios, reciprocity, and indissoluble connection. But it would be erroneous to conclude that the Faculties simply mirror the larger movement in a cause-and-effect relationship, as if Yeats had already formulated his theory of the tinctures and forced the Faculties to fit the same mold. As we have already noted, Yeats believed that the "greater movement" is found not in the solar and lunar cones or tinctures themselves but in gender relations: "I see man and woman as reflecting the greater movement" (149). The Automatic Script makes clear that the Yeatses explored several components simultaneously: the basic movement of opposing tinctures, the Four Faculties, the action of the daimon in the lives of men and women, and the origins of sex. This combination—opposition, reciprocal pairs, daimon, and gender—is self-infusing, and insures that opposition never collapses into sheer antithesis; instead, it maintains the dynamic that I have called complementarity.

Second, through the Faculties, the interaction between human and daimon becomes discernible in the external order. Yeats uses an intricate system to classify the ascendancy of any of the Four Faculties, a system that involves the twenty-eight Phases broken into types: the "Four Perfections," the "Four Types of Wisdom," the "Four Contests," the "Four Automatonisms," and the "Elemental Attributions" (*VA* 33–36). In theory, an observer would recognize when the daimon gains ascendancy within the psyche if the particular phase of the human host is already known. This facet of the Phases is more than another eccentric component of Yeats's occult system. It directs our attention to the necessary connection between the Faculty of the Mask and the focus of this study—the mask as aesthetic and textual construct. Yeats's spirit guides emphasized that the mask as aesthetic device and the Mask as Faculty were distinct phenomena. In defining the Faculty, the spirits insisted that "it is nothing to do with any form of artistic or practical genius—it is the form assumed (as a rule) by the ego as I described before and concerns life and not creation—it is a figure of destiny" (*AS I* 161). While the spirits warn against becoming obsessed "by the idea of artistic self" (162), that was obviously Yeats's only understanding of "mask" when the term was first introduced as part of the discussion of the Faculties. I would argue that the mask as textual reality reflects the deeper and more universal phenomenon that the Faculty of the Mask circumscribes. The Faculty of the Mask is synonymous with both "role" and "image," the exact terms Yeats used to define the aesthetic mask earlier in his career. The Faculty is "a revelation of *soul*" (162) insofar as it dramatizes the self (*VA* 19). But as Yeats makes clear, the drama does not consist of a single actor—the ego alone (later called the Will)—but of the daimon as well. The Faculty of the Mask universalizes what in *PASL* Yeats imagined to be the interaction of poet and daimon in the aesthetic act. Every human host interacts with a daimon in a deep psychological and ontological dramatization wherein a role or image is embraced. That dramatization can exist apart from any aesthetic representation. But once manifested via artistic expression, the mask as textual reality mirrors the deeper and more universal drama associated with the Faculty of the Mask.

Finally, the Faculties encapsulate the intricate and complex makeup of the person, which Yeats defines from a variety of perspectives—sometimes speaking of the simple self (the emotional subjective mind), the individual (the Will analyzed in relation to itself), and the personality (the Will analyzed in relation to the Mask) (20). Because the Faculty of the Mask is a dramatization of the self, the personality, "no matter how habitual, is a constantly renewed choice" (18). Each person can embrace a panoply of images or roles during a given incarnation.

Yeats is able to conceive of the person in such a radical way only at the point in time when he envisions the sexual, psychological, and ontological dynamics between host and gendered daimon. Readers face a seemingly endless series of paradoxes: gender is substantive and pervasive, yet the soul can sustain alternating masculine or feminine incarnations without losing its fundamental identity. During each incarnation, the psyche is multigendered, with the person's sexual identity complemented by the sex of the daimon. The conflict between self and daimon is intense and incessant, but their "knitting together" is both cosmic and intimate. The enmity generates a never-ending passion to the death, but it does not rend the psyche apart. Instead, it generates moments of ecstatic union. Through the scripting process, as Yeats synthesized his aesthetic, occult, and personal interests, he came to his final (and favorite) definition of the Mask as "a form created by passion to unite us to ourselves" (18).

CHAPTER 2

THE SEXUAL DAIMON

"The Yeatsian system is . . . not merely a pot-pourri like Theosophy . . . in the end everything is stamped with his personality and brought into line with his work."

Richard Ellmann, *Masks* (230–31)

"Take up the line she offers—be subservient to that opening."

The spirit guide, *AS I* (328)

The gendering of Yeats's daimonology occurs in the earliest years of his marriage and is documented in the Automatic Script. My interest in the automatic writing sessions centers on Yeats's reconceptualization of the daimon and the mask through inquiry into the "universal masculine & feminine in soul" (*AS I* 109). Focusing on this development means encountering an equally significant facet of Yeats's aesthetic: the explicit, deliberate, and literal connection between mystical reality and sexual love, what I will refer to as Yeats's sexual dynamic. This chapter examines how this sexual dynamic shapes the poet's daimonology and mask theory as developed during the early years of his marriage. Yeats called this system a "myth," and believed that "even my simplest poems will be the better for it" (*Letters* 781).[1]

It is difficult not to feel awash in the three volumes of the Automatic Script—over 450 sittings, 3,600 pages and responses to more than 9,000 questions. And it would be foolhardy to marshal one's scholarly energies to master the Automatic Script by itself. It is not an isolated phenomenon but the completion of earlier and more tentative experiments in the occult in general and in automatic writing in particular, exercises that involved both W. B. Yeats and Georgie Hyde-Lees. More importantly, the Automatic Script is the initial phase of the *Vision* materials, which developed in three stages: the series of questions and answers recorded between W. B. and Georgie Yeats (what we now refer to as the Automatic Script); the privately distributed edition of *A Vision*, referred to throughout this study as *A Vision A* (completed in 1925); and the second, more familiar edition, referred to as *A Vision B* (revised in 1934, published in 1937). I will analyze the evolution of *Vision* material in reverse order, moving from *A Vision B* and *A Vision A* to the Automatic Script. A chronological discussion seems more logical, certainly. But my purpose is to give readers a sense of the dominance of sex—unabashed and untempered—at the heart of this system. Concluding with *A Vision B* would implicitly emphasize just the opposite—a daimonology that is polished, philosophical, and degendered.

This reverse chronology reveals a continuum wherein the authorial voice is consistently monologic in content and form *(A Vision B)*, then dialogic in content but monologic in form *(A Vision A)*, and finally archetypically dialogic in content and form (the Automatic Script). The expository monologues in the *Vision* texts give way to collaborative dialogue in the scripting material, and the relative amount of gender material increases as we move from *A Vision B* to the Automatic Script. That is, the Automatic Script is saturated with discussion of sexual relations. *A Vision A* retains much of the gendered features of the symbol system, while *A Vision B* effaces the sexual dimensions of incarnate and discarnate existence.

Use of gender as a measure to analyze the three stages of the *Vision* material is unprecedented, despite lengthy and sustained debate as to the relative merits of the *Vision* editions. Yet an emphasis on gender will prove fruitful and justify obvious omissions. For instance, I will not address the philosophic clarifications of the 1934 version (for such arguments, I defer to James Olney, "W. B. Yeats's Daimonic Memory"; Colin McDowell, "The Completed Symbol"; and Rosemary Puglia Ritvo), but rather the heightened degree of abstraction and lack of metaphoric and symbolic language in the second edition, as noted by George Bornstein, Giorgio Melchiori, and Virginia Moore, among others.

The cause of that shift is problematic. Yeats himself provides few answers. It is obvious that he was frustrated by the first edition of *A Vision* almost immediately after its publication. In March 1926, he admitted: "'I see now that section XII Book IV in *A Vision* ["The Spirits at Fifteen and at One"] should have been the most important in the book & it is the slightest & worst.' It must be reworked and the whole system 'symbolized in a study of the relation of man and woman'" (qtd. in Hood 37). Yeats is clearly unhappy with the focus of the text, not because it lacks those meaty philosophical abstractions he later prizes in the second edition but because it falls short in elucidating his sexual dynamic, i.e., applying sex ("the relation of man and woman") to the symbol system—a surprising reflection when we consider how much gender material saturates the 1925 version.

If in 1926 Yeats affirms the sexual dynamic as pivotal to his symbol system, his later reaction registers a distinct change of heart. Yeats laments, the earlier edition "fills me with shame" (*VB* 19). The reasons are not altogether self-evident, nor are Yeats's motives in making such an admission. Publicly, he mentions misinterpreting the geometry of the system and of being ignorant about the philosophy that provided the basis of many of its principles (19). Privately he explains:

> Four or five years' reading has given me some knowledge of metaphysics and time to clear up endless errors in my understanding of the script. My conviction of the truth of it all has grown also and that makes one clear. (*Letters* 768)

The kinds of revisions (including wholesale elimination of sections and poems) suggest that Yeats was chagrined by the personal and sexual focus of the 1925 edition, forcing him to reshape *A Vision* into a more abstract, monologic, and consciously posed tome, as is clear from his rationale for the second edition:

> Day after day I have sat in my chair turning a symbol over in my mind, exploring all its details, defining and again defining its elements, testing my convictions and those of others by its unity, attempting to substitute particulars for an abstraction like that of algebra. (*VB* 301)

This choice, to depend upon abstractions rather than particulars, changed not only his style of exposition but also the focus of his discourse. "They [necessary abstractions or "stylistic arrangements of experience"] have helped me to hold in a single thought reality and justice" (25). These two elements, reality and justice, mark a significant departure from the first edition and its intent to explain the working opposition between solar and lunar, light and dark. In 1925, Yeats recognized all opposition as the manifestation of gender conflict: "It was as though the first act of being, after creating limit, was to divide itself into male and female, each dying the other's life living the other's death" (*VA* 130). Contrast this emphasis with the 1937 edition: "'Concord' diminishes as that of 'Discord' increases . . . one gyre within the other always. Here the thought of Heraclitus dominates all: 'Dying each other's life, living each other's death'" (*VB* 68). In both cases, Yeats describes opposition, but in *A Vision B* according to the abstract configuration of concord/discord rather than male/female.[2]

With little indication from Yeats himself as to the real cause of this shift, scholars are left to work out their own explanations of the emphasis on philosophical abstraction in the second edition. One of the most helpful is advanced by Virginia Moore, who argues that Yeats reached the pinnacle of his own personal search for spiritual truth during the late 1920s and early 1930s after becoming immersed in Whitehead, Plotinus, Croce, and Gentile. Along the way, the *Vision* text was transformed into a "dramatic apprehension of truth" (370), a startling claim compared to the intent originally defined by W. B. and Georgie Yeats in the Automatic Script, as will become clear. Moore's explanation is supported by Yeats's frustration with his own ignorance of the philosophical basis of the system. Yet I would argue that what is striking about *A Vision B* is not its philosophic fertility but its aesthetic sterility. It generates no new poetic style, no fresh inspiration, no revolutionary insight into the mask.

My intent is not to minimize the possibility of Moore's hypothesis or the impact of whatever new insights Yeats achieved during the final decade of his life. Nor would I discount Moore's conclusion that *A Vision* is "much more than just the perverse or quaint system. . . . it is a philosophy worthy of some consideration" (378). My argument is this: the second edition of *A Vision* is *only* philosophical; the first is mystical, sexual, and aesthetic. *A Vision B,* the version intended for public consumption, is a heavily philosophical work compared to the original, privately distributed first edition. As such, it departs from the original design of the *Vision* material, which was neither developed nor advertised as a philosophic system but as a very personal insight into reality generated by and specific to W. B. and Georgie Yeats. The second edition also marks a shift in idiom. The 1925 edition is fundamentally mystical, symbolic, and metaphoric; above all, it is gendered. In *A Vision A* the two elements—sex and mystical reality—are irrevocably joined, just as they are in the Automatic Script material. It is this sexual dynamic that transforms Yeats's aesthetic and generates radical, double-voiced verse. If Moore is correct and Yeats later considered *A Vision B* as primarily a philosophical (rather than mystical) work, it is equally true that the 1937 edition does not generate a comparable transformation of the mask.

But it is precisely this second, public edition that is better known and more thoroughly used by scholars. For decades Yeats's double-voiced verse seemed tenuously related to the abstractions of the *Vision* material, or, more accurately, Yeats's daimonology appeared untraceable as the root of the feminine mask. Insofar as *A Vision B* has shaped our reading of Yeats's mature verse, it has contributed to a significant misreading of that verse. Thus, my emphasis is not the sections Yeats added to the second edition but the sections he eliminated, not the philosophical accuracy of the revisions but the sexual dynamic of the original. This focus will bring us back to the Script itself. By receding from *A Vision B*, we will unpeel layers of polish and pose to discover a personal, candid, unguarded window into that critical moment of transition when Yeats's daimon is defined as female. As I compare the *Vision A* and *Vision B* texts, I will argue that the first maintains the sexual dynamic as defined in the Automatic Script and thereby unequivocally bears the imprint of the two voices of W. B. and Georgie Yeats in collaboration. It is with this stipulation that I refer in the next several pages to the author of *A Vision A* as "Yeats."

The pivotal shift in the continuum between gendered/dialogic and de-gendered/monologic texts is most evident in the three key passages of the 1925 edition that were systematically eliminated from the 1937 edition. The first case: in a section of *A Vision A* dedicated to "The Daimon, the Sexes, Unity of Being, Natural and Supernatural Unity" in the chapter called "The Great Wheel," Yeats explores the psychological reality of human and daimonic interaction. This section disappears without a trace in the later edition—a substantive loss to his explanation of the daimon, for in it Yeats not only reveals how human and daimon function as complements to each other but also depicts their relational opposition as shearing through the very depths of the psyche. Their bond is intimate and archetypal, conscious and unconscious, and, above all, sexual. Just as important, this embrace explains, even evokes, artistic expression.

Yeats divides the Four Faculties of man into light and dark forces. (Yeats uses the term "man" and subsequently refers to the daimon as "she" throughout this section and elsewhere. I will retain the same terms, in part for simplicity, in part because Yeats clearly envisioned the daimon as "she" because his own was female.) Will and Creative Mind exist in the light (consciousness), while Body of Fate works "through accident, in dark" (*VA* 26), and Mask "swims up from the dark portion of the mind" (27).

In addition to the way these Four Faculties fall into light and dark (or conscious and unconscious), there is another division within each man wherein light and dark are relative. For man is literally of two minds, his own and his daimon's. From the man's point of view, the daimon's mind is of the dark (unknown, secret, and mysterious); to the daimon, the man's mind is of the dark, and her own is of the light. The Four Faculties of man and daimon intersect like complementary oppositions, "the *Will* of the man being the *Mask* of the *Daimon,* the *Creative Mind* of the man being the *Body of Fate* of the *Daimon* and so on" (27). With the Faculties of the man and daimon so intertwined, it is a simple step to speak of them as facing each other "in a perpetual conflict or embrace" (27). This image is especially appropriate because the daimon is "of the opposite sex to that of man," and so "may create a passion like that of sexual love" (27).

After describing the complementarity of man and daimon, Yeats explores the implications that "my daimon is female" (*AS II* 245). It is not the gender of the two that makes the union sexual but the presence of passion: "The relation of man and woman, in so far as it is passionate, reproduces the relation of man and *Daimon*, and becomes an element where man and *Daimon* sport, pursue one another, and do one another good or evil" (*VA* 27). The course of this pursuit can be plotted by a formula: "every man is, in the right of his sex, a wheel, or group of *Four Faculties*, and . . . every woman is, in the right of her sex, a wheel which reverses the masculine wheel" (27). These wheels are gender specific; just as man and daimon are joined in complementary opposition, so also are masculine and feminine faculties. If men and women are "swayed by their sex" (i.e., acting in truly male and female ways), they "interact as man and *Daimon* interact" (27–28).

And what is the nature of that interaction? The daimon controls the dark side of a man's mind. His dreams are the action of her Creative Mind; the movement of his Creative Mind comprises her Body of Fate. If a man desires to live totally in the light and quench the "entire dark of the mind," the daimon will rise up and engulf his light, which to her is utter darkness (28). But when the two allow each other to "flow" and "animate," there is Unity of Being.

Through a man's passion, the daimon's thought becomes luminous. This daimonic/feminine light "creates a very personal form of heroism or of poetry" (28). For this reason, man must ever remain passionate, energized by conflict with his daimon (and with her, his fate), and be content "that he should so struggle with no final conquest" (28). Being compelled to seek out conflict with his opposite moves a man toward his daimon, intertwines their Faculties, and creates the potential for an experience valued above all else— Unity of Being—and its precursive language form, poetry. This same "purely instinctive & cosmic quality in man which seeks completion in its opposite" (*AS I* 65) also compels him first to seek the feminine within him, since the daimon is feminine and comprises his "dark side." It also moves him to seek the female on a purely human level to further complete his conscious and subconscious existence. For these three movements are linked as long as Yeats identifies his daimon with the feminine: man to daimon, man to his own feminine darkness, and man to women. In a world where temporal and after-life experiences are imprinted with opposition, gender is both the primary manifestation of relational opposites and the only hope of harmony: "two complete opposites never unite except in man & woman" (*AS I* 68).

The second case: in the section of the 1925 edition entitled "The Soul in Judgment," Yeats extends this interaction between male and female into his description of the afterlife. Building on the work of Swedenborg, Yeats describes the correlation between the Four Faculties of the human being (Will, Mask, Creative Mind, and Body of Fate) and the four principles of the departed soul (Husk, Passionate Body, Spirit, and Celestial Body) interacting as the soul works its way through six discarnate states to Beatific Vision. Yeats spends a great deal of time describing how men and women must revisit their loves in the Shiftings—obviously a comforting prospect, since this stage would provide him with an opportunity to find compensation and satisfaction in his relationship with Maud Gonne. The process in Shiftings necessitates the interaction of men and women, for the purpose is a moral one—to "exhaust good and evil themselves," which can only be done by separating what truly belongs to the primary or antithetical self "from that which seems to be" (*VA* 230). This purpose is accomplished by entering once again into those relationships wherein the primary and antithetical principles, the sun and moon, masculine and feminine, brought the soul "to a comprehension of good and evil" (230).

The stage of Shiftings brings back the total spectrum of gendered loves, from light loves, "loves without mutual recognition" that involved only passing experiences of pleasure or pain, to strong loves, "love given in ignorance" that encompassed happy or tragic circumstances (231). As the soul grapples with these past loves, it enters into a state of intellectual ecstasy wherein truth turns the "most horrible tragedy" into "a figure in a dance" (231). Men and women are thereby vehicles of each other's advancement into a more integrated, spiritualized state that is signified by Yeats's favorite image of wholeness, the dance itself.[3]

In *A Vision B,* just as he degenders his discussion of man and daimon in temporal life, Yeats eliminates gender from his exploration of discarnate experience. The stage of Shiftings remains a stage of moral purification but is not tied directly to coming to terms with past loves. Yeats focuses instead on the interrelation among the Four Principles during the stages of the soul between incarnations. The daimon's most significant function appears synchronic: "the *Daimon* . . . contains within it, co-existing in its eternal moment, all the events of our life, all that we have known of other lives, or that it can discover within itself" (*VB* 192). The daimon's inherent gendered and sexual identity is all but forgotten. The soul's journey through the afterlife is fragmented into movements of Husk and Passionate Body, Spirit and Celestial Body, rather than *this* man or *this* woman coming to terms with a lover from the life just concluded.

These two sections of *A Vision A,* "The Daimon, the Sexes, Unity of Being, Natural and Supernatural Unity" and "The Soul in Judgment," encompass all of mortal existence—temporal life and discarnate purification—which are projected as gendered experiences. Like the second edition, the original analyzes the junctures of cones, the rise and fall of civilizations, the cycles of personality types. But in *A Vision A* there is a subtext that accounts for all of mortal life on gendered terms, with opposition instilling conflict but guaranteeing the ultimate beatitude of Unity of Being.

There is, of course, one final, glaring omission in the 1937 edition—the elimination of "Desert Geometry or the Gift of Harun Al-Raschid," the poem that opens book 2 in *A Vision A* text. This poetic narrative clearly embarrassed Yeats, who in the 1930s denounced the "unnatural story of an Arabian traveller" about which he was "fool enough to write half a dozen poems" (*VB* 19). Its inclusion in *A Vision A* is of no small consequence. This poem is one of the few texts that describe the role of Georgie Yeats in the scripting process and reveal that period of transition wherein the mask becomes gendered. It deserves detailed discussion because it encapsulates the very purpose of *A Vision A* by plumbing the source and nature of timeless truth sought for centuries by the greatest philosophers.

The poem opens with a deceptively casual setting. Kusta ben Luka (clearly Yeats's representation of himself) has discovered wisdom and seeks a means of preserving it. He sends the precious text (literally the poem, figuratively the *Vision* material) to his fellow roisterer, Abd Al-Rabban, the caliph's treasurer. Instructions dictate that Al-Rabban hide the letter either in the "great book" of Sappho's poetry or in the treatise of Parmenides. Sappho's poetry does not promise adequate shelter, for it is frequented by lovelorn boys who would discard the letter with "indifferent hands" since the contents do not apply directly to human love, and so the manuscript would "fall unnoticed to the floor" (*VA* 121). Parmenides' treatise is doubly safe. The caliph will treasure it for its wisdom (as he must keep Sappho's poetry for its fame), and the letter will not be bothered by boys in love—perhaps by no one except some nameless, learned man in the future.

Buried in this introduction is a clear message: ben Luka's experience will be discounted by those who are interested only in sexual passion (one extreme) or by those who limit true wisdom to abstract philosophy (a second extreme). The content of the letter is superior to Parmenides alone and to Sappho alone, for it brings together sexual love and mystical reality. Preserving the document is no small task, and it is with ironic humor that ben Luka depends upon the treatise of Parmenides for keeping it safe. Recall that Parmenides divided the world into two halves: being and nonbeing. These two mutually exclusive categories form an adamant, unforgiving symmetry. Within the parameters of being, there is no differentiation. Being is one, whole, and perfect, a sphere with no particulars where nothing changes, nothing dies, nothing is generated: "what is is without beginning, indestructible, entire, single, unshakable, endless" (Nahm 93). Ben Luka hopes for such permanency for his own text. That is, within Parmenides' text, which describes a static monolithic condition, he attempts to shelter reproductions of emblems drawn in the shifting desert sand. The "mystery" that ben Luka strives to safeguard needs protection precisely because things change. The sand blows, the Bedouin moves on, memory lapses, stories are lost.[4]

The specific story ben Luka seeks to preserve concerns a gift from Caliph Harun Al-Raschid to ben Luka: a young bride who shares ben Luka's faith in the afterlife and yet has not forsaken this one. "Herself can seem youth's very fountain,/Being all brimmed with life." In marriage, ben Luka discovers a spiritual and physical soul mate, "the best that life can give." He finds not only physical pleasure but companionship in such mysteries "that make a man's soul or a woman's soul/Itself and not some other soul" (*VA* 124). It becomes clear to ben Luka that she was drawn to him because of the faith they share (just as Georgie Hyde-Lees experimented with Yeats in the occult before their marriage), for she had hardly acquainted herself with his garden paths and rooms before she "spread a book upon her knees" and moved her hand over the pages as if they "were some dear cheek," though she held "old dry writing" on "old dry faggots" (125).

Now for the heart of the drama. The girl is possessed by "some great Djinn"—Yeats's figurative description of what happened during the automatic writing sessions. The djinn does not speak through the girl but uses her white finger to trace "emblems on the sand." (This process parallels Yeats's own experience, since the spirits' responses in the first few sessions went unrecorded. Only after several sessions did Georgie take to writing down their messages). Ben Luka thinks of himself as the child and of her as the "learned man" because the girl imparts truths that transcend any book or thought that could be credited to either of them. They are "self-born, high-born, and solitary truths," which when ben Luka's bones are dust "must drive the Arabian host" (125). But wonder of wonders, the girl has no memory of these night visitations. She sweeps the house "in childish ignorance of all that passed" (125).

Seven years have elapsed between those first visitations and ben Luka's narrative, just as seven years had passed between the first writing experiments (1917) and the publication of this poem (1924). Now ben Luka turns to his fellow student Abd Al-Rabban with a problem that has nothing to do with the content of the writings, the message of the voice, or even his responsibility to impart these secret truths. Rather, it is a problem of the heart: "It seems I must buy knowledge with my peace" (126). This gift of spiritual communication has not come without cost. What if the girl realizes that she has been used as a channel and concludes that ben Luka loves her only for "that midnight voice" from beyond the grave, so precious to an aging man? Ben Luka does not want the girl to lose her innocence about her mysterious power or her confidence in his love for her apart from her role as medium. Ben Luka is convinced that, despite whatever first drew the girl to him, she has now cast away "that first unnatural interest in my books." "It seems enough that I am there," he observes (126). In the same way, he does not love her "only for that voice," but he fears that he might lose her trusting love, "voice and all" (126). It appears an uneven bargain: her love is purified of occult attachments while his remains grounded in both the girl and her voice. Yet for ben Luka, the voice is steeped in the girl's personal and physical identity: "The voice has drawn/A quality of wisdom from her love's/Particular quality," as well as from "the bitter-sweetness of her youth" (126, 127). Indeed, all the "signs and shapes" in the sand,

> All those abstractions that you fancied were
> From the great Treatise of Parmenides;
> All, all those gyres and cubes and midnight things
> Are but a new expression of her body. (126)

For this channeling of "midnight voices" to take place, the girl's love, youth, passion, innocence, and confidence must remain intact. This is one of the most significant ramifications of Yeats's sexual dynamic. It isn't simply that the spirits need a human body to act out their message. The highest truths and deepest mysteries of reason and faith are peculiar to this unique girl, and, just as important, they are contained in and expressed through her body—not her soul but her body. All the books guarded in the caliph's treasure house are worth nothing compared to her body, the vessel containing a wisdom more lofty than any book could express. Neither the caliph's perception of a body ripe for love in the proper season nor ben Luka's perception of a body aging past love's season does justice to the truth.

Thus, ben Luka's understanding of the "utmost mystery" is not of abstract philosophical wisdom but of the wisdom of the female body: "A woman's beauty is a storm-tossed banner;/Under it wisdom stands" (127). Body is again the focus, in this case not the individuated body of his lover but the female body in general or beauty distilled from every woman. Ben Luka likens the beauty of the female body to the banners in the caliph's treasure house because its beauty contains wisdom beyond Parmenides himself. Instead of gathering dust, the banners of beauty are fully arrayed on the battlefield of life. There, beauty channels another voice—ben Luka "can hear the armed man speak" (127). The "armed man" is wisdom. The poet ben Luka becomes a kind of warrior, equipped to wage battle much like the caliph who carries "the ringed mail upon [his] back" (123). While the language may seem to enhance his personal sense of importance and power, ben Luka asserts a more reflective purpose to his story. To all chroniclers of the official history of the caliph's reign, he recommends inclusion of this story: "To show how violent great hearts can lose/Their bitterness and find the honeycomb" (122). The honeyed lesson bestowed upon ben Luka (and Yeats) includes both philosophic and sexual wisdom, the wisdom of the mind via the wisdom of the body.

The signs traced in the drifting sand cannot be preserved. Even the letter remains mysterious and unknown. What prevails, what is truly subject to Parmenides' law, is the poem itself, sheltered in the treatise of Parmenides, preserved and unchanging. But Yeats is not suggesting that ben Luka's poem (his "body" of text) transcends the wisdom embodied in the young girl. Words alone cannot last. The girl's voice fades as the sun rises. Her words are lost like "those emblems on the sand" (126). The poem itself is composed of transitory words and will survive only in disuse. To emphasize his point, Yeats structures the poem so that it "circles" around, beginning and ending with mention of Parmenides. How ironic that Yeats would refute Parmenides and use the great philosopher's own name in doing so. The truths revealed in the night through the unknowing mouth of the girl may fall into "terrible implacable straight lines" (125), but human actions, human speech, even human poetry can only circle around the terrible truth, as if approximating its message.

What is unchanging is the law of change itself, those endless gyres of civilization and reincarnations of the human self. The poem's context helps formulate this final interpretation. "The Gift of Harun Al-Raschid" serves as an introductory piece to book 2 of *Vision A:* "The Geometrical Foundation of the Wheel." This book details the movement of the gyres and cones and defines the Four Faculties and Four Principles of the human person, as I have noted. According to the Four Principles, the body is more than the physical embodiment of a soul in any given incarnation. What we term body, meaning physical body, Yeats calls the Husk, one of three manifestations of body associated with a person. There are also the Passionate Body (PB) and the Celestial Body (CB), also called spiritual or immortal (*AS I* 313). The Husk is connected to a specific ego and is dissolved soon after death. The Passionate Body (equated to "sex") (414) can outlive the physical body by centuries (313). The Celestial Body is the "founder & fashioner of the spirit" (499). Thus, to interpret the wisdom of the body as ephemeral and fleeting is a mistake, according to Yeats's system. A person's "body" (in one of three forms) endures and is continually rejuvenated through the Great Wheel.

In the poem, then, the girl's body—this temporal body, this daily manifestation of beauty—will pass away. But her unique identity, what "makes a man's soul or a woman's soul/Itself and not some other soul" (*VA* 124), will always have a body in this temporal existence, in the purification process after death, and in the next incarnation. Body endures when words blow away like desert sand. Each night visitation (like each successive life) is but a "new expression of her body" (126). Thus, the girl's wisdom consists of "truths without father" (125), outliving both ben Luka and (we must add) Yeats himself.

The presence of "The Gift of Harun Al-Raschid" in *A Vision A* both complements and enlarges the gendered nature of the entire symbol system. The poem is more than a romantic/autobiographical account of the sexual and mystical adventures of a young girl (Georgie Yeats) and an aged courtier (W. B. Yeats). It encapsulates the very purpose of *A Vision A* by posing the question: what is the source and nature of timeless truth sought for centuries by the greatest philosophers? The poem narrates ben Luka's insight, one discovered with the help of his new bride: the highest truths and deepest mysteries of reason and faith are contained in and expressed through the lover's body—not her soul or her mind but her body. Wisdom of the body (in this case, the female body) transcends mere book wisdom because it neither vanishes like words traced in the sand nor petrifies from neglect like the manuscripts of Parmenides. Through this poem, Yeats celebrates the female body and sexual relations as the means of accessing wisdom. That is, he asserts the central role of sexual experience and, moreover, lauds the wisdom of beauty and the female body above philosophic abstractions, an ironic insight considering his later editorial changes.

There are, of course, numerous minor differences distinguishing the first and second editions. But the shift in content—sexual to philosophical—is obvious as we retrace the continuum to the source. The differences between *A Vision A* and the Automatic Script are startling as well, primarily in form (moving from monologic to dialogic) and, to a lesser degree, in content, as the automatic writing material includes the personal content that underpins the sexual dynamic. The differences between the first *Vision* text and the Automatic Script are caused in part by the intimate nature of the personal references in the Script, in part by the artistic necessity of condensing and reshaping major blocks of information from this mammoth amount of inconsistent material, some already labeled bogus by the Yeatses. It is a fair generalization that in *A Vision A* Yeats retained descriptions of daimonic activity but deleted himself and his wife as the human actors and sexual agents in the drama.

Before examining the continuity of content (i.e., the sexual dynamic), I will first address the shift in form, from exposition in *A Vision A* to dialogue in the Automatic Script. My purpose is not to analyze the automatic writing process itself but to uncover the active and formative role of Georgie Yeats. For years scholars had only hints of the role Georgie Yeats played in the automatic writing that generated the text of *A Vision*. Our understanding was limited to the cryptic account W. B. Yeats offered to open *A Vision B:* "my wife surprised me by attempting automatic writing" (8). But her role is portrayed as passive medium (similar, we must note, to the version of spirit visitations in "The Gift of Harun Al-Raschid"):

> My wife's interests are musical, literary, practical, she seldom comments upon what I dictate except upon the turn of a phrase; she can no more correct it than she could her automatic script at a time when a slight error brought her new fatigue. (21)

Not until the publication in 1987 of George Mills Harper's two-volume history of the automatic writing experiments did it become clear how important and active was Georgie Yeats's role in the scripting sessions. With the public release of the complete Automatic Script, Dream Notebooks, and Card File in 1992, the full mystery is revealed behind Yeats's veiled confession: "the whole system is the creation of my wife's Daimon and of mine" (22). What the full Automatic Script text reveals is not only the origins of gendered daimonology but also its *cause*—not a newly discovered text from Berkeley or Hegel, not a new understanding of the Upanishads, but the needs and designs of the newlywed Georgie Yeats.

Georgie Yeats initiated the automatic writing sessions to distract her brooding husband during their honeymoon. Still filled with longings for Maud Gonne, guilty about his break with Iseult, her daughter, and uncertain about his marriage, Yeats was in sore need of assurance that he had chosen the right woman and taken the correct course. On 24 October 1917, Georgie Yeats initiated a series of communication sessions between her husband and spirit "controls" and "guides."[5] In a letter to Olivia Shakespear, Yeats relates the initial incident.

> Two days ago I was in great gloom, (of which I hope, and believe, George knew nothing). I was saying to myself 'I have betrayed three people,' then I thought 'I have lived all through this before.' Then George spoke of the sensation of having lived through something before (she knew nothing of my thought). Then she said she felt that something was to be written through her. She got a piece of paper, and talking to me all the while so that her thoughts would not affect what she wrote, wrote these words (which she did not understand) 'with the bird' (Iseult) 'all is well at heart. Your action was right for both but in London you mistook its meaning.' I had begun to believe just before my marriage that I had acted, not as I thought more for Iseult's sake than for my own, but because my mind was unhinged by strain. The strange thing was that within half an hour after writing of this message . . . I was very happy. From being more miserable than I ever remember being since Maud Gonne's marriage I became extremely happy. That sense of happiness has lasted ever since. (*Letters* 633)

The scripting sessions ended on 4 June 1921, with Georgie Yeats acting initially as "medium" and later as "interpreter" between Yeats and the spirits, who took turns leading the poet through various phases of understanding about the workings of the solar/lunar symbol system and the reality that system expresses: free will, fate and destiny, life after death, and the rise and fall of civilizations.

The Automatic Script is an extraordinary dialogue involving two people, William Butler and Georgie Yeats, as joint authors in whose text it is impossible to distinguish between the finger and the clay. As Margaret Mills Harper notes, neither the subsequent vision of history nor the corresponding insight into individual personalities disclosed in *A Vision* can be understood as wholly W. B. Yeats's own. Georgie Yeats rejected all ties to authorship during her life. For personal and professional reasons, her presence is muted and masked throughout the Script—muted, yet so undeniable that Harper labels the material "unremittingly gender-coded" in purpose, content, and expression to such an extent that the text precludes labels such as "dominant" and "subordinate" writer (36–37).

As obvious as these observations seem when examining the Script material, they run counter to established tenets of *Vision* scholarship. For example, Richard Ellmann insists that despite Georgie Yeats's participation, "the Yeatsian system is . . . not merely a pot-pourri like Theosophy." Although he credits "the influence of the unconscious mind of Mrs. Yeats in building up images" to be "almost as important" as W. B. Yeats's efforts to unify "the fragmentary theoretical revelations," Ellmann concludes that "in the end everything is stamped with *his* personality and brought into line with *his* work" (emphasis added) (Ellmann, *Masks* 230, 231).

Not so. It is impossible here to exhaust the evidence of Georgie Yeats's influence in the full text of the Automatic Script, but her critical role is evident on three levels: in shaping the content of the solar/lunar symbol system, in defining the format, schedule, and topics of individual writing sessions, and, most importantly, in bringing to light the complex designs of the daimon in human life.

The dialogue format of the automatic writing sessions put the burden of information upon Georgie Yeats rather than her husband. As respondent, she not only articulated the major contraries of the system (sun and moon, primary and antithetical, space and time), but she also labored with him through sketches and exploratory commentary to define the workings of these contraries. She becomes exasperated with her husband's occasional density: "You must get this clear," she scolds him during a discussion of primary and antithetical phases (*AS I* 140). They select and discard a series of possibilities to serve as metaphors for the system: "funnel," "shuttle spiral," "spindle," "hourglass," "cycle cone." She eventually warns her husband against his obsession to define the system too precisely: "your mechanics destroy the image" (396). Such metaphors are helpful only in describing rather than defining the system, she insists; the system itself is only a metaphor for the workings of reality. Its complexities often confused them, but Georgie Yeats advises: "use it creatively not as exposition" (399).

It is Georgie Yeats who defines the Four Faculties and identifies their manifestations according to twenty-eight Phases. See, for example, her detailed list of the Phases generated on 23 November 1917, less than one month after their marriage (115–16). It is Georgie rather than W. B. Yeats who identifies major historical and literary figures according to phasal type; for example, "Where do you put Keats," the poet asks. "Keats at 12," is his wife's reply (146). When he cannot keep the phases and types straight, she chides her husband: "What about your formula—you are very forgetful" (152). Such command of content is apparent through the entire script corpus, as evident in the dialogue of 23 December 1920—one of the final automatic writing sessions—when Georgie Yeats outlines the phasal manifestations of Creative Genius and Personality [Body] of Fate (*AS II* 522).

The second level of influence—the actual format and schedule of the writing sessions—reveals the amount of control Georgie Yeats exerted. W. B.'s energy and obsessive interest were all-consuming, and his wife soon set limits to the number and duration of the sessions. As early as November 1917, she advises: "The fatigue is the safeguard against excess" (*AS I* 64). At times, the fatigue made work impossible: "you are both too flat to go on," the spirits complain; "flat is the word" (69). At other times, Georgie Yeats limited the number of questions: "I will answer 3 questions now—no more till tomorrow" (110) or simply begged off: "I am sorry—I am too tired" (195; see also *AS II* 100).[6] She eventually scheduled set times ("Tomorrow I want to come at 5:30") (*AS I* 321) and refused daily communication ("I do not wish to write for 3 days") (343). A year into the writing sessions, she insists: "script is bad for medium especially if she refuses to rest" (*AS II* 124). Sometimes her needs were simple: "Let medium take a hot bath then write" (270). When the poet asks what kind of fatigue his wife should avoid, the answer is "mental." "Sexually?" he wonders. "That is part of mental fatigue," comes the response, but Georgie Yeats refuses to limit sexual activity: "only when otherwise tired" (*AS I* 209). More significant is her vigilance to assure that her husband did not neglect his marital duty. In the dialogue of 31 July 1919, she warns him that infrequency might lead to "declining power." Her husband observes: "I have been under the impression that we have been too irregular lately." The reply: "*Yes certainly*" (emphasis in original). But Georgie Yeats hastens to assure him: "your power will always be amply sufficient" (*AS II* 349). In the closing days of the writing sessions, she describes the toll of the experiment upon the medium: "used up—nothing else—intellectually tired" (499).

Georgie Yeats learned to look after not only her own needs but her husband's as well. She exhibits concern for his health: "you will be better now [if] you drink more & you should take more exercise . . . this is to the man not the medium" (*AS I* 80). She urges him to simplify his life and limit public appearances (208) and insists on a diversified schedule of writing poetry, reading, contacting the spirits, codifying previous script material, and exercising (159, 443; *AS II* 123). Occasionally Georgie Yeats even resorts to threats: "For every public speech or lecture you give after tomorrow during the next 6 months I shall stop script one month" (*AS II* 222). Frequently she refuses to dialogue and instead directs him to his art: "do no writing on it [the system] unless poems" (117; also 387: "you *must* write poetry").

Even more notable is Georgie Yeats's control of the protocol and subject matter of the dialogues. She invariably insists on secrecy, displaying reluctance to engage in dialogue if there is a visitor in the house and refusing to let anyone else participate in their sessions: *"I said alone was better"* (49, 476; *AS I* 242). Within a month of their marriage, she warns her husband: "Do not talk [to] psychics too much—you draw strangers in I do not like" (*AS II* 97; *AS I* 175). The reasons for secrecy are explained on 4 March 1918: "because [if] you speak to unbelievers you destroy our help . . . I do not *wish* the spirit source revealed" (*AS I* 369). Clearly there are two separate concerns expressed here. As George Mills Harper points out, W. B. Yeats was in continual correspondence with friends (John Quinn and Lady Gregory, for instance) who did not approve of such experimentation, a fact Georgie Yeats knew well (13). Secrecy allowed her to sustain the process without undue conflict and interference. Indeed, the more exclusive the dialogues, the more Georgie Yeats was assured of her husband's undivided attention and dedication to his new relationship. As the spirits insisted, the success of the entire enterprise depended "on the perfection of the psychic link" between husband and wife (311). As the subject matter of the dialogues became more personal, the spirits were increasingly adamant: "personal secrecy *always*" (378; also 346 and 369).

An outsider, particularly an unbeliever, might also question the authenticity of the experiments. Throughout the dialogues, W. B. Yeats sought to verify the reliability of his spirit guides. His wife was just as eager to make no outlandish claims about the Script's universal application or objective validity. Several months into their sessions, W. B. Yeats asked the spirits about the source of their knowledge (whether to placate his doubts about the entire process or to validate the universality of the information). The answer makes it clear that the solar/lunar system does not exist apart from himself and his wife:

> it is developed and created by us & by you two or you three now from a preexisting psychology—all the bones are *in* the world—we only select and our selection is subordinate to *you both*—therefore *we* are dependent on you & you influence our ability to develop & create by every small detail of your joint life. (*AS II* 240)

For W. B. Yeats, this explanation clarified why other philosophers and poets had not happened upon the same answers in their search for ultimate truth. But it was also a means by which Georgie Yeats could emphasize the distinct properties of their occult discoveries. The content of the Script could not be generated in the same way with two different individuals (notably, W. B. and any other woman).

The channeling process itself is only loosely defined: automatic images "must have been part of some personal experience though now quite altered by the automatic faculty" (39). But beyond that, Georgie Yeats has little to explain her gift except to say that "the subconscious should be emptied absolutely—that is what the medium wants badly" (*AS I* 81). She had few words of praise about her capacity as interpreter for the spirits, who describe her as "more a seer than a philosopher." But they assure the poet: "you may get much from her more than you will appreciate" (327).

Georgie Yeats did not shy away from holding her husband accountable for the success or failure of their psychic link. She could be gentle, as in this comment during a discussion of Shiftings: "Wait a little longer for medium—great difficulty—your mind is away" (148). Her constant command to reflect on the dialogue from the previous evening and to codify material before pushing further into the system stems in part from her fear that her husband was assuming a passive role: "you are not critical enough of this script" (415). She complains of his hurry to acquire information, his meandering questions, his fixation on the personal rather than the archetypal, his lack of preparation for sessions, and his lapses in understanding: "do please think" (*AS II* 251). At other times, she becomes completely exasperated with him. When W. B. asks about the possibility of lies being generated through automatic writing, there comes this response: "Perfectly fruitless and very useless—I am upset by this stupid subject" (*AS I* 238). Yet Georgie Yeats always insisted on their psychic partnership, which sometimes demanded that he acquiesce to her lead: "Take up the line she offers—be subservient to that opening" (328). And she advises him with words that guarantee not only a successful script but a happy marriage: "The more you keep this medium emotionally and intellectually happy the more will script be possible now" (*AS II* 119).

In his general introduction to the Automatic Script, George Mills Harper ruminates: "George's bewildering ingenuity was remarkable" (*AS I* 34). We will never know the extent to which Georgie Yeats manipulated her husband's interest in the occult or misled him in this process. Nor can we be sure of W. B. Yeats's motives in keeping hidden his wife's formative role in the *Vision* system, her insistence on secrecy notwithstanding. At some point, he must have taken the words of the spirits literally: "You can say it is a sequence & your original thought—that is to a degree true" (123). But it is also to a great degree untrue. As Margaret Mills Harper indicates, the Automatic Script reveals that the experiments

> were being weaned away from the model of a male source of power
> and female receptivity with which they began: Yeats asking ques-

tions, the spirits answering, and Georgie passively relaying information between them, her own words effaced. No longer even in pro-
cedural details would she be an empty vessel for a male text, a female body bearing the offspring of male minds. (47)

Without question, the Automatic Script was actively shaped by two individuals, sometimes more directly by Georgie Yeats than by her husband. But
my point is not whether one or the other controlled the writing experiment
but that both parties manipulated the direction of inquiry and molded the
gist of the revelations. The Script is a true dialogue of two voices, voices that
reflect W. B. Yeats's rapacious appetite for knowledge and assurance as well
as reveal the ever-present personality of Georgie Yeats—intelligent, imaginative, uncertain, even irascible when necessary.

But there is another, more dominant design to the Automatic Script that
I believe is not an outgrowth of Georgie Yeats's subconscious or her capacity as medium to generate automatic images. This design comprises a critical subtext that makes Margaret Mills Harper's description of the Script as
"gender-coded" particularly apt (36–37); it is embedded in the personal material woven through nearly every dialogue wherein the poet attempts to
sort out his sexual alliances. Out of this exploration comes a new, revolutionary understanding of the daimon in human life. Georgie Yeats takes the
leading role in this subtext and therefore in the eventual reconfiguration of
her husband's daimonology and theory of the mask.

Personal issues pervade the Automatic Script. They serve the purpose of W.
B. Yeats, who wanted to interrogate spirit guides about universal and personal
matters of historical and spiritual significance, and of Georgie Yeats, who was
determined to help shape her husband's understanding of reality, particularly
his stormy history with Maud Gonne. The amount of text in the Automatic
Script dedicated to unraveling the psychological, mystical, and sexual course
of W. B. Yeats's life is formidable, and for good reason. On the one hand,
there was W. B.'s preoccupation with Maud Gonne: "Why had I so wild a passion of M[aud] G[onne]?" he queried the spirits on 4 January 1918 (*AS I*
200).[7] In part, the subsequent material dedicated to understanding Initiatory
and Critical Moments, as well as efforts to define the nature and actions of daimons, is rooted in this initial inquiry into the passions in the poet's personal
life. But Yeats's obsession with Maud Gonne does not mean that *his* gender
imprint dominates the content and scope of the dialogues. As the Script un-
folds, it is clear that Georgie Yeats is leading him, not merely placating him.

Obviously, it was in Georgie Yeats's best interest to affirm the validity of
their legal marriage, since it was not the first marriage of W. B. Yeats's life:
he had committed himself to Gonne in a spiritual union years before. Gonne
describes the nature of this union as revealed to her in a dream (July 1908):
"We melted into one another till we formed only *one being, a being greater
than ourselves,* who felt all & knew all with double intensity . . . material

union is but a pale shadow compared to it" (*Gonne-Yeats Letters* 257). However, in the automatic writing process, the guides reveal that his union with
Georgie Hyde-Lees is unique and proper precisely because it is *sexual*. Thus,
rather than minimize her husband's brooding inquiries into his previous relationships, Georgie Yeats fuels his interest by exploring both the role of
those relationships in his life and their contrast to his present marriage, a
marriage that plays into the hands of a spiritual and sexual design not of the
poet's making.

There are literally hundreds of pages (particularly in volume 2) that explore
W. B. Yeats's sexual experiences in terms of Initiatory and Critical Moments,
either directly in reference to Maud Gonne or masked in the historical exploration of the life of Anne Hyde. Adjacent to this interchange runs another dialogue about the importance of sexual relations—between man and daimon,
man and sweetheart—in both this life and subsequent incarnations.

These two dialogues converge into what is clearly a strategic focus of the
Automatic Script, a focus that builds upon and fuels the poet's long-standing interest in "universal masculine & feminine." Early on in the writing sessions, W. B. Yeats sought that primordial knowledge of the origins of male
and female. On 12 January 1918, he asks: "Can you tell me what makes a
soul incarnate as a man or woman?" The guide refused to answer (*AS I*
250). A casual question at the outset, perhaps, but one that assumes in-
creasing importance as sexuality itself attains dominance in the dialogue and
discussion of the origins of sex is postponed. And so the poet persisted. On
19 January W. B. Yeats asks: "Can you go into what decides sex." The guide
replies: "No/Much further on" (271). On 24 January: "Has time come to
go into riches & poverty and determination of sex?" The reply: "Sex much
later[—]also other questions" (283). Finally, on 6 February, "Rose" is sent
for a special purpose: to describe the origin of sex (338). It is more than a
year later when Georgie Yeats ceases to postpone the critical discussion.
Buried in a series of sessions dedicated to unraveling the history of Initiatory
and Critical Moments (events directly related to Gonne) are a simple question and its even simpler answer (6 April 1919):

> Is daimon of opposite sex to ego.
> Yes. (*AS II* 235)

The couple then explores the ramifications of the fact that the husband's
daimon is female. The guides reveal that W. B. Yeats's female daimon collects knowledge differently than does his wife's male daimon. While his daimon collects ideas from "*the thought of*," hers collects ideas from the thinker
(246). That is, daimons operate in gender-specific ways: the daimon united
to the male ego works in abstractions; the daimon of a female ego, in personalities. But the importance of daimonic sexuality goes much deeper than

gender-specific modes of operation. The dialogues of 1919, when sexuality assumed center stage, reveal that a man's daimon uses all the faculties (senses) of the body, but particularly the sixth sense, which is sexual (243). Through the sixth sense, the daimon accesses the *Anima Mundi* and the Personal *Anima Mundi* (244). In addition, W. B. Yeats's daimon collects ideas from Georgie Yeats's (and vice versa) in ordinary sex relations "in accordance with the unity & harmony of the moment" (249). The connection of daimon to sexuality is absolute: "Have we no consciousness of daimon apart from sex?" "None," the guide replies (259).

While men and women become conscious of the daimon in sexual relations, their lives are manipulated by the daimon during what Yeats calls Initiatory and Critical Moments. Daimons use these moments for their own purposes, with Initiatory Moments functioning as overtures (producing changes in the mind, heart, and will) leading up to the Critical Moments when a man's life or a woman's life is significantly changed through events (213). During Initiatory Moments the daimon shocks the self, "luring" it through a sequence of events from inaction and abstract dreaming to objective emotion and action (*AS III* 194). The lure to a man is always a woman (194), for the daimon must entice another daimon to itself in order to be sexually activated. That is, because daimons have no senses of their own, they can be sexual with other daimons only through contact with their human hosts (*AS II* 245). In this way, the sexual life (the sequence of Initiatory Moments before a Critical Moment) "is a perpetual drama, which has for its real theme the nature of the unborn child, for whom the daimons have laid their plans" (*AS III* 115). Through the union of Yeats's daimon with his wife's, their daughter, Anne, is conceived (*AS II* 255). Thus, the drama of temporal life is composed of sexual experiences involving man, woman, and daimon(s). Such experiences are not confined to temporal existence. If a prior sexual relationship is not resolved and if an attraction between a man and woman persists even to the moment of death, it will continue into their next lives (454).

These revelations could only have fueled the poet's interest in human sexual relations, surpassing as they do the power of the poet's own imagination to "divine an analogy" between a man's daimon and his sweetheart (*Myth* 336). The advancement in daimonology builds upon both the analogy Yeats formulated in *Per Amica Silentia Lunae* and his personal and philosophical interests in the origins of sex that are obvious even at the outset of the automatic writing sessions. More importantly, while Maud Gonne speaks of "that lovely world which we so seldom see but that must be for some future time" (*Gonne-Yeats Letters* 62), Georgie Yeats is creating with W. B. Yeats a metaphysical system that emphasizes the here and now and opens up man's spiritual consciousness through sexuality. Indeed, new wisdom is generated only when there is an "equal balance" of contraries (instinct and emotion, male and female), and there is "equal balance in sexual intercourse" (*AS II* 289). Occult and personal desires are fulfilled simultaneously. The daimon cannot function outside of the sexual faculty, performs most fully in the act of sexual intercourse (is "fed," as the guides express it) (*AS II* 282), and is recognized only in sexual relations.

Even this abbreviated analysis of the Automatic Script reveals the central position of Yeats's sexual dynamic—the connection between sexuality and mystical reality—in the solar/lunar system and in the context of its articulation. What is equally unmistakable is that the scripting process itself—W. B. Yeats's dependence on and trust in his wife's capacity to channel wisdom from beyond—-enacts the mystical dimension of his female daimon instructing him and intervening in his life. Whether it be his wife or his daimon, this male poet is open to the influence and wisdom of the feminine.

The three stages of *Vision* material, the Automatic Script, *A Vision A,* and *A Vision B,* make several conclusions clear. For one, the crucial shift in daimonology occurs in the context of what plainly is Georgie Yeats's effort to strengthen her new marriage. Given her husband's appetite for spiritualism, his dejection about Iseult Gonne, and his loyalty to his spiritual union with Maud Gonne, Georgie Yeats set out to convince him that the spirit world was infusing *their* relationship, not only in the scripting sessions but also in their marriage bed. Second, the voice of Georgie Yeats disappears from the 1937 edition. By degendering the second edition, W. B. Yeats makes his lone authorial presence dominate the text, while his interpreter/collaborator becomes a transparent shadow, her imprint effaced and her voice silenced. No wonder "The Gift of Harun Al-Raschid" had to go. And third, with the presence of Georgie Yeats eliminated, the sexual dynamic is severely muted, and as a consequence, scholarly readings of subsequent poetry to a large extent have overlooked the pivotal place of Yeats's gendered daimonology and "the poetry it seems to have made possible" (*VA* xii). None of the later verses have been fully read with the premise that a gendered daimon has helped produce them through Yeats's sexual life.

But it should be. Later chapters deal with works written during and after his apparent retrenchment of his conception of the daimon in *A Vision B.* These chapters will show that, while Yeats elected to mute the sexual dynamic in his mystical exposition, it is still the controlling dynamic in plays *(The Death of Cuchulain)* and in poetry (the sequences "A Man Young and Old," "A Woman Young and Old," and "Crazy Jane"). Whatever the reasons for his more philosophical and less gendered discussion of the daimon, Yeats does not forsake the sexual dynamic in his work. Thus, *A Vision B* is not the penultimate expression of Yeats's metaphysics, nor is it a generative force in his aesthetic effort. It is only the third stage in a continuum comprised of gendered exposition of mystical reality.

The Automatic Script does more than contribute to our understanding of a major poet's private interest in daimonology. Through dialogic exploration it articulates a major event in Yeats's artistic life—the convergence of spiritualism and gender, or, as he would later express it, of the Beatific Vision and sexual love (xii). The Automatic Script freezes in text a formative period in the life of the poet: newly married, examining his past, demanding answers beyond temporal authority, redefining his identity on sexual and textual levels as he collaborates with his wife.

In fact, "a reconfiguration of the concept of identity itself" (M. Harper 36) in the automatic writing experiments works as an analogy for the mask as Yeats conceived it after 1917. The dialogic voice in the Script models the double-voice of the ensuing masks, with verse now an arena wherein the double-voice of the universal masculine and feminine is released. And we must add, reading the mask generated by this sexual dynamic is an insistence upon the joining of male and female in the poetic process. Just as Georgie Yeats helped to free her husband from doubts about his marriage, the female daimon frees him from a monologic poetics, or as Yeats came to appreciate: "The daimon drives us from the self made prison" (AS III 194).

CHAPTER 3

THE FEMININE AND THE HEROIC

"We need not of course believe with him—in his
elaborate angelology, for instance, or in his theory of
a transcendental and divine intersexual love in
heaven—but I can see no reason why the informed
reader should be unsympathetic."
F. A. C. Wilson, *W. B. Yeats and Tradition* (25)

"My 'private philosophy' is there but there must be
no sign of it. . . . It guides me to certain conclusions
and gives me precision but I do not write it."
W. B. Yeats, *Letters* (918)

W. B. Yeats began drafting the third play of his Cuchulain cycle, *The Only
Jealousy of Emer,* on 3 November 1917—less than a month after his marriage
to Georgie Hyde-Lees and only days after her initiation of the automatic
writing experiment. Because *Emer* literally grew with the Automatic Script,
there is no better candidate to test the immediate and substantive impact of
Yeats's evolving daimonology upon his art. With this chapter, I will argue
that *Emer* is Yeats's first attempt at enacting his sexual dynamic—the intimate
connection between the mystical life and sexual relations. While this initial effort is limited in its success, the full scope of the sexual dynamic can be seen

in *Emer's* sequel, *The Death of Cuchulain,* written nearly twenty years later. Not only is the sexual dynamic immediately infused into Yeats's work with *Emer,* but it is also sustained and explored to the very end of his life.

Emer is one of the very few aesthetic works that appear as a subject in the Script itself. Yeats asked his spirit guides to clarify the symbolic significance of characters and events, and even asked midstream how the play might develop (*AS I* 91). What is perhaps most striking about the *Emer* dialogues of the Script is Yeats's personal investment in the Cuchulain figure. Rather than relating to Cuchulain as his anti-self—the contemplative poet at odds with the man of action—Yeats identified with Cuchulain as his alter ego: "Do my own sins exactly correspond to those of C[uchulain]," he asks the spirits. "Given different conditions," they respond (167). Yeats understood the journey of Cuchulain's soul to be his own and composed *Emer* with that connection in mind.

Interpreting *Emer* according to the sexual dynamic makes the key to the play evident. That key is the intersexual relations between Cuchulain and the female characters. But I would make a more ambitious claim: the same key helps solve the riddles hitherto unresolved about the entire Cuchulain cycle. First, there is the riddle of dramatic style. The first play of the cycle, *On Baile's Strand* (1904), requires a stage full of characters with vivid, colorful backdrops and garish costumes designed to suggest the heroic age. The final play, *The Death of Cuchulain* (1938), consists of a handful of characters on "a bare stage of any period" with props consisting of a dark cloth that can signify anything—a waterless, enchanted well or the head of a dead hero. Richard Londraville maintains that such different styles detract from the unity of the cycle (169). Along with the spartan setting comes sparse and eclectic dialogue, which in the crucial scene between Cuchulain and his assassin in *Death* makes communication "inadequate," according to F. A. C. Wilson (*Tradition* 193). What is the rationale for such simplicity, and does it undermine Yeats's dramatic impact?

The obvious response leads to another riddle, that in mid-cycle Yeats adopted the Noh form of drama in the third play, *At the Hawk's Well* (1916).[1] Londraville believes that this decision changed his drama "absolutely" after 1916. But he also concedes that *Hawk* is the purest example and that perhaps Yeats did not understand the Noh well enough to maintain it consistently (171–72). Okifumi Komesu argues that even *Hawk* is a failure as a Noh drama because "Yeats's play depends for its effect on the conflict that develops between characters" (104). Conflict creates plot, and plot undermines the stylized dramatization of universal emotion at the core of the Noh ritual. Why would conflict remain so important to Yeats that he sabotaged his efforts to duplicate the Noh?

Again, the obvious answer poses yet another riddle. Yeats is working within the heroic tradition. Cuchulain is a man of action: a leader of men, a lover of women, and a gallant warrior. The cycle opens with the hero at the height of his power at the age of forty, about to make the tragic mistake of his life (the murder of his own son), going head-to-head with King Conchubar. Yeats describes these two men as "those combatants who turn the wheel of life" (noted in Wilson, *Tradition* 39). Following Yeats's lead, critics have generally assumed that Conchubar and Cuchulain form the primary antinomial pair (Bornstein), interpreting them as complementary sides of Yeats's own personality (Skene), and seeing in their conflict the tension between materialism and imagination (Friedman). The second play, *The Green Helmet* (1908), pits the cunning and courage of Cuchulain against the Red Man, who comes to claim his due. But at this point in the cycle, Yeats appears to reverse course. In the next three plays, he discards all representations of physical courage or of armed and cunning males poised for battle. He also moves out of the temporal order. In *Hawk,* Cuchulain's arch foe is Fand, witch of the Sidhe. In *Emer,* Fand is transmuted into a discarnate spirit from the otherworld. And in *Death,* Cuchulain is set upon by the two witches, Morrigu and Maeve. Why this evolution from romantic heroism to esoteric symbolism?

The answer to all these riddles is the same: the gradual gendering of conflict through the course of these five plays. With each play, Yeats progressed to a deeper understanding of real drama, the sort of interior or underplayed action that reveals Cuchulain's heroism as well as his wrongdoing. In *Emer,* Yeats finally achieves the necessary frame for such drama: Cuchulain's relationships with females. In *Baile* and *Green,* Cuchulain engages in a clear adversarial relationship with female characters, although these conflicts appear secondary to more dramatic action. The remaining three plays depict Cuchulain in a series of encounters with female characters, encounters conspicuously devoid of epic deeds. In *Hawk,* he is defeated by Fand; in *Emer,* he is nearly lost to Fand but is rescued by Emer. In *Death,* Cuchulain is confronted and defeated by a host of enemies—all female.

In brief, I believe that Yeats's sense of epic heroism is transformed into prolonged moments of stasis and sexual tension as the poet consciously explores masculine and feminine relations. To support this argument, I will briefly comment on the first three plays, with particular emphasis on the women who act as foils to Cuchulain's character; then I will detail the critical shift in *Emer* and *Death,* when Yeats amplifies gender conflict to enact the convergence of mystical and sexual reality.

The Cuchulain cycle of plays reveals a playwright searching for the explanation to his own life via his hero's mythic past. How conscious Yeats was of this transference before the automatic writing experiment is not clear. But the key he was seeking does not directly pertain to the nature of heroism or to the anatomy of courage. It has more to do with gender relations, a concern of paramount importance since "the troubling" of his life began with his meeting Maud Gonne (*Memoirs* 40). In the same year that Gonne married John MacBride, Yeats wrote *Baile*. Through the relationship between Cuchulain and Aoife, the great warrior queen, Yeats affirms what in 1904 was one of the foundational tenets of his worldview: that love and war go hand in hand and that love brings misfortune (*Myth* 30).

The true oppositional pair in *Baile* are not Cuchulain and Conchubar, I would contend, but Cuchulain and Aoife, who conceives his son after being defeated by Cuchulain in battle. Aoife is a worthy foe. She has raised her son (named Conlaech, according to legend) to seek revenge upon the man who took her body and her pride. Unaware of the existence of his offspring, Cuchulain remembers Aoife with admiration precisely because she has a wild heart, like Cuchulain himself:

> Ah! Conchubar, had you seen her
> With that high, laughing, turbulent head of hers
> Thrown backward, and the bowstring at her ear,
> Or sitting at the first with those grave eyes
> Full of good counsel as it were with wine,
> Or when love ran through all the lineaments
> Of her wild body. (*VPL* 487)

Yeats remains true to the original myth, yet he clearly shapes the character of Aoife into a figure for Maud Gonne: "With that high, laughing, turbulent head of hers/Thrown backward."[2] These lines repeat Yeats's ruminations about Maud Gonne in "The Trembling of the Veil" (1922), wherein he remembers her "look of exultation as she walks with her laughing head thrown back."

Embedded in the Aoife character is Gonne's adamant rejection of domestic life and conventional social ties, her sense of fierce dedication to Ireland's political cause, and her single-minded focus that subordinated all else to her sense of mission. In *Baile*, this character is lauded for that spirit that cannot be beaten down, in part because Cuchulain is elevated by such a worthy foe. But in *Green* (subtitled "An Heroic Farce"), the hero's choice of spouse is far from noble. The character of Emer is vain and petty, yet she tolerates her husband's public rebuke ("Do you dare . . . Bear children and sweep the house") and his philandering ("Live and be faithless still") (452). In fact, Yeats frames Aoife's fierce strength in a domestic setting, ultimately making a farce of that wild, feminine spirit and turning hardened steel into brittle vanity.[3]

Does Emer's subservient position, the dependence of her social status upon the fame and power of her husband alone, poison her heart, so restricted and so dominated? An important question, one that Cuchulain does not consider but Yeats certainly weighs. Cuchulain's courage is a vibrancy encased in a dull world. Such vibrancy is lessened not by the merits of the hero's own response to the dramatic situation but by the nature of his love, the character of Emer, and the vitality of their passion. Aoife risks the life of her son to satisfy her honor. But Emer, despite her vanity, is not offended by Cuchulain's condescension or his faithlessness. With Aoife refashioned into this Emer, Yeats etches Cuchulain's stature against an inferior foe—hence, the farce.

Viewed from this perspective, *Green* is a conciliatory tale for Yeats himself. He is the Cuchulain who futilely loves an Aoife. He admonishes his own heart not to grow bitter through betrayal by telling himself that he would really prefer not to make an Emer of her because that would lessen his own act of courage. It is clear that in *Green*, as in *Baile*, Yeats is indeed dramatizing himself and does so in relation to the mask of the feminine in general and of Maud Gonne in particular. This dramatization is an obvious two-way exchange: Yeats shaping the Cuchulain myth to reflect his own experience, and Yeats reflecting on his life according to his reading of the myth.

In *Hawk*, Yeats regains his sense of the true heroic, not by enlarging on his hero's deeds of prowess but by stripping the stage, the action, and the characters to bare essentials in a conscious attempt to isolate the nature of Cuchulain's courage and the cause of his downfall. Yeats sends Cuchulain "back to the beginning" in time, to the root of his misfortune. The Noh style adds to the austere, archetypal setting wherein the hero is initially cursed with the "troubling" of his life: his encounter with the Sidhe.

Cuchulain arrives at the well of eternal waters, impatient, confident, and fearless. But he should not be fearless, for his foe is no earthly king but Fand, the guardian of the well. Fand first appears in the form of a "great grey hawk," the likes of which Cuchulain has never seen: "It flew/As though it would have torn me with its beak/Or blinded me, smiting with that great wing" (406). The attack does not daunt him: "Could I but find a means to bring it down/I'd hood it," he declares (407).[4] But this is no temporal creature. The Old Man who has wasted his life at the well knows her, "the Woman of the Sidhe herself/The mountain witch, the unappeasable shadow" (407). He bids Cuchulain flee, for her curse is to be feared:

> Never to win a woman's love and keep it;
> Or always to mix hatred in the love;
> Or it may be that she will kill your children,
> That you will find them, their throats torn and bloody,
> Or you will be so maddened that you kill them
> With your own hand. (407–8)

As Fand begins her dance, Cuchulain boasts, "Run where you will,/Grey bird, you shall be perched upon my wrist./Some were called queens and yet have been perched there" (410). In a quasi-orgasmic moment, the water runs in the well ("it comes, it comes"), and though Cuchulain hears the splash, he forsakes the well to follow the guardian, who has disappeared from the stage. But the curse has fallen. Already Fand has "roused up the fierce women of the hills,/Aoife, and all her troop, to take [his] life,/and never till [he is] lying in the earth/Can [he] know rest" (411–12). Rather than flee, Cuchulain rushes to meet them: "He comes! Cuchulain, son of Sualtim, comes!" (412). He throws himself to his fate, brave to the end— what Yeats would later call "doom eager" (571).

No matter how *Hawk* is read, as a Noh drama, as a parable in Zen-like resignation, as a classic tragedy, or as an episode in gender conflict, it falls short of the mark. Yeats is caught not by any impairment of his art but by the limits of his mystical vision. Let me explain. The dance of the Hawk Woman, along with Cuchulain's boast to tame her, enhances the sexual innuendo in the play. Certainly this encounter evokes sufficient conflict to undermine its Noh elements. But the sexual dimensions are finally flaccid; they remain overshadowed by the mystical scope of the play's theme. Yeats seems most concerned with depicting Cuchulain's destiny: his foolhardy eagerness and his attempts to challenge the spirit realm and throw off the fate of mortal men. Certainly Yeats's criticism is tempered by admiration: "The heroic act, as it descends through tradition, is an act done because a man is himself, because, being himself, he can ask nothing of other men but room amid remembered tragedies; a sacrifice of himself to himself" (569). Still, beneath these words about the heroic type is a vision of unalterable destiny that is theosophical at root. Indeed, heroism and destiny cannot be separated, as this passage from *Per Amica Silentia Lunae* (written a few months after *Hawk*) clearly illustrates: "In an Anglo-Saxon poem a certain man is called, as though to call him something that summed up all heroism, 'doom eager'" (*Myth* 336).

Yeats applies these same words ("doom eager") to Cuchulain because in *Hawk* he heroically pursues his destiny with single-minded courage. The meeting ground between man and destiny is marked by the well. The agent of destiny is Fand. Or more correctly, Fand is the analogic representation of the agent of destiny, for in truth, "the Daimon is our destiny." Yeats is adamant on this point: "I am persuaded that the Daimon [not the Sidhe] delivers and deceives us, and that he wove that netting from the stars and threw the net from his shoulder" (336). Then come those critical lines we have previously examined: "Then my imagination runs from Daimon to sweetheart, and I divine an analogy that evades the intellect . . . it may be 'sexual love,' which is 'founded upon spiritual hate,' is an image of the warfare of man and Daimon" (336). Fand is simply a stand-in for the daimon, and Yeats still conceives of the daimon as "he." The connection between Cuchulain's destiny and Fand of the Sidhe is only analogous, just as the similarity between daimon and sweetheart is only imaginary.

In this way, the sexual conflict in the play rings hollow. Certainly Cuchulain is netted in the doom that will haunt him to his final moments. But it is only incidental that destiny's tools (Fand and Aoife) are female. Furthermore, Fand is not the real object of love or hate. Such passion is reserved to man and daimon: "I understand why there is deep enmity between a man and his destiny, and why a man loves nothing but his destiny" (336).

The point would be moot except that Yeats himself has introduced the issue of gender relations by shaping the action of the play around the adversarial encounter between Cuchulain and Fand and by defining Cuchulain's doom as explicitly tied to the feminine: "Never to win a woman's love and keep it;/Or always to mix hatred in the love" (*VPL* 407). While the overt theme of destiny remains on the mystical level, masculine/feminine conflict that keeps generating the action is neither addressed nor resolved, yet at the same time it is defined as the core of that very doom that the hero must face. Yeats is finally defeated, unable to merge the mystical theme and the sexual tension that animates the play.

A year after drafting *Hawk,* Yeats developed the tools to bring the spiritual and the sexual together. In early November 1917, he was in the throes of a deeply dispirited mood as he began *Emer.* As George Mills Harper observes, the play quickly became an obsession or, more accurately, a vehicle by which Yeats articulated and sublimated his guilt about offending three women: Maud and Iseult Gonne, and his wife, Georgie (*Making* 1:83). Each of these women materializes into a character: Cuchulain's wife, Emer the True, is formed into a mask for Georgie. Eithne Inguba the Good, Cuchulain's mistress, represents Iseult Gonne, and Maud Gonne remains masked as Fand the Beautiful.

Along with these personal concerns, W. B. and Georgie Yeats were completing their map of the stages of the moon, already understood to comprise twenty-eight separate manifestations yet to be named as "Phases." Each Phase expresses a specific proportion or balance of contraries: sun and moon, primary and antithetical, masculine and feminine. As the Yeatses explored the meaning of the twenty-eight Phases, W. B. became increasingly frustrated with his personal balance of contraries. He believed that his primary self, the objective/solar side, had gained ascendancy over his anti-self or subjective/lunar side. "I have nothing but the embittered sun," he lamented (*VP* 344). To achieve his true state of genius required a new balance of temporal and ideal self, of sun and moon, of masculine and feminine. To realize his lunar or subjective side, Yeats turned to Cuchulain, the solar hero, now set at phase 12. But instead of defining Cuchulain through adversarial opposition as in the earlier plays—male against male or masculine confronting feminine—Yeats positions his hero in relation to a complementary ensemble of female characters who signify distinct elements yet comprise a single nature.

The spirit guides assisted Yeats in charting the complex configuration of characters in terms of his mystical system, which was evolving simultaneously with the play itself. Fand signifies love, Emer race, and Eithne Inguba passion (*AS I* 166). Or interpreted from a different perspective, Eithne Inguba symbolizes danger, Emer peace, Fand both danger and peace (521). Or again: Fand is intellect, Emer emotion, Eithne Inguba desire, and Cuchulain instinct (*AS III* 172); Fand is air, Emer fire, Eithne Inguba water, Cuchulain earth (*AS I* 217, 526); Fand is head, Emer loins, Eithne Inguba heart, and Cuchulain soul (*AS III* 172); or from another perspective, Cuchulain is physical body, Emer Passionate Body, Eithne Inguba Spirit, Fand Celestial Body (*AS I* 217). Yeats even aligns the characters with the Four Faculties: Cuchulain with Ego [Will], Fand with Genius [Creative Mind], Emer with Persona of Fate [Body of Fate], and Eithne Inguba with Mask (*AS III* 216).

Working from a series of philosophical axes that would later typify his worldview (the four "elemental attributions," the Four Principles, the Four Quarters, the Four Faculties, and what approximates the four conditions of the will), Yeats conceives of this cluster of characters as together signifying wholeness—of physical matter, of the psyche, of the temporal process, of the cosmos itself. This is the first breakthrough of the *Emer* play: the three women join with Cuchulain to form a unity: "all three are phases of one that should be—they should not be separate—the three are all through one nature but divided" (*AS I* 166). The division "is caused by nature of Cuchulain himself" (166). On a symbolic level then, *Emer* manifests Yeats's exploration of solar/lunar phases, but it is also a psychoanalytic enactment of wholeness founded on the principle of masculine/feminine complementarity.

Indeed, phasality and complementarity go hand in hand, as noted in the first chapter. Because of this metaphysical breakthrough, *Emer* works as a watershed in the cycle, finally crossing the line in gender relations between adversarial conflict and complementary interaction. These new insights also provide Yeats with a more exact and powerful idiom (not Donoghue's "idiom of combat" but the idiom of the sexual dynamic) in order to capture the real drama of life: the necessary connection between daimonic activity and sexual relations.

Although the Yeatses are months away from their insight that the daimon is female (April 1919), the role of Fand has already evolved. In *Emer,* she is not simply a symbol for destiny; she is a phasal being. And she is not simply a phasal being but a discarnate being (much like the daimon) of phase 15, the feminine, lunar principle in full power.[5] In *Emer,* her gender is nothing less than dominant, and her designs on Cuchulain are quintessentially sexual, as the Script reveals. As a being of phase 15, Fand is "near perfection" and thus self-sufficient, which means that she has "no desire for any but *self*" (239). Yet she needs the help of a mortal man to find peace and equilibrium and reach the next phase (209, 215). She selects Cuchulain because he has a "degree of seership" and because he is a solar phase (211). Sending an antithetical image, Fand manipulates her victim so he will actualize that "anti image" through his primary personality, thereby "creating" the image and "objectifying" Fand herself (214, 215). In a word, Yeats has projected onto Fand his personal search for completion of his own primary phase via the antithetical; because of her absolute subjectivity, Fand must seek an objective type. Both "being incomplete they need the other half" (216).[6]

To dramatize the situation, Yeats takes significant risks. It is not enough that he enacts two concepts: first, the sexual tie between a female spirit and a mortal man, and second, the ramifications of temporal acts in the spiritual realm. He must also persuade his audience into taking the otherworld seriously and treat what we normally consider "dramatic" (physical acts in the temporal order) as anticlimactic. He opens the play with the hero's demise, picking up the action where *Baile* leaves off. Cuchulain has just slain his son:

> And thereupon, knowing what man he had killed,
> And being mad with sorrow, he ran out;
> And after, to his middle in the foam,
> With shield before him and with sword in hand,
> He fought the deathless sea. (*VPL* 535)

The hero's body is laid out in grave clothes; the face is covered with an heroic mask. At the foot of the bed crouches the ghost of Cuchulain, also in grave clothes, with an identical mask. His wife, Emer, sits beside the bed along with his young lover, Eithne Inguba. Two dramas will unfold: Cuchulain's soul meeting Fand in the afterlife, and Emer's decisions and desires determining the outcome of that meeting.

Yeats takes a second gamble. For reasons I will presently make clear, he deviates from his early Irish sources by minimizing the audience's view of the otherworld. As Rosalind E. Clark points out, the narrator in the original *Serglige Con Culainn* is equally privy to both the human and spirit realms. The audience witnesses Fand's torment, identifies with her struggle, beholds her human appearance, and watches her commiserate with her rival, Emer. Yeats deliberately remakes Fand into a more alien, less womanly character and closes all windows into the otherworld (44). What readers lose is a persuasive portrayal of the spirits at phase 15 as well as any sympathy for Fand. What we gain, as Clark points out, is the story viewed through the eyes of Emer: "The play becomes her play" (45). This shift is crucial, for in the ensemble of female characters, Emer signifies Georgie Yeats, who is now at the helm of her husband's search for the key to his sexual past.

Precisely how does this play become Emer's? First, Fand's predicament directly impacts Emer's life. If Cuchulain yields to Fand's seductive power,

Emer will lose him forever because when the spirit women

> find our men asleep, weary with war,
> Lap them in cloudy hair or kiss their lips;
> Our men awake in ignorance of it all,
> But when we take them in our arms at night
> We cannot break their solitude. (*VPL* 549, 551)

Second, Emer is doubly tested, both in her love for Cuchulain and in her desire to be the "apple of his eye again" (545). Doubting her own power to rescue her husband, she commands Eithne Inguba to call her husband's spirit: "I am but his wife, but if you cry aloud/With the sweet voice that is so dear to him/He cannot help but listen" (537). With Eithne Inguba's kiss, the body stirs—not with Cuchulain's spirit but with another being, Bricriu of phase 1, maker of discord, and Fand's enemy.[7] Bricriu reveals that Emer must "pay the price" to save her husband from Fand's cunning by renouncing the hope that "some day somewhere/We'll sit together at the hearth again" (537).

This renunciation entails no small sacrifice, as Bricriu understands: "you loved your mastery, when but newly married" (545). Emer's predicament demands that she exchange one state of hopelessness for another. If she renounces her hope (one of the "two things I prize"), she will never again know Cuchulain's love. If she does not, he will love the Sidhe, and mortal men never tire of such a love. "You've watched his loves and you have not been jealous,/Knowing that he would tire," Bricriu reminds her (547). As Emer struggles with her choice, Cuchulain's soul encounters Fand. The sexual overtones of the spirit's dance are accentuated by Fand's movements. She catches him in the net of her hair, claiming to be "all woman now" (555). Yet Cuchulain lowers his eyes, not from the splendor of her appearance but from "old memories" of Emer:

> There we stand;
> Side by side and hand in hand
> Tread the threshold of the house
> As when our parents married us. (555, 557)

Fand bids him kiss her, for "though memory/Be beauty's bitterest enemy/I have no dread, for at my kiss/Memory on the moment vanishes" (555). Once Cuchulain is hers, her "round shall be complete" and her soul freed from its present phase. At the last moment, as Cuchulain's foot reaches Fand's chariot, Emer makes her choice. Rather than let Fand enjoy her man, Emer frees him from the Hawk Woman, in effect giving him back to Eithne Inguba, who is not an object of her jealousy. "I renounce Cuchulain's love for ever" (561).

In a word, while there are two lines of action—Emer's choice and Cuchulain's—there is only one act of heroism. While the man seems momentarily torn between the perfect embodiment of feminine beauty in Fand and the memory of his marriage to Emer, in the end he succumbs to the lure of the spirit. This spells disaster. If Fand succeeds, Cuchulain is doomed to "either isolation or a continual search for the ideal in mortal life" (*AS I* 211). Emer's sacrifice saves him. At the end of the play, however, he is claimed not by his selfless and heroic wife but by Eithne Inguba, who along with Emer has "loved him best" (*VPL* 533). This woman is placed at phase 14, only a sliver of the moon away from Fand. For Yeats, this means Eithne Inguba is self-centered (nearly self-sufficing) and unstable (almost entirely subjective). She knows that she holds only a passing power over Cuchulain and will soon be "flung into some corner like old nut-shells" (539). So she makes the most of her present opportunity, even lying to Cuchulain that "It is I that won him from the sea,/That brought him back to life" (561, 563).

Three women, one man. Their lives are woven together in this world and the next. The bonds between them are unbreakable, whether those bonds be of memory, of physical desire, or of complementary phase. Yeats succeeds in staging a centripetal energy that by the end of the play creates a sense of unity among these characters, so interdependent have they become in their sexual interaction. Without cashiering the importance of the temporal realm, Yeats has dramatized the condition of spirits at phase 15 and depicted their sexual encounters with humans during the expiation process.

Yeats has also resolved his personal concerns, at least in part, for Fand, not Emer, is the real victim in the play. Fand has the most to lose. Her atemporal future depends upon Cuchulain's choice to love her or not. Emer's action revokes Fand's chance for rest; she must continue in her labors through phase 15. Clearly, Yeats has Maud Gonne in mind. For the sake of expiation, Fand will crave to inflict "upon herself [changing the original pronouns] that which she has inflicted" upon others (*VA* 242). If a soul fails to return love in this life, she will be denied love in the next. Thus, the tale of Fand and Cuchulain, two spirits meeting in the afterlife, captures what Yeats believes will be the destiny of himself and Maud Gonne. In this way, *Emer* is a companion piece for *Hawk*, conciliatory in much the same way as *Green* is to *Baile*.

In this way, too, the play becomes Emer's play, not only because her character dominates the stage but also because of the way Georgie Yeats controls its outcome. Here the importance of the Automatic Script proves pivotal. F. A. C. Wilson depreciates the significance of Yeats's "elaborate angelology," though he urges readers to be sympathetic (*Tradition* 25). He also regards Yeats's claims about his wife's talents to be "peripheral" (19)—a true statement insofar as we must deal with W. B. Yeats's mysticism and art, whether or not Georgie Yeats was truly a medium to the spirits. But the Automatic

Script reveals Georgie Yeats as an active agent in the formulation of her husband's worldview, which therefore bears the imprint of her interests as well as his. The resolution in *Emer* serves as a case in point. While W. B. Yeats struggles to sort out his identity in relation to these women both here and in the afterlife, Georgie Yeats writes herself into the selfless and noble character of Emer by shaping the fate of Maud Gonne (as Fand) in the afterlife and by emerging as heroine (not victim) in the present.

Emer is a success on many levels. The mystical and the sexual no longer work at cross-purposes as in *Hawk* because the Yeatses have enlarged their understanding of spirit activities both in the temporal order and the afterlife. The gender conflicts that have hovered in the shadows in the first two plays now dominate the action—action that is still mystical but now effectively integrated with the sexual. In a word, Yeats has enacted his sexual dynamic for the first time.

Yet there are difficulties with the play as well. The most obvious is Yeats's strict adherence to the revelations of his spirit guides, which dictate that Emer must renounce Cuchulain's love to deliver him from Fand. Yeats himself asks the spirits why that must be. Their answer: "play is 3 before beauty" (*AS I* 166)—an explanation too closely tied to the workings of the Phases to make dramatic sense. This difficulty may stem from a more critical shortcoming. Yeats's daimonology is still underdeveloped. Indeed, the frantic few months during which he drafted *Emer* and formulated with his wife the Phases of the Great Wheel left little time as yet for the crucial discoveries made in the latter half of 1918 and the early months of 1919. For now, Yeats understands that discarnate females at phase 15 can enter into sexual relations of a kind with earthly males, but this is a far cry from the complex love-hate relation between human and daimon that is yet to be defined.

Because the daimon is not sufficiently understood (not even defined as sexual, as yet), the feminine in *Emer* remains undeveloped. Compared to the earlier plays—when Aoife never appears and is known only by reputation, or when Emer is petulant and vain, or when Fand silently dances as the Hawk Woman—the female characters in *Emer* are more complex and more convincing. Yet each of the women is still one-dimensional: Fand is only monstrous, Eithne Inguba only self-serving, Emer only self-sacrificing. Such limitations become obvious when we compare *Emer* to the final play of the cycle, *Death*, when females become full-fledged participants, both as complements and as adversaries.

Death describes the hero in the closing moments of his life. The play consists of a series of encounters between Cuchulain and his former lovers, who are also his archenemies.[8] Alone, Cuchulain faces the women assembled for his death; they are agents of his destiny and lovers whom "neither hate nor despair can destroy" (*VPL* 571). First comes Eithne Inguba, ambassador of Emer but bearer of her own advice. She bids Cuchulain to arm himself against Maeve—queen of Connaught, former lover to Cuchulain, source of many a ruined mortal—who advances with her own forces against his army: "The scene is set and you must out and fight" (1053). For Eithne Inguba, to do nothing is a moral failure; it is better for Cuchulain to "ride out and fight. . . no matter though/Your death may come of it" (1053). That is, she speaks for "life-in-death"—immortality and fame through glory in battle. But as ambassador, she carries a letter from Emer, who advances different counsel. Wait for reinforcements to even the odds, Emer writes. Wait and live—Eithne Inguba will be your bedfellow. But Cuchulain prefers Eithne Inguba's advice: "I am for the fight" (1054), he exclaims, rather than a death-in-life fate of ignominy.

Cuchulain cannot win, given these two alternatives. His destiny is unforgiving, but so too is Yeats, who is utterly consistent in his enactment of the heroic character.[9] Eithne Inguba will always relate to Cuchulain as hero. To her, he is fighter and jealous lover, "that violent man [who] forgave no treachery," as she describes him (1055). But that is the man she loves and fears; any softer feelings on his part, like forgiveness, would make him a lesser man. In their encounter, Cuchulain recognizes Eithne Inguba's treachery but chooses to save her "from her own wild words" by ensuring that her life will be protected and that she will be given to Conall Caernach, reputed to be a good lover (1056).

Like the Old Man at the Hawk's Well, Eithne Inguba can discern the presence of the two spirit women, Maeve (with the eye in the middle of her forehead) and Morrigu (with the head of a crow). Both bear old grudges against Cuchulain. He had slain Morrigu's father and her twenty-seven brothers. After their deaths, Morrigu and her two sisters were adopted by Queen Maeve, who schooled them in sorcery "and imbued them with her hatred for Cuchulain" (Jeffares and Knowland 301). Like Aoife, Maeve had slept with Cuchulain and bitterly cursed him for rejecting her.

Although their magical powers are drawing an invisible net of doom around Cuchulain, only one woman has the courage to appear before him as he stands mortally wounded, strapped to a pillar. That woman is Aoife. In a scene that dominates the play by its pathos and tension, she converses with Cuchulain as she helps him strap himself to a stone pillar with her own veil that is laced with gold threads.[10] They relive their first meeting, her reasons for hating him, and the events leading up to their son's death. Time is suspended as these lifelong lovers and enemies appear oblivious of the battle raging around them. Here male and female speak without bitterness, although Aoife is intent upon his death. They speak without deception, although Cuchulain admits he cannot understand.[11] But he knows full well that Aoife is the one with "a right to kill me" (*VPL* 1057).

Of all the women who seek his death, only Emer "had nothing monstrous" about her (1055). She appears after Cuchulain's death, dancing like

Salome.[12] The stage directions are deliberately ambiguous:

> She so moves that she seems to rage against the heads of those that
> had wounded Cuchulain, perhaps makes movements as though to
> strike them, going three times round the circle of the heads. She
> then moves towards the head of Cuchulain. . . . She moves as if in
> adoration or triumph. She is about to prostrate herself before it,
> perhaps does so, then rises, looking up as if listening. (1062)

These directions are more than an echo from the image of Salome in deca-
dent art. Throughout this cycle of plays, the character of Emer has been almost protean: first she is a domesticated Maud Gonne, then an heroic
Georgie Yeats. It is fitting that she turns enigmatic, perhaps too enigmatic
for Richard Londraville's hopeful reading. Londraville sees her movement as
emerging "from the logic of the play at the point when words will not suffice to express the emotion aroused" (184). True, the emotion she expresses
is powerful. But its truth teeters on the edge of possibility. Perhaps Emer
adores her lover; perhaps she gloats over his demise. Is it love or is it hate?

Yeats's rhetorical gesture—creating a puzzling sense of ambiguity and
mystery—is an answer of its own. Emer's dance marks the high wire of paradox where love and hate, life and death, cannot be distinguished. Men and
women die each other's life, live each other's death—this is the heart of
Yeats's vision. In commenting on the play, Yeats wrote in October 1938:
"My 'private philosophy' is there but there must be no sign of it . . . It
guides me to certain conclusions and gives me precision but I do not write
it" (*Letters* 917–18). One of these "certain conclusions" is that love and
loathing exist side by side "upon the same neck," just as the Old Man
promised at the opening of the play (*VPL* 1052).

At the point of Cuchulain's own transition from a temporal to a discarnate phase of existence, then, the female characters tend to dissolve into one
collective appetite for destruction. As Cuchulain gazes at his own soul ("a
soft feathery shape,/And is not that a strange shape for the soul/Of a great
fighting-man?"), the females gather as birds of prey (1060). Emer dances
like the spirits of the Sidhe, those "deceivers of *men*" (emphasis added)
(405). Cuchulain is truly "one whom the dancers cheat," to echo the Old
Man's bitter words at the well (405). Yet at this very point in *Death,* when
all seems hopeless, there is a prospect of illumination after all. While Cuchulain's character in phase 12 ("that amorous, violent man," as described in
Emer) cannot be modified, his very death will move him into another phase,
signaling a fundamental transformation. Death is a process, not an end
point. Although Cuchulain's character has remained constant in this heroic
phase, his soul will enter another body and thereby alter its character type.
This next body will be female, as Yeats defines the pattern of reincarnation

along the Great Wheel. Yeats's expectation that Cuchulain, himself, and every individual will cross the barrier between male and female in each incarnation is a radical means of bringing masculine and feminine together, but it guarantees the ultimate resolution of old wounds and reckless faults.

"Everything sublunary must change," Cuchulain remarks (1055). Insofar as he is engaged in the phases of the moon, he will progress through a series of bodily forms; the resulting self or character is fixed until death. At the same time, life is not just a stage or a condition to be endured but also a stepping-stone to a new character type, a new gender, and a new level of awareness. Because he is leaving the heroic phase, Cuchulain can forgive a traitor. But it is only "because [he is] about to die," whereas his lovers remain grounded in temporal existence and retain the "passion necessary to life" (1055).

The closing lines of *Death* pose a fundamental question: "Are those things that men adore and loathe/Their sole reality?" (1063). Do the ambivalence of sexual relations and the complementarity of contraries comprise all of reality? Yes, Yeats insists, in this life. But temporal existence is not "their sole reality." Contraries will be made whole when "time and times are done" and the soul completes its journey through the twenty-eight Phases. Until then, the pathos of Cuchulain's death is tempered by the impetus of the full cycle of plays coming to completion. This is the moment that the young Cuchulain in *Baile* longed for, "a brief forgiveness between opposites/That have been hatreds for three times the age" (478).

The Cuchulain cycle, then, ends far afield from its beginnings. True, Cuchulain's nature is consistently maintained as a man of action with his stubborn resolve, his impetuous and disastrous choices, his bravado, his callousness, his unfaithfulness, on the one hand—his courage, his nobility, even his wisdom, on the other. But with each successive play, his personal fate becomes inextricably linked not to great kings and events but to women, who are both wounded by his sins and elevated by his goodness. The adversarial nature of gender relationships in the opening plays is tempered by the added mystery of complementarity in the two final plays.

As sexual relations assume center stage, Yeats's depiction of the feminine becomes more complex and convincing. The feminine is manifested in a wide range of characters: fierce warrior, domesticated wife, young lover, selfless spouse, absolute beauty, and vengeful spirit. But in the end, very earthly women (Aoife and Emer) enact their power and passion to the fullest and thereby reveal the full depths of Cuchulain's heroic heart. Yeats's female characters do not counterbalance Cuchulain's personality so much as heighten, provoke, and reveal interior action within the heroic figure. This allows Yeats to hone his dramatic focus to an ever-refined point of simplicity, particularly in *Emer*, where the core of dramatic tension resides in the choices made by Emer, and in *Death*, where the true dénouement occurs when all action is suspended and Aoife and Cuchulain meet face-to-face. In sum, the riddles of style, simplicity, and heroism make sense if we understand that Yeats is pruning away all peripheral elements to lay bare the drama of hearts as male and female encounter their destinies through each other.

With *Emer*, W. B. and Georgie Yeats together establish that a man's search for meaning is bound up with women. At the end of his own life, as he drafts *Death*, the poet enacts his hero's resolve to face destiny by lining the threshold of this world with his array of lovers. Cuchulain, like Yeats himself, is irrevocably linked to the feminine, both here and in the world to come.

CHAPTER 4

THE WISDOM OF THE BODY

"Robartes' argument—which Yeats has by now often enunciated—is that beautiful women who
achieve Unity of Being . . . must learn to think with
the whole body rather than with the mind."

> John Unterecker, *A Reader's Guide to William*
> *Butler Yeats* (158)

"If Michael Robartes had been away in the desert
for twenty years, Yeats had not, and the comically
urbane tone of "Michael Robartes and the Dancer,"
together with the deflating simplicity of the young
girl's rejoinders . . . and her determination to have
the last word . . . combine to suggest that we have
here the portrait of an attitude rather than a portrait
of the artist."

> Elizabeth Cullingford, "Yeats and Women" (33)

The Only Jealousy of Emer registers the immediate impact of W. B. Yeats's
sexual dynamic and developing daimonology. The transformation of his poetry is also direct and dramatic. Like *Emer* in relation to earlier Cuchulain
plays, the poems generated during the scripting sessions differ significantly

from previous verse, with the volume *Michael Robartes and the Dancer* (published in 1921) marking the beginning of the shift.

By the closing months of 1918, W. B. and Georgie Yeats had already established major elements of their metaphysical system through the scripting process. They had explored the parameters of the primary and antithetical cones, the personality types associated with the twenty-eight Phases of the moon, and the Four Faculties. They had queried their spirit guides about the theme and symbolism in *Emer*, about daimonic activity in human lives (both during and between incarnate states), and about the origins of sex. They had established the existence of "universal masculine & feminine in soul" (*AS I* 109) and the tenet that "two complete opposites never unite except in man & woman" (68). More importantly, the Yeatses believed that their daughter, Anne, born in early 1919, was the product of daimonic design (*AS II* 255). Through the later months of 1918 and the first half of 1919, they would discover and explore the workings of the daimon in human sexual relations in what they called the Moments of Crisis.

While functioning as medium throughout this critical period, Georgie Yeats continually urged her husband to spend his days writing, and not simply to codify ideas from the Script. Indeed, as early as February 1919, the spirits were clear: "I do not want you to write on system[.] I would like you to write something *through which* I can give you ideas" (*AS II* 197). A month later, the command was repeated: "you must begin writing" (223). By August, the spirits were adamant: "you *must* write poetry" (387). It would seem that Georgie Yeats sensed what W. B. Yeats would discover, that the process of writing verse would not only order and internalize their metaphysical discoveries; it would also mark a significant achievement in Yeats's aesthetic development.

I will use three of the handful of verses Yeats drafted in 1918 and 1919 as examples of this development: "Solomon to Sheba" (drafted in March 1918), "Michael Robartes and the Dancer" (1919), and "Solomon and the Witch" (1919). Previously considered as minor works by most critics, these poems reveal radical innovations in Yeats's art. In style and form, the female voice emerges in Yeats's initial attempts to articulate the "woman in me." In content, sex becomes the avenue to intellectual enlightenment, and gendered relations become an appropriate pathway to spiritual wisdom, an insight possible only as Georgie and W. B. Yeats identify sexual relations as the link between human and daimonic existence. Finally, in his development as a poet, these poems refine and integrate three critical tenets in Yeats's thinking: his veneration of the feminine as a privileged avenue to the sacred, his association of the act of loving with the act of masking, and his vision of daimonic and human interaction.

A brief summary of the first two tenets will be useful in demonstrating the innovation of Yeats's lyrical style that emerges between 1918 and 1919.

First, the feminine and the sacred. Yeats's theory of the mask is rooted in a broader aesthetic vision, which in turn was shaped by his rebellion against the materialism of his own society. Yeats found modern civilization fragmented, despiritualized, and dominated by the spell of Lockean metaphysics. He believed that a poet could directly counteract this "growing murderousness of the world" (*AU* 130) by conjuring archetypal reality from the *Anima Mundi* through the use of symbols: "Every symbol is an invocation which produces its equivalent expression in all worlds" (326). The poet could transmute—the alchemical parallel is deliberate on Yeats's part—the weary heart into a "weariless spirit" (*Myth* 269) through language that is "subtle, complex, full of mysterious life as the body of a flower or of a woman" (*Collected VI* 199). Here the sacred, the physical, and the feminine converge in what is clearly a formative value. In describing a woman's body as subtle, complex, full of mystery, Yeats reveals his reverence for the female, both her psyche and her body. He insists that in Western culture "all power is from the body" and that "religion and magic insist on power and therefore on body" (*AU* 326).

It is a natural step in logic for Yeats to associate the female with magic and mystery, since he believed that women are naturally in harmony with nature and her secrets—closer to body, in that sense. The natural and supernatural are knit together, and women are particularly sensitive to that bond. In fact, Yeats envies the way women are in tune with the presence of spirits. When it comes to embracing and understanding ancient lore, "women come more easily than men to that wisdom which ancient peoples, and all wild peoples even now, think the only wisdom" (*Myth* 115). There is a kind of madness to such wisdom, he goes on to acknowledge in true Platonic style. Fools may have it, but women "do get of a certainty" an intuitive kind of insight about ultimate reality that reason and sanity can find only at the end of a "painful journey" (115). Through his experience in the Theosophical Society and the Golden Dawn, along with his study of Irish folklore and his friendships with rustics who were in tune with spirits, Yeats concluded that "miracle is mostly a woman's privilege" (*AU* 125). She commands it and recognizes it—none better than Yeats's own wife, who gathered up an "entire web of influences" in her automatic writing (326).

There is a touch of irony in how Yeats revered the sacred and doggedly pursued occult activities while all along believing himself at a disadvantage compared to women with their natural sensitivity and inherent power. In a journal entry from 1912, Yeats expresses respect for the feminine mixed with envy and fear:

> I give God praise for woman, what is a man's friendship worth beside
> hers? I praise God because she is a woman, and in her our minds our

bodies find rest. I praise first for her mind where she covers our vague thoughts with the substance of her revery, for Solomon grew wise in talking to her and then for her body and the pleasure that comes with sleep; and because in her the vague desires of the dim sky meet the violent, and the curtain shivers; O God, grant me for my gift, not in this life for I begin to grow [old], but somewhere, that I shall love some woman so that every passion, pity, cruel desire, the affection that is full of tears, the abasement as before an image in a savage tent, hatred even it may be, shall find its prey. O God, it is a pity that even you cannot [grant] this to the old, in whom only the heart is insatiable.

> No longer the moon
> Sends me dark leopards
> Green eyed, and wavering (?) in the body
> Nor longer her white hares
> And that holy centaur of the hills
> And the young witches with lofty dissolute faces
> Now that I grow old
> I have nothing but the harsh sun
> I no longer climb in the white mountain valleys
> Our heroic mother the moon has vanished
> I am alone with the timid sun.
> (qtd. in Bradford, *Yeats at Work.* abr. ed. 6)

These entries reveal two tendencies in the speaker: first, he praises woman for the consolation of her friendship, for the tranquility of her "revery," and for the pleasure of her body. But equal to the speaker's celebration is a kind of futile, embittered longing. Indeed, the passage is primarily a prayer with little hope of fulfillment, since the speaker is old and beyond his prime. So the supplication extends even to the afterlife. If not now, then later. And for what? To fulfill "every passion, pity, cruel desire," pain, humiliation, even hatred. In the meantime, the speaker is stranded: "I have nothing but the harsh sun . . . I am alone with the timid sun." That is, he must do without woman, without the feminine or lunar principle. In his isolation, he finds the solar or masculine principle to be insufficient by itself, "harsh" and "timid." The implication is that once joined with the feminine, the masculine experience would be more complete. The speaker states as much, associating woman with wisdom and citing Solomon's experience as an example: "Solomon grew wise in talking to her."

One of the problems with the passage is that Yeats provides no groundwork to prepare the reader for the implied connection between the feminine and wisdom. How are man's "vague thoughts" transmuted into wisdom as woman covers them "with the substance of her revery"? The passage may assert that the feminine and the sacred fuse, but Yeats does not demonstrate how or why. Two years later, as he reshapes these entries into the poem "On Woman," Yeats still struggles for a philosophic foundation to his theme.

In the opening lines of "On Woman," the speaker is again on the outside looking in: old, despairing, and longing. In the first part of the poem, the speaker lauds a certain type of woman, one who "gives up all her mind" and does not quarrel "with a thought/Because it is not her own" (*VP* 345). He values women who give up not only their bodies but also their minds. A man's thoughts can fill a woman; his "word" can become incarnated through her flesh as she "covers all he has brought/As with her flesh and bone" (345). Such a woman offers a type of friendship that surpasses what could ever be offered man-to-man, for men can only produce but not receive a thought. This woman can *receive* and *conceive*. She is a madonna, a lifegiver, the means whereby an idea can become manifest in the physical through the process of word-made-flesh.

In the second part of the poem, the speaker treads a fine line, not expecting a woman to be literally empty-headed but to open herself to thoughts "not her own." Women are sources of wisdom, it seems, for "Solomon grew wise/While talking with his queens" (345).[1] But the King was most wise "when Sheba was his lass"—Sheba, the cool moon likened to the waves of night, who encloses Solomon the sun.

> When she the iron wrought, or
> When from the smithy fire
> It shuddered in the water . . .
> Shudder that made them one. (345–46)

As Sheba receives his seed (literally his physical seed, metaphorically his intellectual seed), Solomon grows wise, both by knowing her intimately through sexual union and by tempering his thoughts in the cool waters of her body. His thoughts take on form (are enfleshed) through his queen. Sheba becomes the channel of Solomon's sexual and intellectual vitality, and her means of doing so is entirely physical.

In the final section, the speaker harbors hope for his next life, his own reincarnation, when the cool darkness of the moon will reform the thought of him into a new manifestation—a word refleshed. He desires a wisdom like Solomon's: "To find what once I had/And know what once I have known" (346). This prayer is double-edged; he yearns to be like Solomon in yet another way and to succeed in better loving the woman he once desired above all else. The speaker seeks that "perverse creature of chance," a woman like Sheba to lead him "a dance" (346). He believes that he had such a woman and such an experience in this present life, but his advancing age precludes a successful ending.[2]

With this poem, Yeats articulates a desire for the wisdom of sexual union as much as for escape from "an aching head,/Gnashing of teeth, despair" (346). But Yeats does not establish a necessary link between the feminine and wisdom or between the feminine and the sacred; specifically, he has yet to establish a metaphysical dimension to sexual relations. Thus, the male speaker here is in the same boat as the speaker in Yeats's journal entries: both only assume that Solomon grew wise with Sheba. In 1914, Yeats struggles to find a pathway between human and divine, between sexual and mystical. As yet, there is none.

This same struggle occurred as Yeats attempted to connect the concepts of loving and masking. Well before his marriage to Georgie Hyde-Lees, Yeats concluded that men and women must mask in order to love. In 1909 he argued that love depends upon difference, not harmony, and that the lovers must select a mask to inflame a full, passionate response in the beloved.

> It seems to me that true love is a discipline, and it needs so much wisdom that the love of Solomon and Sheba must have lasted, for all the silence of the Scriptures. Each divines the secret self of the other, and refusing to believe in the mere daily self, creates a mirror where the lover or the beloved sees an image to copy in daily life; for love also creates the Mask. (*AU* 313)

When Yeats says that love sees beyond the daily self to the secret self, he is saying that love is not directed to the temporal, real self but to the ideal, anti-self. The purpose of love is to create passion, not to inspire the hope of union. The mask is chosen to evoke passion, while the mere "daily self" of the lover is set aside in favor of the secret self.[3]

It is one thing to assert the connection between loving and masking, quite another to demonstrate it convincingly. One of his best known, pre-Script attempts to do so is "Ego Dominus Tuus" (1915). As noted earlier, "Ego Dominus Tuus" deals directly with Yeats's early daimonic theory, dramatizing the process of seeking the image or anti-self, and this is the level that most scholarship addresses. The characters Hic and Ille stand for opposite ways of describing the artistic process. Hic voices the modern expectation that poetry expresses the authentic self. Ille argues that poets mask themselves by assuming an image, their antithetical self. Ille's search for his anti-self is not only in process but occurring even within the poem. That the piece is written as a dialogue indicates that even a discussion with Hic, who voices many assumptions and opinions opposed to Ille's values, is an instrument that aids Ille in his search. Without such interaction, the "mysterious one" might never appear. And who is this "mysterious one"? Here Yeats's own uncertainty muddles the poem, for in 1915 he has not yet personified the anti-self as the daimon.[4] There are really two anti-selves here. The first is an image of an opposite, either in personality (Hic would be Ille's anti-self) or as an interior faculty of the same self (the subconscious would be the anti-self of the conscious). The second type of anti-self is the "image"—a presence that seems to be more than a second self or pose but a being of separate and distinct ontological existence.

Yeats thus displays inner reality from two complementary views. With one perspective, he is projecting opposing dispositions within a single psyche as separate characters to dramatize their tension and their necessity to work together, or fight against each other, in order to progress toward an integrated personality and (ultimately) to produce great art. With the other perspective, Yeats is using that same projection to stand for a yet deeper and more mysterious opposition: the juxtaposition between man and image or mask. This is precisely the encounter that Ille seeks. The image, the "mysterious one," has not yet walked "the wet sands by the edge of the stream," but Ille waits with confidence (*VP* 371). Their encounter will create "a vision of reality" that will allow Ille to become a great poet like Keats and Dante. Ille will also transcend his two-dimensional, temporal self and flesh out that three-dimensional contour as the real and anti-self are joined.

But there are serious limitations to this depiction. According to "Ego Dominus Tuus," the action of masking appears to be entirely an aesthetic process. This depiction not only limits the mask but also belies the title of the poem itself, which Yeats explains in "Anima Hominis."

> At times I remember that place in Dante where he sees in his chamber the 'Lord of Terrible Aspect,' and how, seeming 'to rejoice inwardly that it was a marvel to see, speaking, he said many things among the which I could understand but a few, and of these this: ego dominus tuus.' (*Myth* 326)

This "Lord of Terrible Aspect" comes from Dante's *La Vita Nuova,* where the lord in question is "Love as a Daimon" (Langbaum, *The Mysteries of Identity* 163). Love is the master; this is why Dante's search ends when he finds "unpersuadable justice . . . The most exalted lady loved by a man" (*VP* 369). But Yeats does not follow through with the allusion in "Ego Dominus Tuus," leaving the reader to wonder what love has to do with what is otherwise presented as the purely aesthetic function of masking. To compound the problem, Yeats deliberately chooses to minimize reference to the gender of this "mysterious one."

> I call to the mysterious one who yet
> Shall walk the wet sands by the edge of the stream
> And look most like me, being indeed my double,
> And prove of all imaginable things

The most unlike, being my anti-self,
And, standing by these characters, disclose
All that I seek; and whisper it as though
He were afraid the birds, who cry aloud
Their momentary cries before it is dawn,
Would carry it away to blasphemous men. (371)[5]

The anti-self is given no pronoun referent until line eight, and the reader is forced to move through a maze of verbs ("walk," "look," "prove," "standing," "disclose," "whisper"), creating the illusion that the future event has come to pass but at the same time veiling the gendered presence of the mysterious one himself. And the gendered pronoun is especially significant here. For the anti-self is still a "he," and passion is only a topic of discussion. Passion does not underpin the relationship between Hic and Ille (as anti-self and real self), between Ille and the mysterious one (man and image), nor does it animate the hunger that should in theory spark Ille's search along the gray shore. This trivially gendered version of the relation between man and anti-self makes a crucial difference in "Ego Dominus Tuus," provoking Yeats's ultimate judgment that the poem is too abstract: "I need no longer write poems like 'The Phases of the Moon' nor 'Ego Dominus Tuus,' nor spend barren years . . . striving with abstractions" (*VA* xii). These poems are "abstract" precisely because they have no metaphorical way to express the passionate interaction between contraries, to establish an avenue for union, or to enact an attraction between poet and anti-self.[6]

Four years later, Yeats is married to Georgie Hyde-Lees and is deeply involved in sessions of Automatic Scripting. In 1918 and 1919, he will write and publish three poems, dialogic in form, that pull together not only masculine and feminine voices but also the mystical life and sexual relations. That is, Yeats will finally make sense of what he believed all along to be the connection between woman and wisdom, and between loving and masking—in large part because he genders the daimon and thereby makes explicit the link between supernatural infusion and sexual relations.

As noted in the beginning of the chapter, W. B. and Georgie Yeats were steeped in material that yoked the spirit realm and human existence, a union made possible through their own marriage, i.e., their occult experiments and intimate relations. It is no accident, then, that W. B. Yeats's poetic efforts would revolve around dramatizing the process whereby a man is enlightened by his lover. In "Solomon to Sheba," the male speaker no longer talks about Solomon as in "On Woman"; he assumes the mask of Solomon himself. The setting of "Solomon to Sheba" demonstrates that he has found his love, who leads him "a dance." But the poem does more than vindicate the prayers of the suppliant speaker in "On Woman." It reveals significant changes in style and form to accommodate a dramatic shift in focus. No longer is Yeats interested in the lone voice of a male speaker who suffers because love is denied to him. The poet himself has firsthand knowledge of how sexual union and spiritual enlightenment come together. Using the dialogue format of "Ego Dominus Tuus" (and of the Automatic Script itself), Yeats sets out to enact, not assert, his theme. The subsequent dialectic exchange—an affectionate conversation wherein the lovers question, correct, and instruct each other—performs a second critical function by giving voice to Sheba herself.

Not surprisingly, the topic that sparks the occasion is the subject of love itself. The first stanza in "Solomon to Sheba" displays a man who is weary-hearted, not from futile love—after all, Sheba is planted on his knee—but only from speaking "in the narrow theme of love" since "mid-day" (*VP* 333). Solomon feels confined by the singularity of the topic and longs for the approaching night, for night signifies not a threat but a fulfillment, as Sheba's "dusky" face promises. Yet for Solomon and Sheba, love is not just a theme. It is a space, a location; ideas are being actualized in the "flesh and bones" of the woman. Thus, they have "talked in the one place" and "gone round and round/In the narrow theme of love" (332–33). If, as Yeats writes in his autobiography, love is a discipline (*AU* 313), then Solomon has been learning his "lesson" or "themes" from Sheba. And like any schoolboy, he chafes at the restriction of sitting in one place "Like an old horse in a pound" (*VP* 333). The dialogue format reveals the action of Solomon's schooling. The primary exchange is sung—an activity that reinforces the schoolhouse setting wherein lessons are "sing-sung." But it also suggests that learning about love is poetic song, a thing of beauty. As Solomon grows in wisdom (or learns his themes), he does so via poetic exchange.

Just what does Solomon's schooling consist of? This particular lesson is found in stanza two, as Sheba responds to her lover's complaint. What we have addressed, she sings, is not considered "wise" by learned men. Had they studied conventional wisdom on traditional themes, Sheba's ignorance would have been clear to Solomon "before the sun had thrown/Our shadows on the ground" (333). But her thoughts are limited only in comparison to the reality they attempt to articulate. That is, her own thoughts "are but a narrow pound" because they are focused on love (333). Sheba is also admitting something else: matters that please learned men are no concern of hers. Her mind is indeed emptied of issues, opinions, and philosophical learning—the very condition advocated by the speaker in "On Woman." She is wise beyond all pedantry. Her own thoughts are narrow only compared to the reality they express; "like an old horse in a pound," her mind is surrounded by the vast and complex reality of love.

In stanza three, Solomon is wise enough to recognize the meaning of Sheba's words. For the reality of love dwarfs the world. Its vastness is wider than all the temporal order, greater than the pedantry of scholars, deeper than his own thoughts. The conjoint labor of Solomon and Sheba ("us two")—male and female, two minds and two bodies, the wealth and abundance of masculine and feminine joined, all of reality pooled—is vaster than all other aspects of life that are essentially splintered and fragmented into separate realms. Indeed, their efforts at learning and lovemaking signify a movement toward spherical wholeness, a condition of completion in which all else is contained. This experience, in turn, produces an understanding far superior to any reasoned insight or book learning.

But with this poem Yeats's journey is only half-finished. His mystical explorations are yet to be completed, and while he has enacted the connection between the feminine and the sacred to a more satisfactory degree, he has yet to wed the acts of loving and masking in a convincing way. In the early months of 1919, the Yeatses made critical headway in their exploration of daimonic activity. They had established that "my daimon [is] part of me" (*AS II* 211), and while the ego may successfully refuse to communicate with the daimon, ego and daimon cannot exist apart from each other (252). They also know that W. B. Yeats's daimon is female (245), that they have no consciousness of their daimons apart from sex (259), and that intimate relations feed their daimons (282).

Interwoven with the Yeatses' exploration of the daimon is the ongoing discussion of W. B.'s obsession with Maud Gonne. By 1919 he was willing to face the truth:

[Question:] Do you mean that I clung artfully to a delusion?
[Answer:] Yes because *you* built up the delusion. (228)

The delusion stemmed from false pity rooted in a conflicted interaction of Faculties between Yeats and Gonne so that the Creative Genius deceived "the ego by objectifying the mask" (229). In a word, Yeats was duped, or duped himself, into creating and responding to an image that belied the reality. Herein resides the pitfall of associating the acts of loving and masking. To wean himself from his delusion about Maud Gonne, Yeats pursued long discussions about Initiatory and Critical Moments in the Automatic Script (I will take up this concept in more detail in chapter 5). He also wrote two poems, "Solomon and the Witch" and "Michael Robartes and the Dancer," on the importance of "image" in the process of masking. These poems are drastically different from their prototype, "Ego Dominus Tuus," because they are grounded in explicitly sexual contexts.[7]

Roughly two months after establishing that his daimon is female, Yeats entered into a prolonged exploration of the "image," specifically, how the daimon manipulates images in human sexual encounters. The Script reveals that Yeats himself struggled for many months to understand the images that lovers devise for each other. In June 1919, the spirit guide distinguished between a woman's image of an ideal lover and her image of an actual man.

The difference has nothing to do with the lovers; rather, it depends upon which stage of "Moments of Crisis" the woman is experiencing. Yeats tries to clarify for himself:

> [Question]: When you say 'image' do you confine 'image' to the actual physical form
> [Answer]: Yes but remember I said in the IM [Initiatory Moment] the woman realises the objective image is the *subjective* image of the particular man
> [Q]:You mean that physical image in womans mind is the mask of the man
> [A]:Yes. (316)

Still searching for clarification, Yeats restates masking as he understands it:

> [Q]: John Smith falls in love with Maria because Maria is symbol of his own anti. His genius has found Maria Having found Maria he tries to think thoughts worthy of her This is finding mask
> [A]: Oh no no no no . . . you haven't found right key
> Generally Generally. (319)

By December that same year, Yeats asks:

> [Q]: How do you distinguish between the Physical Image & the Real Image?
> [A]: The physical image is the sensuous form of intellectual perception The Real image is the emotional form of sexual image
> The Ideal image is the Supernatural desire form of sexual image. (520)

In the midst of this search, Yeats drafts "Solomon and the Witch." On the surface, this poem appears simply to be the sequel to "Solomon to Sheba." In the "Witch," Sheba is possessed of a spirit from the nether world. Because Solomon can understand all tongues in both this world and the hidden realm, he takes it upon himself to interpret when his Sheba cries out "in a strange tongue/Not his, not mine" (*VP* 387). Although their conversation is playful, shaped as an affectionate exchange of lovers, the theme is philosophic at its root, addressing the workings of choice and chance and the interaction of the temporal and spiritual realms. It is as abstract in content as "Ego Dominus Tuus." However, the dramatization of the protagonists into a male and female pair and the recasting of the spiritual subject matter into gendered terms both clarify and concretize the theme.

In Yeats's worldview, the temporal world is composed of human beings who can, if they wish, freely choose to love each other, just as Solomon and Sheba, William Butler and Georgie, have done. Each act of sexual union marks an attempt to make two things—oil and wick, water and iron, female and male—into "a single light" (388). When these separate entities "burn as one," that is, achieve a state of peace, of perfect repose and harmony, then time will cease and eternity dawn: "this foul world were dead at last" (388).

Solomon and Sheba's lovemaking comes so close to perfection that the cockerel that announced the first turn of the gyre and "crowed out eternity" "three hundred years before the Fall" has been fooled into crowing once again (388), this time to welcome in eternity and announce yet another turn of the gyre. But Sheba adds a dose of reality therapy. There is something wrong with Solomon's interpretation, for eternity has not dawned: "Yet the world stays" (388). It is an amusing scene, as if the lovers could judge the quality of their union not by the degree of personal bliss but by a quick check of their surroundings. The world is still with them, Sheba confirms. "O! Solomon! let us try again" (389).

Levity quickly gives way to deeper reflection. This dialogue enacts many truths Yeats considers fundamental to his worldview and pivotal in his symbol system. As F. A. C. Wilson notes, the cockerel is a beast of Hermetic lore, the traditional "harbinger of all the cycles" (*Iconography* 281). The bird's usual habitat is the Tree of Life, in cabalistic lore symbolized by the apple tree. But Yeats's cockerel also has roots in Christian Scripture. In the Old Testament, the apple tree is the tree of the knowledge of good and evil; the first man and woman will die from eating its fruit. In the New Testament, the cock crows in response to an act of abject treachery, when Peter denies the Christ for the third time. In both cases, ages will fall (paradise) and rise (the Christian period) through acts of betrayal. This somber tone is only partially lifted by the farcical betrayal—the lovers' bliss tricking the cock to crow "a blessed moon" ("he thought it worth a crow," Solomon ruminates) (*VP* 388).

But the chance of life-threatening betrayal is embedded in the choice to love. One of the things that make this life so "foul" is the pain that love can bring:

> Love has a spider's eye
> To find out some appropriate pain—. (388)

Pain is only an overture to a more violent confrontation involving "cruelties of Choice and Chance" that end in despair—the death of the heart. This is the cruel lesson of Yeats's obsession with Maud Gonne. Such cruelty is part and parcel of life, and for a critical reason:

> For each an imagined image brings
> And finds a real image there. (388)

Recall again Yeats's interpretation of Solomon and Sheba as significant figures because "each divines the secret self of the other, and refusing to believe in the mere daily self, creates a mirror where the lover or the beloved
sees an image to copy in daily life; for love also creates the Mask" (*AU* 313).
Their harmony as lovers depends upon their ability to project the true mask
for the other, one that subsumes the daily self of the beloved.

   The conflict between imagined and real images is crucial, for it is the single cause cited by Solomon of despair in the marriage bed. When expectations clash with experience, when an imagined image reflected in the eyes of
the lover is rejected by the beloved, then spiritual union is not possible, and
love yields only bitter fruit. As Yeats learned in the scripting process, "the
choice of others is chance" (*AS II* 498), and both the act of selecting an image (or mask) and of selecting a lover balance on the cutting edge of choice
and chance, or destiny and fate. This is a critical concern—the issue of free
will and power, the imagined and real image. In this poem, Yeats describes
the best scenario. Solomon and Sheba fail not because they refuse to embrace the imagined image, but because

> Maybe the image is too strong,
> Or maybe is not strong enough. (*VP* 388)

The "slippage" between imagined and real images flows from a failure of
imagination or intellect, with the mind of the lover reflecting an inadequate
image, which is either "too strong" or "not strong enough." Sheba's solution is to try and marry oil and wick once again. Thus, the despair that
Solomon speaks of is not rooted in the bitter emotions of the 1912 journal
entry, where the speaker longs for "the abasement as before an image in a
savage tent, hatred even it may be" (qtd. in Bradford, *Yeats at Work*. abr. ed.
6). Nor is it like the speaker's lament in "On Woman":

> Pity, an aching head,
> Gnashing of teeth, despair;
> And all because of some one
> Perverse creature of chance. (346)

Here there is only a muted sense of a battle to the death between the sexes.
For Solomon and Sheba, love despairs not because of cruel acts of dominance, coldheartedness, or perverse manipulation. Love despairs "because it
is always unsatisfied" (*AS I* 269). Whatever tension still exists will dissipate
into the world:

> The night has fallen; not a sound
> In the forbidden sacred grove

Unless a petal hit the ground,
Nor any human sight within it
But the crushed grass where we have lain. (*VP* 389)

The reality is that the lovers Solomon and Sheba (or W. B. and Georgie Yeats) have the power to yoke the gyres, direct their turns, and shape destiny in the course of their lovemaking as daimons meet and plot the course of human events. True, this particular act fails to intersect with eternity. But the lovers share a kind of quixotic resignation: it is better to be on the road than to arrive at the inn. These lovers will little notice the true turn of the gyre.

Clearly, this poem describes both the difficulties in achieving lasting union in the temporal order and in finding and donning a mask to reflect a lover's freedom and to accommodate the partner's needs. With "Solomon and the Witch," Yeats has gone well beyond the limitations of "Ego Dominus Tuus," a poem also enacting the search for an image, also dialogic in form, also seeking a solution through a dialectical process. He has successfully melded the idea of loving and masking, passion and image, by using gender to express mystical phenomena as well as to depict the spiritual dimensions of sexual relations. But "Solomon and the Witch" goes further than deepening Yeats's own understanding—it expands and personalizes his association of loving and masking. Here I believe the real genius of the poem emerges.

What we are seeing, both in the Automatic Script and the poems from 1918 and 1919, is a process wherein the original meaning of mask—as aesthetic construct—is broadened and complicated. In chapter 1, I discussed the first stage of that process, when Yeats defined mask as one of the Four Faculties. Mask as aesthetic action and Mask as Faculty are both terrains of the daimon. Now in "Solomon and the Witch" Yeats's use of the term "mask" is again expanded, this time applied to Nietzsche's notion of divining the secret self of the lover. As Yeats writes poetry about this action, he adapts wholesale the concepts he has learned from the spirit guides. He is forced, as it were, to map out how daimon and lover vie for ascendancy in selecting the image of the beloved, just as daimon and poet war against each other in selecting the image of a poem.

Consequently, a scenario more problematic than the love scene in "Solomon and the Witch" haunts the poet. What happens when someone attempts to impose a false image on a resistant partner or an unwelcome image upon a reluctant partner? The danger is clear: power too quickly enters into the arena of sex (and by extension) into the mask. In the poem "Michael Robartes and the Dancer," Yeats directly addresses this issue.

In "Michael Robartes," the rhetorical situation appears on the surface to have nothing to do with the act of masking. Robartes and a nameless young woman argue about her future education. Scholars have extended this situation to a more serious issue: what is the place of women in society? The poem tends to force readers to side either with Robartes or the girl in diametrically opposite views. As a case in point, John Unterecker argues that the woman and Robartes are at loggerheads because she is "incapable of understanding his ingenious explication of the allegory of the altarpiece" and reduces everything to simpleminded platitudes (158). The dancer is "eminently physical" but desires education in "the most modern way" (158). Unterecker concludes: "Too stupid to realize that she does not need the sort of education she would have, the lady coyly rejects the only education that could possibly be of value to her" (159). Unterecker finds in Robartes' words Yeats's own perspective: "Robartes' argument—which Yeats has by now often enunciated—is that beautiful women who achieve Unity of Being . . . must learn to think with the whole body rather than with the mind" (158).

Elizabeth Cullingford, however, decries Robartes' speeches as "outrageous sophistry that clearly reveals his double standards" ("Yeats and Women" 33). She strongly disagrees with the type of reading advanced by Unterecker[8]:

> If Michael Robartes had been away in the desert for twenty years, Yeats had not, and the comically urbane tone of "Michael Robartes and the Dancer," together with the deflating simplicity of the young girl's rejoinders . . . and her determination to have the last word . . . combine to suggest that we have here the portrait of an attitude rather than a portrait of the artist. (33)

These diverging views address what in this discussion is the critical issue of the poem: whether Yeats's voice and Robartes' voice are one. That is, which position in the poem serves Yeats's own beliefs?

To answer this question, I propose dealing with the poem not as a sociological debate but in terms of the groundwork of the Solomon and Sheba poems—as a study in gender relations revolving around the connection between image and mask. True, on the surface the conflict centers on whether the girl should attend school: "And must no beautiful woman be/Learned like a man?" (*VP* 386). Robartes insists that she attend to things physical; indeed, her name in the title of the poem is an ironic imposition of the role Robartes would have her assume. But the core issue runs deeper than roles or careers. Yeats attempts to dramatize and solve the conflict between freedom and power, sex and the mask, and to do so according to principles learned from his spirit guides.

The image of "dancer" conveys more than Robartes intends. The dancer is one of the most important images of Yeats's poetry. Even his early work consistently connected the spirit world (the ever-living ones) with the dance.

THE WISDOM OF THE BODY 87

The Sidhe could be recognized by their dancing feet as they kept time to the rhythm of the wheel of eternity (*Myth* 77, 286). This magical, spiritual phenomenon gradually evolved into a useful image for Yeats's cosmic vision, which, as Kathleen Raine points out, is best captured by the Hindu god Shiva, also called Lord of the Dance (*Initiate* 353). Shiva dances in a ring of fire; he is crowned by the crescent of the moon and directs the movements of time and space in all material things. His dance signifies the union of inner and outer worlds, matter and spirit. This image of the dancer in a ring of fire suggests Yeats's own eternal wheel, the cyclic motion of primary and antithetical cones, the balance of contraries, the elusive state called Unity of Being in which all elements are harmonized.

In "Michael Robartes and the Dancer," Robartes seems to harbor this Shiva-like vision as he joins the concepts of physical beauty and wholeness: "all beautiful women may/Live in uncomposite blessedness,/And lead us to the like" (*VP* 387). But also implicit in the Shiva-as-Dancer image are the seeds of another important meaning of the dance. For while Shiva might be depicted alone, he could not survive without Kali, birth-and-death Mother, his feminine energy. Joined with her, he is the "spark of creation," and every human orgasm reflects the creative acts of Shiva and Kali (Walker 936). We have seen Yeats associate the dance with sexual union: "live like Solomon/That Sheba led a dance" ("On Woman"). The image of the dancing couple is more ambiguous than the image of the single dancer and can easily dissolve into blatant decadence, as Yeats knew full well: "When I think of the moment before revelation I think of Salome—she too, delicately tinted or maybe mahogany dark—dancing before Herod and receiving the Prophet's head in her indifferent hands" (*VA* 185; *VB* 273). Rather than whirling toward that still center of the individual psyche as a single dancer is able to do, the dance that yokes male and female signifies the relational movement of contraries—sometimes harmonious, clearly threatening, always seductive.

The sexual dimensions of the dance image are clearly latent in the dialogue between Robartes and the young woman. His tone is aggressive, personal, and suggestive. The poem opens in midstream, with the first words from Robartes being a dismissal of the girl's implied, previously stated position about the altarpiece in question: "Opinion [meaning her opinion] is not worth a rush" (*VP* 385). Speaking as if the image of St. George (or Perseus) were a mask for his own intent and attitude, Robartes describes how the hero "loved the lady" and resented that "the half-dead dragon was her thought" (385). According to Robartes' scenario, the lady refuses to turn away from the beast. If she had but time, Robartes argues, she could look "upon the glass" that reflects (presumably) both his love and the image he has fashioned for her and thereby grow wise. Beware, Robartes warns her, of the knight's displeasure and violent anger "at all that is not pictured there" (385). In a word, Robartes argues that the girl should learn from the image her lover creates for her.

The lady also sustains an image upon which the knight may gaze. That image, he believes, is his by right ("[her] lover's wage") since he has rescued her from the dragon. Rather than shape an image that suits him, she cultivates her own and quite modern design. Thus, Robartes has two rivals, the metaphorical dragon and the lady's desire to "put [herself] to college" (385). As David R. Clark and others have noted, while Robartes regards the dragon as a source of jeopardy for the lady, it symbolizes the beast of her own sensual appetites that "dug its claws and shrieked and fought" (385). Her wish to have her own ideas and opinions registers her resistance to being dominated; she refuses to "give up all her mind" or to embrace "as with her flesh and bone" (345) what her lover brings ("On Woman"). The dragon of her own physical desires and her resolve to be learned converge in her act of resistance, her refusal "to turn her eyes . . . upon the glass" and accept the image that Robartes would impose upon her. That image is of body alone, of great beauty eliminating intellect and spirit. This would mean becoming the living embodiment of phase 15 when the weight of absolute, pure beauty collapses the distinction between body and mind—she would "live in uncomposite blessedness" or total subjectivity (387).

Were the girl to accept this image, she would also be embracing Robartes' inaccurate equation of phase 15 with Unity of Being. Like Dante, Robartes translates Unity of Being into the symbols of a perfectly proportioned body: "beating breast," "vigorous thigh," "dreaming eye," sinew "pulled tight" (386). But Unity of Being is not body alone; it is only *like* proportioned physical dimensions that signify a harmony of members. Robartes wants the lady to see this erroneous image in the mirror and embrace it as herself; this is the mask Robartes fabricates for the girl. Contrary to Unterecker's analysis, it is Robartes, and not the lady, who is "eminently physical."[9] Moreover, Robartes balks at nothing to convince her, citing great artists of the Renaissance, Latin texts, even the ritual of the Eucharist "To prove [him] right" (386)—all misrepresented in misshaped images.

In unlocking Robartes' duplicity (and thereby disengaging him from the poet's own position), it is tempting to discredit entirely the knight-in-shining armor/lady-in-distress image. But in the next chapter we will encounter a poem written several years later in which Yeats again employs this same image to illustrate a different point. In "Her Triumph" (poem 4 in "A Woman Young and Old" sequence), the woman freely enters into the image of the lady in distress. Her St. George/Perseus rescues her from the dragon coils of casual pleasure by offering a love of both body and soul. Previously, she "did the dragon's will," i.e., prized only physical appetites. Now she is free from the tyranny of mere sensuality. As David R. Clark observes, the distinction between the dragon and her new love is analogous to the oppositional relationship between the body of fate and the mask—those perennial antagonists. And this is a point applicable to the Robartes poem. For the seemingly simple gesture of the man's offering this image or enforcing it upon the woman involves a cosmic process. The body of fate is "the changing human body" (*VA* 15) that can "snatch away" some "object of desire for a representation of the *Mask* as Image" (D. Clark, *Songs* 142). In both poems, the lady's lover (through his creative mind or intellect) fashions a new mask for both of them, casting himself in the image of St. George and her in the image of a lady in distress.[10]

In "Michael Robartes," the girl refuses to assume the image of Andromeda or the lady in need of rescuing. But Robartes is too blind to recognize that this mask is not welcome. We have what Cullingford calls "a knight in shining armour confronting a damsel who refuses to recognize her own distress" ("Yeats and Women" 32). The lady does not want to be rescued from herself. She wants to be "learned like a man" (*VP* 386), to be revered as more than a body, whether that body be her "lover's wage" or not (385). And she will stimulate her intellect so that she is able to decide what mask is appropriate for her.

Robartes would seek as much to control her life as to incite her love, and he betrays his motives through his use of the "looking glass" image, which conjures another damsel in history—the Lady of Shalott, who was forced to view life through her mirror and not her window. Robartes wants to control the woman's perception; he dictates that she view reality only from his mirror, that she see with his eyes, that she look at the world through his mask. The irony is that he desires to reduce the lady to body alone, yet he would deny the woman her own physical appetites. She is confused by the contradiction: "My wretched dragon is perplexed" (386). "Wretched" is used not in the sense of "evil" but in the sense of "unhappy"; the dragon is pushed back into the cave of nonbeing, into the mirror of secondhand reflection, denied the light of day by Robartes who would "push/That dragon through the fading light" (385), out of the mind and gaze of the lady. The mask Robartes offers her is a deadly one; he would replace the pleasure and appetites of her own body with Dantesque proportioned perfection. He means to empty her mind of booklearning and replace it with the wisdom of what he assumes is her type—a cold, ruthless, indrawn subjectivity wherein mind becomes body, body becomes mind ("The Phases of the Moon").

The mask that Robartes tries to force upon the woman is the mask of a dancer—an eminently suitable image for that state of being wherein she could "outdance thought," where her "Body perfection brought," where dancer cannot be known from the dance ("The Double Vision of Michael Robartes" 383, "Among School Children" 446). These are heady images, but they must be counterbalanced by the dark side of this image. The dancer is also like Helen, "Homer's Paragon/Who never gave the burning town a thought" ("The Double Vision of Michael Robartes" 384). Within her, Mask and Body of Fate are identical, thought and will converge, chance and choice are one, contemplation and desire are united (*VA* 69–70; *VB* 135–36). That is, the dancer needs no one else; her vision is turned entirely inward, the Intellect/Creative Mind provides no corrective to the Mask nor the Will to the Body of Fate.

Robartes criticizes the woman for neglecting the wisdom of the body and pursuing an education of the mind. But the girl will not be seduced. In an ironic twist, the woman's own thoughts and appetites (her dragon) save her from this peril, which is perhaps the ultimate defense against the beguiling attraction of Robartes' dancer image. "What but a dragon could dream of thwarting a St. George?" (*VB* 138).

But the lady does more than politely resist. Like the dragon, she actively parries Robartes' attack. In their first exchange, the woman clarifies for herself Robartes' opening lines: "You mean they argued," she comments (*VP* 385). Robartes replies: "Put it so"—i.e., say it that way if you like. But he cannot stop her; the girl rewrites his words, putting the story of St. George and the dragon into a different perspective as seen through her own eyes. She will also "put [herself] to college"—designing an image for herself just as she puts her life into her own words, writes her own text, even rewords and corrects his. She has the final word, too: "They say such different things at school" (387). In this light, Robartes' seduction appears as sophistry born out of Renaissance art or twenty years in the desert—or more accurately— out of the very mask of Michael Robartes. But not out of the mind of W. B. Yeats. The voice of Robartes is not the voice of Yeats. Nor is the girl's voice the voice of the poet. Yeats's position is found through the girl's resistance, working in the metaphysical principles at issue in their debate.

If "Michael Robartes" is ultimately a poem about masking, then it should be placed alongside other metaphysical dialogues like "Ego Dominus Tuus" and the Solomon and Sheba poems. Yeats does not define gender roles in these lyrics, although such roles may become topics in the course of the dialogues and real-life outcomes of masking choices. Instead, Yeats attempts to enact the process of masking as it occurs. Whether "Michael Robartes" succeeds on this level is a separate issue. The character of Michael Robartes is guilty of attempting to control and distort the feminine; Yeats himself is not, and for perhaps one paramount reason: the lady must be free to accept or reject the lover's mask.

Given that loving and masking are inseparable actions, there are inherent dangers. The first has to do with selecting the right mask. Solomon knows that an image may be too strong or not strong enough. Yeats himself speaks of true and false masks and clung "artfully to a delusion" in his own past (*AS II* 228). The appropriate selection does not depend so much on the mask itself as on specific conditions. After all, Yeats does not condemn the woman in "Her Triumph" for embracing the Andromeda mask, the very mask that the "dancer" rejects. He praises Sheba, who by willingly emptying her mind to conceive her Solomon's thoughts engenders a wisdom that transcends their single intellects; he also supports this nameless girl in her designs to become learned. It is not the type of mask (or its practical corollaries) that are at issue in "Michael Robartes" but rather an "attitude," as Cullingford rightly argues ("Yeats and Women" 33). This is the second danger, that one lover will attempt to impose an unwelcome mask and thus to dominate the other with his or her own will. Disagreement, even conflict, is inevitable, but both participants must be free and engaged in the outcome. Robartes violates this tenet by displaying a "mine or nothing" attitude.

It is no accident that the poem Yeats chose to follow "Michael Robartes" in the volume *Michael Robartes and the Dancer* is "Solomon and the Witch," which therefore serves as a corrective to the preceding poem. Solomon is wise enough to admit that "maybe an image is too strong/Or maybe is not strong enough" (*VP* 388). Positioning the two poems back to back, Yeats implies that Robartes could well learn from Solomon.

Reading "Solomon to Sheba," "Solomon and the Witch," and "Michael Robartes and the Dancer" as poems enacting the act of masking clarifies how important they are to Yeats's artistic development. By joining these two major tenets of his worldview—the feminine as an avenue to wisdom, and the connection of loving and masking—to his new understanding of human and daimonic interaction, Yeats has in effect revolutionized both the style and the focus of his poetry. First, he has given the feminine a voice. True, Sheba does not have a coherent presence *per se,* but she is a full partner in a dialogue that enacts the process of finding wisdom through sexual union. She is thus a forerunner to the young bride in "The Gift of Harun Al-Raschid":

> All those abstractions that you fancied were
> From the great Treatise of Parmenides;
> All, all those gyres and cones and midnight things
> Are but a new expression of her body. (*VA* 126)

The young girl in "Michael Robartes" articulates a wisdom of the body of a different kind, one that seeks its own appetites and authority but at the same time insists on being learned in her own right. Her voice, too, is different from Sheba's—more corrective, more critical, but for Yeats a source of wisdom for Robartes, if only he would listen.

Second, these poems reveal that even in midstream, as Yeats and his wife are inundated by massive amounts of provocative and (for them) exhilarating disclosures from the spirit guides, he is not paralyzed by euphoric success. These insights into temporal and spiritual reality challenge both his poetic skills and his own personality type. He refuses to remain trapped by the "harsh" and "timid sun" (qtd. in Bradford, *Yeats at Work*. abr. ed. 6), just as he declines to claim credit for "truths without father" ("The Gift of Harun Al-Raschid"). He continues what he understands as a lifelong struggle to establish peace

> 'Twixt oil and water, candles and dark night,
> Hill-side and hollow, the hot-footed sun,
> And the cold sliding slippery-footed moon. (*VPL* 478)

And he knows full well that loving and masking are a trial-and-error process and in 1919 is already considering the snares.

While it is one thing to contend that the genius of these poems is to designate the act of loving and masking as the terrain of the daimon, it is quite another to find them entirely satisfactory. As he explores how men and women seek images appropriate for the secret self of lover and beloved, Yeats comes nearer to the nerve of his occult dialogues and his poetic verse: his own relationship with the daimon. Yet for all the innovation and insight these three poems represent, I would finally argue that they fall short of the prize. That is, they fail to solve the shortcomings of "Ego Dominus Tuus," where Yeats tries to make the Hic/Ille projection stand for that hidden, nearly indecipherable opposition between the "mysterious one" and the poet. The docility of Sheba, the polite but firm resistance of the nameless girl, may serve his purpose if Yeats intends only to critique human sexual relations. But as insights into the operation of the daimon or as a window into the feminine in his soul, these feminine masks mark a notable beginning to a task not yet completed.

Thus, there is still important ground to cover, in particular, the power and personality of the daimon and her love/hate relationship with her human host. Yeats's feminine mask is still underdeveloped, confined to reactive responses to the masculine and as yet far afield from the daimon as arch foe. Much of Yeats's energies in the early 1920s were dedicated to collating and honing the Automatic Script material into *A Vision*. But in the closing years of the decade, he will further perfect his feminine mask in a voice so complex that it requires a sequence of poems rather than a single lyric to express it.

CHAPTER 5

GENDERED VOICES IN MOMENTS OF CRISIS

"A Man Young and Old works a kind of free fantasia on Yeats's own love life."
> John Unterecker, *A Reader's Guide to William Butler Yeats* (194)

"IMs and CMs are the expression of the Wheel in the life of sexual passion."
> W. B. Yeats, *AS III* (111)

After the publication of *A Vision* in 1925, W. B. Yeats exerted continuous and dedicated effort in writing poetry that not only released the voice of the feminine, as in the Solomon and Sheba poems, but also displayed fully developed feminine masks. With this chapter, I will explore Yeats's double-voiced verse in the sequence "A Woman Young and Old" and in its complement, "A Man Young and Old." These sequences are of special interest for two reasons. First, the power and depth of "The Woman's" mask testify to Yeats's developing skill in creating the feminine in action. This marks an artistic achievement as well as a mystical milestone, measuring not only the lessons Yeats learned in writing *The Only Jealousy of Emer* and the Solomon and Sheba poems but also the contemplation and honing of the Script discoveries as he completed *A Vision*.

The second unique feature of these sequences is that they capture in verse an aspect of daimonic activity called the Moments of Crisis, which permeate much of the Script material. "A Man" and "A Woman" tell the story of sexual passion. It is not two stories but one—told from two perspectives, different yet complementary, which form a unified whole. These sequences have usually been read as autobiographical, often in isolation, sometimes in counterpoint to each other, but never as I propose to read them: as one poem, one continuous plot, one unified treatment of sexual relations and (by extension) human and daimonic interactivity. But why *never*?

For reasons of his own, Yeats appears to have sabotaged the possibility. Consider the publication history of the poems. Both "A Man Young and Old" and "A Woman Young and Old" were written between 1926 and 1929. They were obviously structured to reflect each other, both with eleven poems depicting gender as expressed in youth and age and concluding with choruses from Greek tragedies. Despite these clear parallels, Yeats published the sequences independently, nearly five years apart.[1] "A Man Young and Old" first appeared in two separate sets called "More Songs from an Old Countryman" (1926) and "Four Songs from the Young Countryman" (1927) before appearing as a single collection in *The Tower* (1928) (Jeffares, *Commentary* 259). "A Woman Young and Old" remained unpublished until 1933, when the poems were positioned after the Crazy Jane sequence in *The Winding Stair and Other Poems*, "for some reason I cannot recall," Yeats comments (*VP* 831). The decision is a telling one. Despite Yeats's curious lapse of memory, his rationale to separate the sequences cannot be as casual as he pretends. It is as if Yeats deliberately fragmented "A Man" and removed it from "A Woman" to impede associations between the two in the reader's mind.[2]

There is a second obvious reason why these sequences have not been connected to the Moments of Crisis. Outside of the Automatic Script, there is almost no reference to the Moments of Crisis in Yeats's occult essays. He mentions the phenomenon only briefly in the first edition of *A Vision* (173, 241) and removes it altogether in the second—yet another illustration of Yeats's partial but deliberate elimination of gendered material from the mystical exposition that most scholars have had to depend on for decades.

It is risky business to argue with Yeats's own placement of the sequences. But my reasons make sense in terms of the poems' fit with the Moments of Crisis, as I will show, and in terms of the very rudiments of the solar/lunar system. In the temporal order, gender never exists in pure form.[3] It is known only through its phasal manifestation, which for Yeats meant ever-shifting ratios of masculine and feminine principles coexisting in the same personality. Similarly, personal sexual relations do not emerge, develop, or dissolve in isolation. Neither do men and women fashion a sense of themselves as sexual beings without interacting across gender lines. Just as the twenty-eight

Phases mark the interaction of masculine/feminine in personality types and historical periods, Initiatory Moments (IM) and Critical Moments (CM) define the encounter between masculine and feminine in personal relationships. These Moments "are the expression of the [Great] Wheel in the life of sexual passion" (*AS III* 111).

In brief, "A Woman" and "A Man" sequences capture male and female voices as they proceed through temporal experience, not aging so much as registering Initiatory and Critical Moments in their lives. That is, both voices reflect the consequences of stages outlined in the Automatic Script, stages that for the Woman complement the Man's, for the Man complement the Woman's. Before turning to the poems themselves, a brief synopsis of the Moments of Crisis will prove helpful.

From March to June 1919, the bulk of the Automatic Script dialogues was dedicated to exploring the Moments of Crisis in temporal existence. This discussion generates the fundamental tenets of Yeats's metaphysical system, including the sexual nature of the daimon, the previous incarnate forms of W. B. and Georgie Yeats, and the structure and purgative stages of the afterlife. Initially what attracted the poet to the topic was the prospect of solving the enigma of Maud Gonne in his own sexual history. Readers can glimpse how W. B. Yeats reconstructed the life-changing experiences in his personal past, and to a lesser degree they can do the same for Georgie Yeats.[4] But without question, the couple understood this subject to be philosophical and not personal in nature and were warned away from purely personal applications: "All personal is DANGEROUS" (*AS II* 379, 380).

The belief that underlies this section of the Script is simple. All men and all women will love—this is a philosophic necessity. That an individual should love now, this person, for this reason, is a matter of either fate (another's choice) or destiny (one's own choice). The Yeatses used their own lives to illustrate the course of these choices, which fall into specific and universal patterns. True to the trademark of their vision of gender, the Yeatses define the Moments of Crisis for men and women in a reciprocal and complementary dynamic.[5]

Individuals experience several Initiatory Moments (originally called Impregnating Moments), which produce changes of the mind and prepare them for two Critical Moments, when self-deceit and self-pity are removed (377). Several characteristics are immediately striking about Yeats's vision of Initiatory and Critical Moments. First, they occur by necessity with no apparent means of escape. Second, they describe intense and most often painful experiences (what Yeats calls "shock") that serve the hidden purpose of the daimons and force the individual to undergo a process of self-illumination. And third, the difference between a man's experience and a woman's at any moment can be defined simply by inverting the elements or sequence, since complementarity provides the energy to propel the process to its final end, spiritual revelation.

The Moments of Crisis occur by necessity because they are designed and executed by the daimon (*AS III* 112). The daimon is also at the root of the tragedy of sexual love, which Yeats characterizes as unhappy but not "permanently tragic" (*AS II* 317). The more painful the experience, the more intimately involved is the daimon: "the greater the tragedy the greater the . . . daimonic reaction" (321). The daimon is no mere puppeteer who manipulates men and women to produce a union and progeny of its own. Rather, the daimon can be free or can suffer during a Moment of Crisis. A woman's daimon suffers during her Initiatory Moments but is free in her Critical Moments. The reverse is true for the man's daimon, who is free during his Initiatory Moments but suffers in his Critical Moments (345). If the daimon suffers, the human host is said to be a "victim." If the daimon is free, the human host is "teacher" (345). Thus, the woman is victim, the man is teacher, during Initiatory Moments; the woman is teacher, the man victim, during Critical Moments.[6]

Initiatory Moments help pave the way for Critical Moments. The purpose of Initiatory Moments is "to free from deception" (350) by revealing a weakness (214). These Moments comprise what Yeats calls a "moral rescue" (329). A man suffers "from lack of perception of reality" (*AS III* 274). During the IM experience, he adjusts according to his phase: if objective, he needs to forget self; if subjective, he needs to realize objectivity (270). In the case of a woman, during the first Initiatory Moment she desires to gain experience from the man (*AS II* 329). During the second, she is rescued from "lack of pity—that is to say a rescue from the desire to help the helpless, this becomes a desire to isolate the helpless or real pity" (329). For Yeats, there is a distinction between false and real pity, and between pity and true affection.[7] False pity means desiring to help another, feeling sorry for the other. It is "blind" (i.e., self-deceiving) because while it masquerades as altruism, it entails pronounced egoism: it "is only the analysis of *your ego in their* shoes" (305). Rather than wishing to help, the lover wishes to control (308).

Real pity, on the other hand, allows lovers to feel autonomous. It is "pride of self" achieved by the lover and extended to the beloved. The lover knows that he/she cannot be fundamentally hurt or changed in a relationship. Identity remains: "it says go and I am still I" (330). Thus, the lover is willing to allow the beloved to depart: "it says go if that were better for you—do if it is better for you to do[.] Think as you will" (330). Real pity allows "unity of self with another self"—or the "I" affirming the "you"—which permits the other to approach without "*fear* of hurting or changing" (330).

Achieving real pity is only a stage in the process of self-illumination, evident by its association with the important but insufficient Initiatory Moments. While pity always entails desire (307), it is the contrary of true affection (286, 379). Affection never desires to change the other, but "it is impossible to pity without desiring to change" (379). At best, pity is a precursor to wisdom and love (304), the end points of Critical Moments.

Critical Moments complete the process launched through the Initiatory Moments by eliminating cruelty and deception from relations of passion (*AS III* 113). During her first Critical Moment, the woman learns "that admiration is not necessary to love" (*AS II* 330). She exercises her own "clear reasoning choice" and so holds herself apart from the relationship (330). During her second Critical Moment, there is a "harshness coming"; she is purged of her own pride and vanity, is able to extend true pity to her lover, and opens herself to chance or blind fate (329, 330). She also achieves "pride of identity" by discovering the "isolation of identity" (329), in effect internalizing that autonomous sense of self that makes real pity possible. This pattern is reversed for the man. In his first Critical Moment, he desires to be chosen; in his second, he desires to choose. He first feels autonomous and self-sufficient and only later realizes "the necessity for identity merged in another" (329). So while the second Critical Moment is a "cutting apart" for the woman, it is "a link" for the man (329).[8]

The complementarity of these patterns surfaces with every comparison between the experiences of men and women. It is found in comparing the Initiatory Moments: for the woman, unlikeness is harmonized; for the man, unlikeness is accentuated (341). It is found in comparing the Critical Moments: for the woman, unlikeness is accentuated, choice yields to chance; for the man, unlikeness is harmonized, chance yields to choice. It is found in the reciprocal alignment of Faculties: for the woman in Critical Moments, the mask is first freed from the Personality of Fate (later called the Body of Fate in *A Vision*); then Creative Genius (later called Creative Mind) is freed from the Ego (later called the Will). For the man, his Creative Genius is first freed from the Ego; then his Mask is freed from the Personality of Fate (*AS III* 123).

As with much of the Script material, the Moments of Crisis seem only occult abstractions. But in "A Man" and "A Woman," the concept takes on depth and substance as masculine and feminine voices enact these experiences, which Yeats believed were intrinsic to sexual relations. In reading the sequences in this way, I am not asserting that Yeats's metaphysical interests dominate his aesthetic purpose. On the contrary, these poems do not strike readers as abstract renditions of spiritual principles in the same way that prompted Yeats to denounce "The Phases of the Moon" and "Ego Dominus Tuus." Nor will I argue that each of the eleven poems in the sequences marches lockstep through the various Moments. Initiatory and Critical Moments provide a framework, not a formula, for reading.

Interpreting "A Man Young and Old" and "A Woman Young and Old" against the backdrop of Yeats's conception of human sexual relations has two direct benefits. First, it allows the speakers of these poems to take on a depth and complexity previously ignored by critics, who too often overlook everything but the personal parallels to Yeats's own past.[9] The Moments of

Crisis help readers better understand the archetypal dimensions of gender as enacted in these sequences. Second, Moments of Crisis help explain the adamant differences between the male and female speakers—I will refer to them as the Man and the Woman—who appear profoundly alienated, frustrated, even embittered by their attempts at loving. Indeed, the Man and the Woman are out of sync, but not because love is hopeless or because masculine and feminine genders are irreparably flawed or alienated. Rather, the speakers move through reciprocal stages, working toward a purpose that for each as an individual marks significant achievement, even completion.

To dramatize the difference between the sexual experiences of the Man and the Woman, Yeats first distinguishes their preferences. The Man values the power of speech or song and measures his impact according to the efficacy of his voice. The Woman values the power of sight. She is profoundly affected by what she sees and seeks to lure her lovers by her physical appearance. This contrast in preference does not encase the speakers in separate realms in an absolute sense, but it does accent their unique and sometimes opposing reactions to sexual relations.

"A Man Young and Old" relates the sexual experiences of the male speaker through a series of phases: his youth ("First Love," "Human Dignity," and "The Mermaid"), young adulthood ("The Death of the Hare" and "The Empty Cup"), maturity ("His Memories," "The Friends of His Youth," and "Summer and Spring"), and old age ("The Secrets of the Old" and "His Wildness"). In each of these phases, the speaker is obsessed with the power of speech. In his youth, the Man believes that voice can heal his heart by expressing his anguish: "I could recover if I shrieked" (*VP* 452). Voice can also express intense pleasure, but one of his most painful memories is the refusal of his lover to make his sexual prowess known. "Strike me if I shriek," she cries into his ear (455). The Man feels betrayed by the Woman's willful silence. By crying out, she would admit his success as a lover. He is angered by that withholding of her cry of pleasure, her denial of his success to the world.

> The women take so little stock
> In what I do or say
> They'd sooner leave their cosseting
> To hear a jackass bray. (455)

As he ages, the Man complains that his voice is cracked, destroyed by "laughter not time" (455), and compares his early loves to "an old song" (457). Finally, he feels intimately bound to two women who alone "know the stories that we know/Or say the things we say" (458). By the end of his life, he longs to "have a peacock cry" but must settle to "nurse a stone/And sing it lullaby" (459).

What is most striking is the tone of these poems, which is shaped by a character who is "self-tormented, nostalgic, and bitter," as Hazard Adams describes him (121).[10] The Moments of Crisis provide an insight into both the mind of this character and the path he follows—bitter, besieged, and empty as he is. If there is one word that characterizes the Man's perspective, it is "adversarial." The three poems of his youth address the catastrophe of his life—an encounter with a Woman (his "first love") who is spawned by the moon "in beauty's murderous brood." This is not the "blessed moon" of Solomon but a lunar force that lashes beauty to its service and drives mortal lovers "lunatic." In "Human Dignity," the speaker accuses the Woman of having a heart of stone and of generating kindness that "has no comprehension in't" (*VP* 452). In "The Mermaid," the Man likens himself to a "swimming lad" who is selected by a creature from the seas "for her own" and "plunging down/Forgot in cruel happiness/That even lovers drown" (453). Behind such bitterness lies intense suffering. Clearly, the Man longs for comfort and completion. Instead, he encounters rejection and disappointment, the kind of pain ("shock" is the term used in the Script) that typifies sexual relations in Moments of Crisis.

The Man also experiences the seductive power of the "lure" (*AS II* 448). He believes that the Woman deliberately chooses to appear in his life to further her own ends: "She walked awhile and blushed awhile/And on my pathway stood." He sees himself as her victim, losing the very power to direct his own actions with any success: "I have attempted many things/And not a thing is done," for she has "left me but a lout,/Maundering here, and maundering there/Emptier of thought/Than the heavenly circuit of its stars/When the moon sails out" (*VP* 451). With "The Death of the Hare," the metaphor of the hunt makes the adversarial nature of love explicit. Here the role of pursuer/pursued is reversed as the speaker rejoices "as lover should/At the drooping of an eye,/At the mantling of the blood" (453). These words are particularly revealing because they disclose the Man's own heartlessness and self-absorption.

In "The Empty Cup," the speaker has imbibed the cup of sexual union but is still parched. The experience duplicates the lesson of the hunt. Throughout his youth, the speaker desired love without attaining it. Now he achieves his goal but remains unsatisfied—victim once again: "for that reason am I crazed/And my sleep is gone" (454). The experience underlying the metaphor is not unrequited, but instead unsatisfying, love. Deprived of the very power he curses, he moves away from lamenting its loss to renouncing its value altogether.

Thus, in the poems of youth and early adulthood, Yeats has created a masculine mask that is quintessentially "objective" in type. The Man operates entirely within his own mind; he is continually self-conscious but unaware of the limitations of his own perspective. The Man may feel *lured* by feminine beauty, but he is *trapped* by his own "lack of perception of reality"

(*AS III* 274). This psyche shapes the voices in these poems and saturates their style and syntactic structure. "First Love" serves as a perfect example of how that psyche works. Each of the three stanzas consists of one sentence. Each sentence is constructed so that subordinate clauses are paired together. But instead of clarifying or qualifying, these clauses contradict their partners. The Woman is otherworldly yet walks earth's paths. She is murderous but blushes like an innocent. He mistakes her heart to be human, but it is the moon's own cruel heart. He touches her and finds stone instead of flesh and blood. He has since attempted many things but accomplished nothing. Love has transfigured him into a lonely lout with an empty mind and aimless feet.

This binary structure dramatizes more than the disparity between the Man's expectations and the Woman's designs or between his hopes and the subsequent results of the encounter. It reveals the Man's mind at work, a mind that seeks and finds life's contradictions, a voice that through a syntactic structure imposes that vision upon the reader. It is also a victimized voice, one that perceives fate's agents—and they are female—pursuing him to his destruction. According to the Man, women have seduced, spurned, and humiliated him because they are cold, heartless, and foreign, offspring of the crazed and maddening moon. But the truth is that his judgment reflects his feelings alone, his conclusion merely what appears to him to be true. He has neither asked nor listened to the other side.

The solution, to his mind, is to conquer the Woman. But he is either dismayed by her "distracted air" (*VP* 453) or despairs that the cup of sexual union is "dry as bone" (454). Simply put, in the first five poems of the sequence, the Man's own mind has locked him away from all fruitful experience. To attain any level of self-illumination or fulfillment in love, the Man must establish a link between himself and the women he pretends to love. This is the very course that Yeats sets for his character.

At first glance, it appears that the Man makes no headway in his destination. In the poems of maturing manhood—"His Memories," "The Friends of His Youth," and "Summer and Spring"—undisguised enmity gives way to bitter derision. In "His Memories," the Man dwells upon personal humiliation, how women "take so little stock/In what I do or say" (455). His bitterness is not assuaged by the memory (the "cup") of enjoying beauty herself—Helen—"who had brought great Hector down/and put all Troy to wreck." But the destructive powers of his self-deceit have already activated the process of Initiatory Moments. What the Man relates as his lover's cruelty ("Strike me if I shriek") is really a moment of intense self-doubt ("They'd sooner leave their cosseting/To hear a jackass bray"). In the continuum of spiritual revelation, self-doubt may be a far cry from self-illumination, but it marks a progression from the self-deceit that opens the sequence. Indeed, "His Memories" is a culmination of a painful process: not a series of seductions and rejections but rather a prolonged purging of deception. By this midpoint of the sequence, it is clear even to this objective type that "the nature needs something beyond itself" (*AS III* 120). The Man's true "rescue" (*AS II* 329) is therefore not from the Woman's supposed "cruelty" but from his own self-deceit, which requires that he forget himself. This process is already initiated in "The Death of the Hare":

> Then suddenly my heart is wrung
> By her distracted air
> And I remember wildness lost. (*VP* 453)

In "The Friends of His Youth," the Man depicts his former love interest (Madge) as a laughable, comic figure rather than one of the "murderous brood." The image of "old Madge" replaces the female as a powerful, cruel seductress: "She that has been wild/And barren as a breaking wave/Thinks that the stone's a child" (456). The Man's derision reflects his own need to belittle his old foe and prompts him to ridicule his own youthful naiveté. Yet here, too, we can see a striking change in the speaker's attitude. For one, the Woman is no longer regarded either as a nameless female or as an idealized lover. Rather, she is an individual with a name. Madge may be the lover he previously described as Helen of Troy, but now he paints a different picture of her, closer to the real Woman:

> Old Madge comes down the lane,
> A stone upon her breast,
> And a cloak wrapped about the stone,
> And she can get no rest
> With singing hush and hush-a-bye. (456)

The Man has entered into the phase of Critical Moments, becoming partially aware of his lover's true nature so that his new image is "half her half his own thought" (*AS III* 121).

"Summer and Spring" describes the Man's memory of believing that he "halved a soul" with a Woman, only to discover that she had tried to make herself "whole" with someone else. The romance turns into farce; Plato's myth of androgyny is overturned by the Woman's promiscuity and by the seductive ploy used by both men. But instead of lashing out at the Woman's cruelty, the Man exhibits a surprising sense of equanimity:

> O what a bursting out there was,
> And what a blossoming,
> When we had all the summer-time
> And she had all the spring! (*VP* 457)

In a word, he extends what Yeats calls "real pity," which brings with it a "pride of self" as the Man understands he cannot be fundamentally hurt or changed even in a painful relationship: "it says go and I am still I" (*AS II* 330).

In "The Secrets of the Old" and "His Wildness," the speaker loses his air of autonomy and superiority and confesses "the necessity for identity merged in another" (329). He acknowledges the truth of his relationships with Madge and Margery:

> We three make up a solitude;
> For none alive to-day
> Can know the stories that we know
> Or say the things we say. (*VP* 457–58)

This insight into the interdependence, the link with Madge and Margery, marks a milestone in growth and illumination in this character. The Man "lives in memory," "For Peg and Meg and Paris' love/That had so straight a back,/Are gone away" (458). Missing are the bitter ranting and the ambiguous laughter of his former years. His lone desire is to mount to the stars, and "Being all alone I'd nurse a stone/And sing it lullaby" (459).

The Man no longer accentuates the unlikeness. His perception of the moon and "beauty's murderous brood" has shifted. He understands (finally) that there is a different way to describe the relationships of his life. The youthful, terrifying tryst with the mermaid (the subjective siren who seemed to draw him down into her unknowing cruelty) now seems "like an old song" (457). These changes in the Man's awareness mark a new ability to relate to people as individuals, to do more than curse the moon, to raise his voice alongside crazed lullabies and "old women's secrets" (457).

Using the Moments of Crisis as a framework for interpreting the experience of this speaker encourages readers to see beyond the bitterness and self-containment of the poems of youth to the aging lover who frees himself from the prison of his own perspective and acknowledges his connections to the women in his life. This framework also prompts us to read this sequence not merely as the history of Yeats's own sexual past but also as a voice for all men who labor through the turning of the Great Wheel. Such labor is shared by women as well. I now turn to "A Woman Young and Old"—the complementary voice in the life of sexual passion—to discover how the Moments of Crisis provide an insight into this character and into the universal feminine.

This sequence is structured identically to its counterpart. There are poems of youth ("Father and Child," "Before the World Was Made," and "A First Confession"), young adulthood ("Her Triumph" and "Consolation"), maturity ("Chosen," "Parting," and "Her Vision in the Wood") and old age ("A Last Confession" and "Meeting"). Throughout the poems, sight rather than sound assumes center stage. Yeats elects to make these faculties both conflicting and gender-specific by introducing the sequence with "Father and Child." Because father and daughter operate out of distinct senses, they apprehend different realities. The man *strikes* the board; he *tells* his daughter that she is "under ban/Of all good men and women" because he has *heard* her name *mentioned* with a man of ill repute, a target of *gossip* (531). Then he *relates* her *reply*. But though she has *heard* him, her eyes are turned elsewhere, to the man of "the worst of all bad names" (emphasis added). Rumor does not sway her; neither does her father's irritation nor his gesture of insistence and exasperation. She does not deny her interest but explains it: "his hair is beautiful,/Cold as the March wind his eyes" (531). What society *tells* her cannot eclipse what she *sees* with her own eyes.[11]

Appearance and perception are critical, and the Woman's preference for the power of sight is sustained in the subsequent nine poems. In "Before the World Was Made," the young Woman becomes more aware of the interaction between herself and the men around her, and thus appearance becomes more and more important to her. She designs a type of mask, wondering if she should make "the lashes dark/And the eyes more bright/And the lips more scarlet." She wanders "from mirror after mirror," seeking the correct image (531–32). "A First Confession" shows the Woman growing in her understanding of the masking process. The briar tangled in her hair did not injure her, although her "blenching and trembling" suggest it did. It is all an act to entice and seduce, a sort of gendered sleight of hand, "Nothing but dissembling,/Nothing but coquetry" (532). The motive appears simple enough: "For a man's attention/Brings such satisfaction/To the craving in my bones" (533).

The themes of masking and flirtation culminate in "Her Vision in the Wood," when her gaze meets the gaze of her former lover, "all blood and mire, that beast-torn wreck" (537). Now she masks herself in the "wine" of her own blood, matching the "blood-bedabbled breast" of the Adonis-figure who is "no fabulous symbol" but "my heart's victim and its torturer" (537). The Woman assumes her final "masker's cloak and hood" in "Meeting." She stands face-to-face with her lover, both of them withered by old age. They gaze upon each other and hate "what the other loved" (539). It is a kind of self-hatred or a hatred of what they had become, masked in "this beggarly habiliment" (539). But their speech belies the truth; rather, they hurl cruel words against the hideousness of the other. The Woman, so dominated by sight, recognizes that there is a "sweeter word" to describe "such as he" and "such as me" (539). But that word remains unspoken.

Some critics have emphasized what they describe as the Woman's superficiality, her manipulative flirtations, her appetite for sexual pleasure. John Unterecker points to "her own evil nature" that takes a "casual approach to love" (236). He does not comment, however, on the transformation from her flirtations in "A First Confession" to her ability to experience a union of

hearts in "Chosen." Hazard Adams argues that the Woman is "simply beyond reasoning with." In her youth she indulges in "casuistic self-justifica-
tion." As she matures she longs for spiritual union, yet does not care "for
the soul of the afterlife" (209), and finally lapses into a bitter rage at the
sight of her former lover (209, 213). But other critics defend the Woman's
character. Elizabeth Cullingford, for instance, praises the speaker's ability to
outplay the male at his own game, as well as her sense of humor that allows
the Woman to regard love's bitter disappointments less solemnly than the
humorless male speaker of the first sequence (*Gender and History* 215).

While such analyses may help the reader assess the Woman's character,
they do not come to grips with the shifts in the Woman's state of mind. She
flirts, she indulges her physical appetite, she longs for spiritual intimacy.
Even Cullingford's conclusion that the sequence displays the Woman's
"widely different sexual identities" (226) fails to establish an interpretive rationale that makes sense of vignettes that appear disconnected, even contradictory. However, when the framework of Yeats's Moments of Crisis is applied to the sequence, its internal unity is revealed.

In the poems of her youth, the Woman lures her lover by her beauty, but
not to destroy him, as the speaker in "A Man" alleges. Rather, she herself is
captivated by the vision of his physical beauty ("his hair is beautiful") and
his cool spirit ("Cold as the March wind his eyes") (*VP* 531). Her attraction
is stronger than the moralistic ranting of her father. She is drawn to the for-
bidden and longs to experience what this Man has to offer, or in the terms
of the Script, she has "a desire of experience from the man" (*AS II* 329).

Because of her own attraction, the Woman's actions in "Before the World
Was Made" are focused on commanding the Man's attention. She fashions
her snare with great care—the dark lashes, the bright eyes, the scarlet lips—
for she seeks "the face I had/Before the world was made" (*VP* 532). That
is, she seeks literally a cosmetic mask, figuratively an image, that the Man will
love: "I'd have him love the thing that was" (532). This is more than a re-
iteration of the loving/masking theme of the Solomon and Sheba poems.
For the "image" she seeks (Yeats uses the term "lure") is dictated from beyond the Woman's own designs. It comes from outside the temporal order,
determined before she herself was born ("before the world was made"). As
Yeats's spirit guides instructed him, the image that the Woman assumes is
the "symbol of some thing in the nature" of one of the children that the
Man will father (*AS III* 113). It is fashioned by the daimons of "those
women with whom [the Man] has been in a relation of passion in other lives,
who are now in the state between two lives" (113). The Man will love the
symbol itself, not the Woman who lures him.

The Woman understands this, even desires it, and so remains "cold the
while" as she looks "upon a man/As though on my beloved" (*VP* 532). No

wonder the Man finds a "heart of stone" where a "flesh and blood" woman should be. These lovers meet at cross-purposes. He is called by the lure, expecting love, only to find what he thinks is cruelty and betrayal. She attracts him by shaping an image designed by daimons, not one that reflects herself. Yet behind the apparent impasse is the Woman's refusal to deceive the man, ironic as it may sound. If she were cruel, she would lash him to her, control him by extending what Yeats calls false or "self surrendering pity" (*AS II* 330), the desire "to help the helpless" (329). But she refuses to do so. This speaker, who may squander her body, is not so free with her heart: "my blood be cold the while/And my heart unmoved" (*VP* 532).

True, in "A First Confession" their encounter seems a kind of game, "a casual improvisation," even a ritual:

> My blenching and trembling,
> Nothing but dissembling,
> Nothing but coquetry. (532)

Yet just as we identified in the poems of the Man's youth, the Woman is working through Initiatory experiences. While she comes to terms with the temptation to feel sorry for her lover, she must also address a dilemma unique to her sex. The Woman is divided between the desire to disown the false, bright face of her mask/image ("Brightness that I pull back/From the Zodiac") and her obsession with commanding the Man's attention. His admiration is paramount, for it "Brings such satisfaction/To the craving in my bones." If she allows the image to slip, his questioning eyes will surely turn away: "What can they do but shun me" (533).

While the Man must "forget self" in his poems of young adulthood, the Woman must rid herself of this uncontrolled appetite, this insatiable craving for attention, which in "Her Triumph" she calls "the dragon's will" (533). This compulsion is overthrown by a new experience, a union that is not dominated by mere coquetry, simple physical pleasure, or duplicity. The Woman calls this new lover her St. George and her Perseus, acknowledging her need of "moral rescue" (*AS II* 329). Together they stare at the astonishing sea (employing her preferred sense) and hear the shriek of a "miraculous strange bird" (his preferred sense) (*VP* 534). In this moment of enchantment and harmony, when sight and sound are both commanded, this male and female become a Solomon and Sheba of a kind and hear their own cockerel.

The Woman's near-mystical experience of harmonious and balanced union brings her to a new level of wisdom. In "Consolation," she cites the pleasures not of a Man's admiration but of his company. Her invitation may be one of rest or death or pleasure; the gesture is ambiguous. But the end result is fulfillment:

> But stretch that body for a while
> And lay down that head
> Till I have told the sages
> Where man is comforted. (534)

Pleasure and comfort cannot erase the crimes of the fall or of mortality, but they can erase their memory, at least "for a while." Freed from her cravings for attention and from false pity, the Woman achieves a sense of intimacy as the "unlikeness" moves in harmony (*AS II* 341) and her Initiatory stage is complete. Like the Man, she has reached a very different state of mind than she had in her youth. But instead of learning *his* lesson—the necessity of breaking from the prison of his own limited perceptions—she passes through the illusion that love is "a casual/Improvisation, or a settled game" to the wisdom that comes only when male and female share comfort. The Woman understands "that admiration is not necessary to love" (330) and so enters into the process of Critical Moments. The masking and coquetry give way to moments when "his heart my heart did seem."

With "Chosen," the speaker continues her journey through Critical Moments. Her path will be the reverse of the Man's: he will learn that his identity is "merged in another." But she will experience a "cutting apart" (329). Already her experience of harmony is joined to a dawning sense of disparity and isolation. She longs for that moment of "utmost pleasure with a man," a moment that does not stem from admiration or pleasure but comes when

> his heart my heart did seem
> And both adrift on the miraculous stream
> Where . . .
> The Zodiac is changed into a sphere. (*VP* 535)

She marks the departure of her lover in Ptolemaic terms, as if he were the orbiting sun and she the still moon. While she acknowledges the transitory nature of union, she journeys through the reaches of the zodiac, not meandering aimlessly like the speaker in "A Man Young and Old" but searching for that one place wherein she and her lover become truly one, joined as an androgynous being.

But in "Parting," the distance between lovers is already widening as they face "the horror of daybreak." The Man hears a rooster, announcing the dawn; the Woman calls it a night bird that "Bids all true lovers rest" (536). He sees day spreading across the mountaintops; she says it is only the light of the moon. His "dawn" is her "murderous stealth of day" (536). The Woman's antidote to his uneasiness is an invitation to "love's play" in the "dark declivities" of her body (536). Literally, she cannot stop the advance of day; figuratively, she cannot alter his solar nature. Still, she tries to delay its advent by denying its occurrence and masking its light with the recesses of her body. But the Man's silence is a rejection of sorts. Indeed, these two autonomous voices no longer join together in harmonious silence as in "Her Triumph."

What appear to be transition poems, "Chosen" and "Parting," mark significant progress on the road to self-illumination. The Woman's sense of harmony begins to disintegrate, and she suffers a growing sense of the unlikeness (*AS II* 341). Yet she freely embraces the inevitable moment of parting ("The lot of love is chosen") because she cannot change what is fated ("the horror of daybreak" and eventual separation). Even as she throws her lot to chance, she exercises her power of "clear reasoning choice" (330): "I chose it for my lot!"

In "Her Vision in the Woods," the Woman undergoes her second Critical Moment. She imagines a surreal meeting with an Adonis-figure, a former lover, "[her] heart's victim and its torturer" (*VP* 537). She is caught up in the sight of "his blood-bedabbled breast," and moved by empathy, sings her "malediction with the rest." The poem is animated by two equally intense feelings: a sense that she is "too old for a man's love," and the memory of "love's bitter-sweet." While she acknowledges her past connection to the Man, she also knows that her sexual experiences will occur much like this scene itself—only in "imagining men." Purged of her own pride and vanity and resigned to separation, she nonetheless empathizes with his wounds and extends real pity in Yeats's sense: "go and I am still I" (*AS II* 330).

With "Meeting," the Woman completes her journey of sexual passion on the Great Wheel. Undergoing a complete "cutting apart" (*AS II* 329), she offers a very different face to her former lover, not red lips and bright eyes but the mask of old age. Her disparagement of the Man registers a "harshness coming" (330): "I hate/Such a man the most" (*VP* 539). Within herself, she knows there is a "sweeter word" to capture their experience of each other. But his rage does not shatter her own "pride of identity," her sense of autonomy, that contrasts so sharply with her state of mind in her youth when she would do anything to earn his admiration. She has endured a hard exchange: for inner strength she has surrendered all prospect of harmonious connection. But she will suffer less this way and not perpetuate her past mistakes and illusions to the end of her days.

What is ultimately accomplished by using Moments of Crisis as an interpretive framework for "A Man Young and Old" and "A Woman Young and Old"? Simply put, I believe that this reading contributes significantly to our understanding of Yeats's vision of gender. First, readers gain a sense of what Yeats calls the "universal masculine" in action. Equipped with a lens that sees beyond what Cullingford calls the "heavy autobiographical freight" of the male sequence, readers realize that "A Man" is not a repackaging of Yeats's sexual history, although his personal relationships may follow this same course. Rather, it is a study of solar nature and the male experience of self-revelation, which is very different from the lunar nature and the female experience of self-revelation. Men and women endure different paths to illumination as well as different pain and joy. Men need to free themselves from their own nature (the "harsh sun") by connecting to others and by transcending their limited perspective. Women need to realize their own autonomy and achieve a sense of personal value apart from their sexual role.

But Yeats goes beyond difference alone. By insisting on complementarity, he escapes one of the inherent pitfalls of essentialist treatments of gender. That is, he advances a vision of sexual relations that denies the self-sufficiency of a male-dominated standard or male-specific perspective. The Man's story is not the only version or the normative perspective. Neither is the Woman's, for that matter. The separate and unique experiences of men and women, joined together, form a complete truth. Neither mode of experience or expression—masculine or feminine—can stand by itself as a complete rendition of life. If readers hear only the Man's voice or see only through the Woman's eyes, they will settle for an appearance that belies the full truth about sexual relations.

Secondly, we have a detailed account of what Yeats means by wholeness. The spirit guides had informed him: "two complete opposites never unite except in man & woman" (*AS I* 68). I have contended that these sequences should be read not in counterpoint to each other but as a single poem united by an identical plot. In reading these poems according to the Moments of Crisis, we sometimes feel as if the Man's path and the Woman's path seem too disparate, as if these voices haven't shared the same worlds, let alone the same experiences. Yet their paths culminate at the same destination. If we look to the final poems in each sequence (the choruses from *Oedipus at Colonus* and *Antigone*), their crowning illuminations are identical. Both the Man and the Woman lament the loss of "the delights of youth" that now seem as "bitter sweetness" (459, 540). Life's calamities cannot be dimmed by the treasures of memory. Nor does the vision of "laughing dancers," the bride being carried to the bridegroom, change the hard-earned wisdom of these enlightened lovers. "I celebrate the silent kiss that ends short life or long," the Man ruminates. But he recommends "a gay goodnight and quickly turn[ing] away" (459). For her part, the Woman exhibits the same measured caution.

> Pray I will and sing I must,
> And yet I weep—Oedipus' child
> Descends into the loveless dust. (540)

Out of context, these lines seem to vocalize desolation. But contrasted with the coquetry of her youth and the petulance of his, what is salient about them is the calm dignity of two runners who have gained the prize. When Yeats speaks of unity and enacts wholeness, his vision of gender relations compels us to expect something far more complex (and valid) than "they lived happily ever after."

Finally, there is a third insight into gender that is perhaps the most crucial. As the automatic writing dialogues continually remind us, the subject of sexual relations inevitably brings with it a subtext, an underlying motive: to unlock the even more mysterious relation between human and daimon. Yeats is explicit. The Moments of Crisis are not only engineered by the daimon but also involve the daimon directly as a participant. Thus, we have two interactions: daimonic activity in human affairs as well as our knowledge of that activity. In terms of daimonic involvement in sexual relations, we know that the daimon lures a man to a particular woman; the lure suggests the child to be fathered rather than the attractions of the woman herself. Eventually the daimon directs the man to the woman who will conceive the intended child. The woman is selected because her daimon is desired by the man's daimon. During sexual intercourse between the man and woman, the daimons access the Personal *Anima Mundi* and collect ideas from the man or woman "in accordance with the unity & harmony of the moment" (*AS II* 249). In terms of our knowledge of such activity, the usual avenue is the act of sex itself. Yeats believed that we have "no consciousness of daimon apart from sex" (259). This is true in two ways. First, by engaging in sexual relations, the Yeatses are in tune with their daimons. Second, their daimons are able to achieve their goals when (and only when) the Yeatses are sexually united.

Yet there is more to understanding the daimon than reciting these truths from the Script. These two sequences reveal a mystery that can be explored and articulated only through poetry. What is that mystery? The literal answer: what sexual involvement means from two points of view, masculine and feminine. Because these experiences are often reciprocal, even antipathetic, constant communication is imperative. The figurative answer: what the relation between ego and daimon may be, again from two different and complementary points of view that demand both communication and integration. More than any lyrical enactment to this point, these sequences display the dramatic interaction of human and daimon as they converge in the mask. Both are intensely invested in the process. Each follows his/her own distinct path through temporal existence to a spiritual end. Although they move "side by side in the same cycle" (*VA* 221), their purposes and destinies are not aligned. Expressed from the human perspective alone or the daimonic perspective alone, the conflict between them seems pronounced. But understood as two distinct approaches to a single, unified process—ego and daimon working together through a particular phase of the Great Wheel— that sense of dissonance yields to cohesion; their coexistence generates a centripetal energy.

One of Yeats's primary goals in the Script is to understand who this daimon is that shares his psyche. He knows even less about his wife's male daimon. The only way to induce his daimon out of his own darkness is to enact the feminine through his verse, perhaps all the while hoping that once his ego and daimon are in alignment, he will enjoy healthier sexual relationships with the women in his life.

Here Yeats's developing skill in assuming a feminine mask takes on a strategic dimension. This achievement is more than a tribute to what Patrick Keane called Yeats's "empathetic imagination" (304). Yeats is moving closer to apprehending the daimon who is "part of me"—her power, her depth, her autonomy. Indeed, as Yeats proceeds through the post-Script years, he seeks an image for his daimon—not the docile and exotic Sheba, not the ambitious and intelligent dancer, not even this strong and passionate Woman. The ultimate voice of the feminine and the effective image for the daimon will emerge in the mask of Crazy Jane.

CHAPTER 6

ENACTING THE FEMININE
Crazy Jane as Daimon

"[The] 'Crazy Jane' poems . . . and the little group
of love poems that follow are, I think, exciting and
strange. Sexual abstinence fed their fire—I was ill
and yet full of desire. They sometimes came out of
the greatest mental excitement I am capable of."
                        W. B. Yeats, *Letters* (814)

"I want to exorcise that slut, Crazy Jane, whose language has become unendurable."
            W. B. Yeats to Georgie Yeats. Qtd. in Jeffares,
                            New Commentary (307)

In aesthetic achievement, the Crazy Jane mask is the clearest, most compelling of the feminine voices of Yeats. This sequence is also the definitive
enactment of Yeats's sexual dynamic—the merging of mystical and sexual reality. It is no coincidence that Yeats masters the feminine mask and the sexual dynamic together, for they both spring from the same aesthetic and
theosophical principle: the presence of the gendered daimon. In this chapter I will read the mask of Crazy Jane as Yeats's most developed expression
of "the woman in me" and the ultimate study of the daimonic presence. In
a word, Crazy Jane is Yeats's daimon in poetic form.

Notwithstanding Patrick Keane's observation that Yeats's mature poems are distinctive in their "subordinating esoteric doctrine to human drama" (131), I will argue that the mystical informs the aesthetic in the Jane sequence, but in a different way than we have seen in previous works.[1] Yeats does not make a case for the sexual dynamic, as he does in the Solomon and Sheba poems, by demonstrating how a man becomes wise through verbal and physical intercourse with a woman. Neither does he describe the act of masking by explicitly debating the merits of a specific image, as in the Sheba and Michael Robartes poems, nor map out human sexual relations according to the stages on the Great Wheel, as in "A Man" and "A Woman" sequences. Perhaps the closest parallel to the Jane poems is *The Only Jealousy of Emer*, which objectifies an internal drama between facets of a single nature. In "Jane," the drama is mystical (encompassing the daimon), internal (occurring within the poet), and objectified (through female and male personae). Crazy Jane is not merely a woman sighing for wholeness, battling against men who both reject and seduce her. She is daimon; her passionate focus is her "conflict, or friendship with a man" (*VA* 28)—with the Bishop, with Jack the Journeyman, and ultimately with Yeats himself.

If Yeats were a poet of less skill, it would be possible to "prove" Jane's daimonic identity. Indeed, Yeats himself does not attempt to prove it, only to suggest it, by positioning Jane as the prime contrary throughout the seven poems.[2] First, she is the lone female who must deal with three men (much like Cuchulain and his three women). Because she is female, she enacts the lunar principle (also the antithetical, the subjective, and the feminine) in contrast to the men, who are solar, primary, objective, and masculine. Because Jane is lunar, she is associated with the night and with darkness. She wanders to the blasted oak at midnight. She meets the ghost of her lover "on the road that night." She loves "between the dark and the dawn" (*VP* 511). By contrast, Jack's name (the *Jour*neyman) is from the French for "day." He leaves with the "dawning light" (512).

These contraries seem obvious, but from them unravel even deeper dynamics. Jane articulates a kind of gospel that encapsulates Yeats's own vision of the world. She adamantly defends the importance of body, and with it, the dignity of physical pleasure. She isn't ashamed that "Jack had [her] virginity" or that she "had wild Jack for a lover." Her adversary is the Bishop, who claims that Jane and Jack "lived like beast and beast" and calls the woman to "Live in a heavenly mansion,/Not in some foul sty." While Jane defends sexuality, she also affirms spiritual union. She and Jack will meet after death because the skein of love "bound us ghost to ghost" (511). Their lasting union nullifies the Journeyman's habit of taking his pleasure and leaving: "the more I leave the door unlatched/The sooner love is gone." Thus Jane functions as a contrary to both the Bishop (who disdains the body) and Jack (who loves as if union is transitory) by insisting on both wholeness and intimacy. Love must "take the whole/Body and soul" because union depends upon the existence of contraries: "fair and foul are near of kin/And fair needs foul" (513).

Ann Saddlemyer aptly refers to this attitude as Jane's "both/and philosophy" in opposition to the men's "either/or" positions (148). But Jane does more than affirm both matter and spirit—she understands their relationship (they are near of kin, not opposites), and she views them in action (spirit needs matter). In a word, she sees them as complements. The male voices operate from a bipolar position, a philosophy of negation. Both Jack and the Bishop renounce much of the world around them and thereby sacrifice the possibility of wholeness. Not only does Jane argue for complementarity, but her passionate, lusty "praise of the joyous life" (Yeats's words) also functions as the complement to Jack's casualness and the Bishop's prudishness (*Letters* 758). Even more to the point, Jane acts as Yeats's own complement. She is earthy and uncouth, he philosophical and urbane. Although she appears to articulate many of his values ("I approve of her," Yeats wrote to Olivia Shakespear), Jane succeeds in entrenching her own personality at odds with the poet's so that in the end, he is glad to be rid of "that slut, Crazy Jane, whose language has become unendurable" (qtd. in Jeffares, *New Commentary* 307).

Given that Jane is developed as a contrary to the Bishop, Jack, and Yeats, how does her position reflect what we know about the daimon? Yeats's daimonology is subtly woven into each level of complementarity in the same thoughtful way that his mystical beliefs shape *The Death of Cuchulain:* "My 'private philosophy' is there but there must be no sign of it . . . It guides me to certain conclusions and gives me precision but I do not write it" (*Letters* 917–18).[3] Yet that philosophy clearly directs the types of contrary relations at work in the sequence. Just as Jane is female, Yeats's daimon is "of opposite sex to ego" (*AS II* 235). As lunar principle to Yeats's solar nature, she actualizes "the Antithetical position of the Daimon" (*AS III* 107). While Yeats's conscious mind is in the "light," there is another mind which "swims up from the dark portion" of his psyche. It is the daimon, who like Jane is associated with the darkness, "in possession of the entire dark of the mind" (*VA* 28).

Sex is a crucial value for the daimon, as it is for Jane. The "moment of the supreme activity of the daimons" occurs during sexual union (*AS II* 507). The greater the harmony between W. B. and Georgie Yeats, the more successfully the daimon will collect images from his personal memory (249)—the only way that the past is made available to the daimon. The bond between Yeats and his daimon is timeless, like Jane's bond to Jack. The daimon is in contact with "only one living man" (*AS III* 392), and they will be tied to each other during this incarnation and in the afterlife (*AS II* 211, 271). Their destinies are joined for many years: "Daimon & man two beings interlocked for the 12 Cycles" (*AS III* 187), which means that in every phase that W. B. Yeats is incarnated as a man, he is united to this same female daimon.

Over the course of their relationship, Yeats and his daimon work in complementary ways. He retains memories of the past and consciousness of the present; she knows the present and the future but has no sense of the past without him (*AS II* 260). She takes items from his personal memory and incorporates them into her Spiritual Memory. In turn, Yeats has no Spiritual Memory apart from the daimon: "You only have it through him" (271).[4] The two are linked in the Spiritual Memory and can "speak" to each other via the Personal *Anima Mundi* (238). There is also a complementary relation between their senses, as the Yeatses discovered in querying the spirits about their infant daughter. Person and daimon "age" together. "When child begins to talk the daimon begins to hear" in a reversal of the senses (499). Thus when Yeats himself listens, the daimon speaks. When he tastes, she smells. As he touches, she is intellectually awake; as he desires, she emotionally quickens; as he laughs, she is supernaturally energized (500). Yeats summarizes: the daimon "perceives the contrary of objects seen & of desires felt by us" (*AS III* 279).

Jane's passionate nature reflects the daimon's appetite for emotional stimulation. When Yeats's ego "has positive qualities or emotions," the daimon becomes "linked" to him, or in cases of special intensity, "united" to him (*AS II* 241). In fact, his daimon is never influenced by his mind, only by his emotions and instincts (251).[5] "The Daimon therefore seeks to bring Ego into a state of emotional intensity" (*AS III* 39), which is done usually through the Moments of Crisis. In the same way, Jane's irascible and headstrong nature manifests the daimon's own independence. Yeats learns that "the Daimon is not a mere fountain arising out of a pool & falling back into that pool. It has its independent life & we cannot call it" (96).

Defying human control, using her human host to access the past and to feed her passion, operating by a reversal of senses, residing in the dark subconscious of Yeats's mind—the daimon shapes the poet's journey through time, while she herself transcends time. She remains stationary, existing in the Thirteenth Cone, more powerful than the perfected men who share that realm with her (392). Indeed, she is like Jane, a still center, "like a road/That men pass over" (*VP* 512). The daimon acts in practical life only "through the man himself" (*AS I* 71) and is powerless when emotion dwindles (*AS II* 241). Yet she draws the poet out of himself, away from the gravitational pull of his own ego, and supplies stimuli "objectively"—from outside that ego (528).

Yeats fully expected that union with his daimon would enlarge his Four Faculties and enhance his creative power (242, 248). He appears to be right. The Crazy Jane poems are the end of a long journey for Yeats. They allow him a moment of personal unity, to give life to both the man he is and to what he calls "the woman in me." I would go so far as to argue that the simplicity and depth of the Jane mask reveal the ultimate internalization of his gendered daimonology. In Yeats's own terms, his daimon rises out of his darkness and has her say.

And what precisely is her message? The title of the sequence implies it. Crazy Jane, the feminine daimon, defines the feminine principle from the heart of the lunatic moon itself. She enacts facets of her own power and mystery apart from male mediation so that readers encounter a new world, the daimonic world, the masculine world in reverse. This is new and unexplored territory. The following pages describe complementarity from the feminine side of things. No wonder Jane is branded as "crazy"—her attitudes work against the grain of male standards; her actions jar male sensitivities; her vision of life challenges long-standing tenets of social practices and philosophical values. In true contrary fashion, Jane reveals the nature of the "universal masculine" even as she articulates the feminine; she discloses as much about her own perspective as about what kind of thinking stands in its way. But the genius of the Crazy Jane sequence goes beyond this enactment of the daimonic. Yeats executes the full complexity of complementarity between genders and, in doing so, challenges readers to move beyond any single point of view—the Bishop's, Jack's, Jane's, perhaps even Yeats's—to a sense of gender in action as perceived in the round.

First, then, Jane's reversal of the masculine world. The structure of the sequence suggests that Jane enjoys a transcendent sense of time. The poems are only roughly chronological. In the closing poems, Jane describes herself in old age, but otherwise she displays a total disdain for linearity. In "Crazy Jane on the Day of Judgment" (poem 3), Jack is alive and talking. In "Crazy Jane and the Bishop" (1) and "Crazy Jane and Jack the Journeyman" (4), he wanders the world as a discarnate spirit. "Crazy Jane Reproved" (2) and "Crazy Jane on God" (5) give no indication of their fit in linear time. Whatever sense Jane makes of her world, she does not gather up sequential bits but unifies parts synchronously, threading her thoughts together into a theme called "Words for Music Perhaps."

But the men around her have a very difference sense of time. If mortal existence is like a road along which men travel toward death, all men (not just Jack) are "journeymen" or pilgrims in this life. But Jane is not; as a spirit of the Thirteenth Cone, she remains at the still center of a world in motion. "Men come, men go," Jane observes, "Whether I would or no" (VP 512). She compares her body to the road "that men pass over" (512). She is constant, like God, a steady presence in the march of time.

This privileging of stillness applies to space as well as to time. It is as much an ontological state of being as a temporal one—better yet, a truce between Jane and her own feminine identity. To capture in words what the feminine is like, Jane uses the metaphor of a seashell, with an "elaborate whorl/Adorning every secret track/With the delicate mother-of-pearl" (509).⁶ Words like "elaborate," "adorning," "delicate," and "mother-of-pearl" are coupled to the image of a round, whirling receptacle with a "secret track" to indicate beauty, artistry, and hidden mystery that "made the joints of Heaven crack" (509).

Here Jane challenges certain masculine assumptions about power head-on. She holds up the craft and subtlety of the feminine against the "roaring" and "ranting" of the male in motion, dominating and disrupting the stillness

> I care not what the sailors say:
> All those dreadful thunder-stones,
> All that storm that blots the day
> Can but show that Heaven yawns. (509)⁷

The real power of life, the real force of nature, says Jane, is not found in the "roaring, ranting" of nature or of the male (be he Jack or Zeus in his Heaven) but in the hidden darkness of "that shell's elaborate whorl." The divine does not simply craft the shell; the shell contains the divine in its graceful movement, in its "consummate strength" (*AU* 364), and in "every secret track."⁸

In arguing that the feminine surpasses the masculine in true power and divinity, Jane also reverses presumptions about the male nature of the godhead. As David R. Clark demonstrates, in describing thunderstorms as a sign "that Heaven yawns," the sailors interpret the disruptions of nature as manifestations of male sexual desire, almost an overture to intercourse (*Songs* 47–48).⁹ Thunderstones and storms are more than natural forces; they are male passion unleashed. Such a claim is possible only if the sailors regard nature as a physical register of Heaven's sexual desire and thereby equate "Heaven" with masculinity.

When trying to read the sky, sailors interpret events around them as if they were shaped by the male sexual imperative. That is, the sailors recognize the divine according to what makes sense to men. Jane not only sees the divine manifested more perfectly in the feminine but also denies that events, natural or human, erupt from male appetite. Her dismissal of the sailors' point of view casts them in an ironic, almost comic light: the sailors navigate the sea while trying to read the sky. Although the thunderstones and storms can prove disastrous, it is the sea upon which they sail that will either drown the sailors or not. Because their attention is riveted to the sky, the men (travelers like Jack) will never recognize the divine contained in the sea, which hides delicate, elaborate treasures in its "secret track."¹⁰ If we read the sea as a symbol for the subconscious, then there is a ready parable for human/daimonic relations when the ego refuses to link with the daimon—that mystery from the dark, submerged half of the mind.

Considering Jane's rejection of linear time, her affirmation of the divine power of the feminine, and her mockery of a male Heaven, we are not amazed when her proprieties collide with an institutional, male sense of morality. Even before he was a parish priest, the Bishop condemned Jane's sexual involvement with Jack the Journeyman: "he, an old book in his fist/Cried that we lived like beast and beast" (*VP* 508). From his personal perspective, the Bishop censures Jane for her own good. He argues like a spiritual capitalist, urging her to trade in her "uninhabited, ruinous" condition of the flesh and move up to something finer: "Live in a heavenly mansion,/Not in some foul sty" (513). Of course, in his own moral universe, the Bishop is the upright spokesman of moral norms, the "solid man," while Jack is the "coxcomb" (508).

But Jane reverses the images of "coxcomb" and "solid man." The pretentious Bishop is the coxcomb, while Jack is the solid man—both physically vital and sexually aroused—straight and lithe like a birch tree. According to Jane's moral vision, the Bishop's character is deformed, his sense of the spiritual realm narrow and withered, and so she casts the shape of "beast" back upon the cleric:

> The Bishop has a skin, God knows,
> Wrinkled like the foot of a goose . . .
> Nor can he hide in holy black
> The heron's hunch upon his back. (508)

The Bishop's defense of a heavenly mansion does not square with Jane's perception of the godhead: "Love has pitched his mansion in/The place of excrement" (513). If Christ can become incarnate, flesh cannot be the evil void that the Bishop projects. Spirit and flesh must be "near of kin." The Bishop expresses a bipolar philosophy—he not only considers spirit and matter to be opposites but also discredits matter altogether. Jane reverses that view, advancing a philosophy of contraries. Fair and foul, constancy and change, sweet and sour, soul and body, sun and moon, man and woman— these are not exclusive entities. Members of each pair need their contrary, for everything is relative, or rather, everything is relational.

Clearly, Jane's understanding of salvation clashes with the Bishop's. Jane is dedicated to wholeness as a value. But wholeness embodies a paradox: "For nothing can be sole or whole/That has not been rent" (513). Unity depends upon difference. Just as sexual union requires a man and a woman, wholeness (or Unity of Being) requires soul and body: "unity of being cannot exist in separation from the body" (*AS II* 41). Within this blessed state, contraries are not effaced but held in balance, in "complete harmony between physical body intellect & spiritual desire" (41). This balance is the energy behind Jane's exuberant embracing of the physical and her rejection of the cleric's moral frame of reference. For Jane, unity and wholeness do not absorb each contrary in some kind of metaphysical rescrambling of parts to form a composite that erases discrete beings. Love is possible only if Jane and Jack embrace the sweet with the sour, only if male is rent from female, only if body and soul commit the crime of living, only if ego and daimon are distinct ontological beings.

Salvation, morality, divinity, power, time—Jane runs the gamut in how she reverses the masculine perspective. She is a true contrary, as a daimon should be. But that office—the antithetical voice within Yeats's psyche—is not simply oppositional. The feminine may reverse the masculine, but they are near of kin, and female needs male. As daimon, Jane seeks "conflict, or friendship with a man" (*VA* 28) and consistently struggles to bond with her human host or, figuratively, with her male lover. She insists on a deep, integrated love that takes "the whole/Body and soul" (510) so that "when looks meet," she says, "I tremble to the bone" (*VP* 511). Echoing the speaker in "A Woman Young and Old," Jane argues that love is not complete if it does not involve both body and soul. Indeed, this argument is the first corollary to her gospel of complementarity. She refuses to settle for surface compatibility by allowing body to overpower soul to ensure pleasure, or soul to eclipse body to diminish bestial interaction. If given the choice—either to join with God as "a lonely ghost" or to be incarnated in the flesh once again—Jane would elect to "leap into the light lost/In [her] mother's womb" (511).

According to Jane's view, intimacy is a great unraveling of hearts, minds, and senses: "Love is but a skein unwound/Between the dark and dawn."[11] Yet she admits, "The more I leave the door unlatched/The sooner love is gone" (511). She counts on meeting Jack "ghost to ghost" in the afterlife, but in this world there is no reciprocal commitment from her lover. Jane is the one who demands wholeness. She works for it, pursues it, sacrifices for it, despairs of it. But there is no common ground between Jane's expectations and Jack's. Jane ruminates:

> Naked I lay,
> The grass my bed;
> Naked and hidden away,
> That black day. (510)

As David R. Clark explains, "that black day" is an image that refers to the Day of Reckoning ("*The Day of Judgement*" 46–49). Jane has experienced two such reckonings. As discarnate spirit, her soul has been laid bare since the moment of death. As lover, she gave up the "secret track" of her body. Against this impetus to reveal (to lie naked) is a contrary motion: to be "hidden away." These movements occur simultaneously and, Jane would add, tragically. For while she gave her body and would give her mind and soul, she is not permitted to show the whole of herself to an equally eager, embracing "whole" of a man. So the day is indeed black—the sky covered with storm clouds of male desire and Jane's heart darkened by the realization that she is alone even when linked to a man. "What can be shown?/What true love be?" she wonders. While Jack agrees that "All could be known or shown/If Time were but gone," he falls silent when Jane advocates wholeness (510).

For Jane, love turns into an unruly force, equally capable of turning sweet or sour, balancing on the sharp edge of contradiction. "Love is like the lion's tooth," she states; it is a rending as much as an unraveling of hearts, leaving men and women to dance "heart's truth" on the razor's edge of pure love and pure hate. So while Jane is an advocate for wholeness and a "friend" of man, she is simultaneously his most deadly adversary. Jack must "take the sour" if he takes Jane, who can "scoff and lour/And scold for an hour" (510). Jane showers curses on the Bishop, and should he show up under the oak, "I spit" (509). As she watches the dancers—the "chosen youth" winding his partner's own hair around her neck, the woman drawing a knife "to strike him dead," Jane declares: "For no matter what is said/They had all that had their hate" (514). Her perspective again reverses "what is said" about male/female relations. For love and hate are near of kin, and where there is hate, love is close behind.

In this sequence, then, readers view Jane in a series of relationships, one of antagonism with the Bishop (she is admonished but unsilenced), one of union with and alienation from Jack (their bond is timeless yet unsatisfying), and one of kinship with the divine (which she associates with the mystery and power of the feminine). Jane understands love as a union of soul and body, an unveiling of her secret self that too often ends in isolation, a skein unwinding in passion and joining lovers even in the next life, a seductive dance of desire and hate. Jane is headstrong and helpless, bound not only to her lover but also to a complementary process—a never-ending coupling and separation of men and women, masculine and feminine, body and soul.

Yet this mask is more than a poetic creation that captures Yeats's vision of human love. Because the sequence operates on the figurative as well as the literal level, it captures the essence not simply of sexual relations between men and women but also of human-daimonic relations between Yeats and Jane. We could go through the sequence, then, and translate each of these situations into the spirit realm. For instance, Jane's black day of reckoning enacts the dark chasm between herself and Yeats, her mind veiled in darkness from him, his from her, for they are of "two minds (one always light and one always dark)" (*VA* 27). And though their faculties continually interact in an embrace that "may create a passion like that of sexual love" (27), there is no permanent meeting of minds and hearts. After several short months of creative ecstasy, Yeats renounces Jane as "unendurable."

On the daimonic level, the image of love as a "skein unwound/Between the dark and dawn" does not refer to physical union in a moment of time. Rather, it points to a passionate meeting between Yeats and Jane, a spirit waiting to "leap into the light" of temporal existence once again. This meeting occurs in the mental and psychological space between the dark of the subconscious and the light of consciousness, her mind and the poet's. Their fates are adamantly tied together, just as human lovers are bound together in the afterlife. Yeats and Jane "sport, pursue one another, and do one another good or evil" (27). As "two beings interlocked for the 12 Cycles" (AS III 187), they pursue each other across centuries. No wonder Jane feels like the still center—"Men come, men go"—as Yeats's soul appears in a dozen different male guises to do her "good or evil."

Yeats and his daimon relate in conflict or friendship; what matters is not moments of harmony that may be shared but the real, passionate, and resolute bond between them. Although the poet may turn away from his daimon, their fates are locked together: "for she is in possession of the entire dark of the mind" (VA 28). If there is any consolation for Jane either as daimon or as lover, it is this truth: conflict may typify the union of masculine and feminine, but it does not undermine their inevitable future. In the afterlife they will experience together a moral purging that results in "an intellectual ecstasy at the revelation of truth, and the most horrible tragedy in the end can but seem a figure in a dance" (231). As Yeats writes in notes for A Vision:

> all whirling [is] at an end, and unity of being perfectly attained. There are all happiness, all beauty, all thought, their images come to view taking fullness, to such a multiplicity of form that they are to our eyes without form. They do what they please, all [struggle] at an end, daimons and men reconciled, no more figures opposing one another in a demoniac dance, and it is these who create genius in its most radical form and who change the direction of history. (qtd. in Ellmann, Identity 166)

We might well assume that Jane's gospel of complementarity speaks for Yeats. But I would argue that despite the obvious affinity, Yeats forms his own conclusions. He observes Jane's attacks on masculine perspectives, then abstracts from them to reflect on two crucial features of her daimonic vision of the nature of complementarity. In the opening poem, as Jane reverses the Bishop's labels of "solid man" and "coxcomb," the issue for Yeats is not the argument itself—whether the Bishop or Jack is the coxcomb—but the fluid and constant reversal of positions. As the Bishop pontificates upon his view, there is momentary polarity between solid man and coxcomb, but it dissolves as Jane reverses the images. Clearly, the meaning of the terms themselves is relative. Who is a beast: Jack, who had Jane's virginity, or the Bishop, with a back hunched like a heron? Who provides the corrective: the Bishop, who rails with an "old book in his fist," or Jack, who "stood" like a birch tree?

What initially appears to be a clear opposition between solid man and coxcomb proves unstable. It follows that the conflict between Jane and the Bishop, sinful woman and pontificating cleric, is also fluid as Yeats sees it. From Jane's point of view, their conflict is undeniable, her loathing pronounced and adamant. But the reader sees that this fluidity applies to each successive contrary in the sequence: sweet and sour, love and hate, dark and light, masculine and feminine, Jane and the Bishop.

In the same way, the passionate conflict between man and daimon consists of perpetual encounters that result in a momentary ascendancy of male poet, then female daimon, but never in a static dominance of one over the other. Just as fair needs foul and soul needs body, daimon and poet are affirmed and enlivened not by the other's repression but by their continued and passionate engagement. More importantly, such conflict produces the poem itself. "A man becomes passionate and this passion makes the *Daimonic* thought luminous with its peculiar light—this is the object of the *Daimon*—and she so creates a very personal form of heroism or of poetry" (*VA* 28).

The second observation that Yeats makes apart from Jane further defines the nature of complementarity. While opposition is not the sole feature of their relationship, it is essential to the action of contraries. How significant that the theological debate between Jane and the Bishop creates the occasion for her most profound utterances. Without this adversary's condemnation and active confrontation, Jane would not have such an occasion to define her beliefs about the nobility of the body and of sexual love. Thus, conflict with the Bishop allows Jane the opportunity to voice her own eloquent vision of love and passionately affirm its importance, just as the warfare between poet and daimon results in song ("Words for Music Perhaps"). By enacting exterior conflict between Jane and the Bishop, Yeats has established the necessity as well as the complexity of their coexistence.

Yet Yeats does not settle for this ultimately bipolar distinction. Difference must give way to the action of complementarity. It is too easy to define the feminine according to Jane's view of the world, the masculine according to the perspectives she opposes. But Yeats does not regard this oppositional configuration as essentially true, only relatively so. What Jane perceives as the masculine way of things he is careful to associate with specific men in the poems—with the Bishop, with Jack, with the sailors—not with all men, not with Man, not with the essence of masculinity. In truth, there is no such thing, no masculine view, only perceptions held by particular men. Thus, masculinity may look different to another woman's (or daimon's) eyes. More importantly, these men would relate differently, act differently, depending on the female in question. Jack is this Jack in relation to Jane. Jane is this Jane in relation to the Bishop. In each interaction, masculine and feminine take on particular hues and direct their energy in certain ways, relative to the individuals involved.

It takes two sets of eyes in this sequence, Jane's and Yeats's, to see all of what Yeats means by "contraries." The term resonates with such depth and intricacy that words nearly fail. But not quite. Certainly what this sequence expresses about complementarity calls into question the kinds of labels described in chapter 1: Yeats's "consciousness as conflict," his "antithetical theories," his "poetics of hate." Jane as a feminine mask is not "different." That is, she does not diverge from some masculine norm. She is *contrary*, near of kin, crucially necessary to the function, nature, value, and actualization of the masculine.

After making the case for reading Jane as daimon, we are left with two questions. First, what does this interpretive frame add to our vision of the feminine as Yeats portrays it? More than any other work in the Yeats corpus, this sequence reveals what Yeats calls the perpetual "Thermopylae" between masculine and feminine, an opposition that is relational, fluid, and dynamic (*VB* 52). Jane seems never to be free from conflict, either in her bed or in her relations with the world. But she is certainly capable of holding her own in any confrontation. She remains unbested by the Bishop, undefeated by her disappointment in Jack, unconquered by the voice of the poet.[12]

Just as important, Yeats reiterates the integrated wholeness of "A Woman" in the adamant wholeness of Jane. The Woman seeks physical pleasure but also values moments when "his heart [her] heart did seem" and turns from a life of coquetry so that her soul "naked to naked goes." Jane understands that love is satisfying only when it takes "the whole/Body and soul." Unity and fullness require the interaction of contraries. "Fair needs foul," yet the "elaborate whorl" and "delicate mother-of-pearl" of the feminine do not qualify as "foul" in her mind. Indeed, in Jane there is a "pride of identity" that Yeats believes is a critical step in the process of self-illumination (*AS II* 329).

The second question relates to the first: what does interpreting Jane as daimon add to a reader's understanding of the mask or, more specifically, to a new appreciation of Yeats's double-voiced verse? I believe this question approaches the crux of Yeats's daimonology. Simply put, the concept of the gendered daimon—fully enacted in the Crazy Jane mask—reveals in a pivotal way Yeats's understanding of himself and his poetry. Yeats believed himself composed of a masculine nature and a feminine daimon. As the spirit guide insisted: the ego "is aware always of the bisexual element" (285). He saw human life as an ebb and flow of objective and subjective tinctures: "human life is impossible without the strife between the *Tinctures*" (*VA* 14). Perhaps most important, the contrasexual nature of the daimon allows Yeats to transcend his own masculine nature. As Barbara J. Frieling and others have noted, Yeats became more and more critical of the objective element and used the term "objective" with negative connotations (292). He respected the feminine for its proximity to the divine, for its subtlety and complexity, for its ability to intuit wisdom and enjoy the privilege of miracle. Encounters with the feminine drive him from his "self made prison" (*AS III* 194) to experience freedom (*AS II* 19) and unity (*AS I* 68).

Because Yeats acknowledges, understands, and lives this connection with the daimon, he is able to achieve a wholeness of his own, to grow beyond the harsh and timid sun, and to achieve both "solar vision" (a special understanding of the external world via the mind) and "lunar vision" (an understanding of the heart) to bring him closer to the Beatific Vision (an understanding of the soul) (*AS II* 327). But as Yeats himself realized, a female poet can be twice a woman, because of herself and because of the muses. He admitted, "I am but once a woman"—not because of his biology but because of "the muses," or what he can become through the aesthetic act (*Letters* 831). In a word, Yeats can realize his bisexuality only by the action of the mask. Because Yeats writes out of this connection with the daimon in the Crazy Jane sequence, he achieves "the greatest mental excitement I am capable of" (*Letters* 814). As he drafted the poems, he reflects: "I am writing more easily than I ever wrote and I am happy, whereas I have always been unhappy when I wrote and worked with great difficulty" (761). He uses terms such as "ecstasy" and "exuberance" to explain this feeling— an experience unmatched in his life except when he describes his meeting with the daimon: "everything fills me with affection, I have no longer any fears or any needs; I do not even remember that this happy mood must come to an end . . . I am in the place where the Daimon is" (*Myth* 365). A coincidence? Not at all, considering that as Yeats drafted the Jane poems, he was also finishing his final revisions of the second edition of *A Vision* (see *Letters* 768, 788). Thus, although the scripting sessions were nearly a decade in the past, their content was in the forefront of his thoughts.

Such a state, then, such intimacy with the daimon who is "part of me," goes well beyond the credit scholars have previously extended to Yeats for his double-voiced verse. Crazy Jane is not simply "Yeats as he would like to be, in some moods at least," as Lawrence Lipking argues (145). She and the other feminine masks are not merely expressions of Yeats's "empathetic imagination," as Patrick Keane suggests (304). They mark more than the adaptation of "a female subject position which contests and . . . defeats his own prejudices," as Elizabeth Cullingford puts it ("Venus or Mrs. Pankhurst" 21). Rather, as Yeats realizes unity within himself, he reaps the harvest that such freedom engenders—emotional fulfillment and aesthetic consummation.

Make no mistake, poet and daimon are at war. In this sense, Ann Saddlemyer is correct. Jane possesses this poet, and he hates her for it (157). But hate and love are next of kin, and love needs hate. So, too, masculine and feminine are next of kin, and Yeats the masculine poet needs Jane the female daimon. This is at once the ultimate justification and the seminal motivation for the Crazy Jane mask. The feminine perspective provides for Yeats a way of transcending the pitfalls of a male poet attempting to speak from a masculine point of view alone. Rather than feeling fragmented by this oppositional drama taking place within him, Yeats seems to agree with Jane's closing lines:

> . . . I
> Cared not a thraneen for what chanced
> So that I had the limbs to try
> Such a dance as there was danced—. (*VP* 514–15)

And that is what Jane said.

CHAPTER 7

POWER AND THE MASK

"Here is the essential difference between the theoretical potential of *A Vision* and poetic thinking: the basic fundamental questions about Leda . . . are annulled by the violent symmetry of the dominant formula of *A Vision:* 'All things are by antithesis.'"

William Johnsen, "Textual/Sexual
Politics in Yeats's 'Leda and the Swan,'"
Yeats and Postmodernism (84)

". . . The day is far off when the two halves of man can define each its own unity in the other as in a mirror, Sun in Moon, Moon in Sun, and so escape out of the Wheel."

W. B. Yeats, *VA* (215)

I have argued throughout this study that Yeats's gendered daimonology is founded upon his idiosyncratic vision of "universal masculine & feminine in soul." This vision enlarges his use of contraries. No longer does he enact opposites in ceaseless conflict. Instead, he envisions complements that war with, define, and renew each other even to moments of unity. Yeats also holds himself accountable to the "woman in me"—his countersexual daimon—who, in enacting that dialectical dance of contraries "near of kin," moves him toward the wholeness and integrity he seeks. Although readers may not share his worldview or mystical vision, they are still able to explore Yeats's post-Script verse with a new understanding of contraries in action, the dynamics of a world comprised of complements and not mere opposites, and the poet's constant awareness of his female daimon and his "bisexual element" (*AS II* 285).

An understanding of the mask as a gendered and gendering action equips readers with a new reading strategy, as I have argued and demonstrated throughout this study. In this final chapter, I turn to one of the most controversial poems of Yeats's career, "Leda and the Swan," to explore how readers might apply this strategy in fruitful ways to a poem that on the surface does not lend itself to these same principles of complementarity and wholeness. "Leda and the Swan" has prompted passionate responses from a variety of scholars; many of them take gender into account, but none use Yeats's gendered daimonology as an interpretive guide.

Yet "Leda" is a post-Script poem, drafted when Yeats was deeply involved in finalizing the first edition of *A Vision*. In this chapter, I will apply to "Leda and the Swan" the tenets of Yeats's gendered mask theory as identified in the previous chapters. This application has a twofold purpose: first, to see what new interpretations this gendered reading strategy can elicit, and second, to argue against recent objections leveled against the poem. Such attacks have revolved about Yeats's use of rape as the controlling metaphor. The image of rape perforce evokes emotional, social, and scholarly discomfort. Even Elizabeth Cullingford, after establishing the "transgressive intent" of "Leda" and Yeats's desire to attack censorship and prejudice by championing "sexuality and its representation in print," concludes that the rape metaphor objectifies the female, making the poem sexist and pornographic (*Gender and History* 142, 148, 151–52). For my purposes, the issue can be expressed by the following question: how can Yeats be sensitive to the "woman in [him]" and yet depict a woman's sexual victimization as the cornerstone of one of his major poems? The answer will develop through three stages: understanding how the rape image is appropriate, discerning why it was selected, and defining what Yeats is saying by it.

In terms of the suitability of the rape image, Yeats explained his rationale in the following way:

> I wrote Leda and the Swan because the editor of a political review asked me for a poem. I thought, "After the individualist, demagogic movement, founded by Hobbes and popularized by the Encyclopaedists and the French Revolution, we have a soil so exhausted that it cannot grow that crop again for centuries." Then I thought, "Nothing is now possible but some movement from above preceded by some violent annunciation." My fancy began to play with

Leda and the Swan for metaphor, and I began this poem; but as I wrote, bird and lady took such possession of the scene that all politics went out of it, and my friend tells me that his "conservative readers would misunderstand the poem." (*VP* 828)

In his recent poststructuralist analysis, William Johnsen agrees that rape is a suitable metaphor for Yeats's system of historical change. But Johnsen attacks that very system as fated and deterministic, calling it the "violent symmetry of the dominant formula of *A Vision*" that makes brutalized victims of all humankind (84).

In what way does rape accurately describe Yeats's vision of civilizations, and is that vision irreparably flawed? First, Johnsen's argument. In reading "Leda" as an enactment of "the iron law of a new political order overcoming an older one" (81), Johnsen invokes the writings of René Girard. "Leda" displays all of the patterns Girard denounces. The woman is a sacrificial victim; her demise is necessary for the Christian moral/social fabric to emerge out of Greek culture. She is chosen because she is weaker, because she has no champion, because she is socially and sexually marginal, and because she has no means to retaliate (Girard 141–42). In Girard's terms, the Leda myth portrays a constant truth: "Violence is the heart and secret soul of the sacred" (31). There is a corollary: only violence can put an end to violence (26).

Johnsen rejects the association of sexual victimization with social order and opposes any attempt to identify power with fate. His reading of the poem emphasizes Leda's helplessness, not only because she is overpowered but also because she is pitted against gods and against gyres. History and fate are unfolding, and Leda is simply a passive vehicle. Johnsen argues that "these metaphors resist Yeats's system, engendering a hypothetical potential equal in seriousness but superior, both intellectually and morally, to his iron law of antithesis and the 'poetics of hate'" (87). Put another way, what "Leda" really enacts is a patriarchal world in which violence and the sacred are coupled and through which sexual violence habitually victimizes women. What the poem lacks is an antidote to that vision. For Johnsen, the lesson of "Leda" is not that Troy will fall and Christ will ascend from the ashes but that Western man must deconstruct the myth of sacrifice by meeting violence with "positive, nonviolent reciprocity" (85). This is precisely what Yeats refuses to allow Leda to do and why the rape metaphor outgrows Yeats's thematic intent.[1]

Johnsen argues that leaving the story on the level of violence and victimization invites "violent reciprocity," paying back "one movement of resentment with its monstrous double" (87). Yeats's system of antithetical history can thus be reduced to the issue of power merely repeated over and over again, never to be explained or superseded. What Yeats needs, Johnsen concludes, is a vision of a Leda who refuses consent, who "brushes the amorous bird aside" so that Zeus loses "possession of the scene" (88).

But doesn't she already "refuse consent"? This is rape, after all, not se-duction. To imply that she has the option to resist suggests that she coop-erates at some point during the coupling, that on some level she freely chooses to embrace the amorous beak, or that she ceases to struggle because she welcomes the "brute blood of the air." Yeats's point is that Leda has no choices. The act of coupling is forced upon her, along with all its conse-quences: "The broken wall, the burning roof and tower/And Agamemnon dead" (*VA* 179). It would seem that the rape metaphor resists Johnsen's own conclusion.

What of the substance of Johnsen's charges against the solar/lunar sys-tem? I would argue that Yeats has anticipated these objections and built a refutation into his philosophy. The remedy to Zeus and brutes like him re-sides in the mechanics of the Great Wheel itself—the complementarity of contraries. Consider the section of *A Vision* entitled "Dove or Swan," which is introduced by the Leda poem. In this section, Yeats explores the homol-ogy between how the primary and antithetical tinctures and Four Faculties operate within individuals and how they operate within civilizations. Just as the individual is forced through a process of self-illumination via a series of "shocks" (i.e., the Moments of Crisis), cultures are changed through violent disruptions until they achieve a new "revelation." The 1925 and 1937 ver-sions of "Dove or Swan" are nearly identical, save for slight changes in the references to Leda and for the absence in the second edition of Yeats's pre-dictions about the new millennium.

Yeats discusses three millennia, the classical, the Christian, and the ro-mantic. Because the Leda myth develops from the classical world, I will fo-cus on that part of Yeats's analysis. Over the course of 2,000 years and the sequence of twenty-eight Phases, the classical world took root, developed, matured, and decayed through two principal cultures: Greece and Rome. Within this primary cycle are multitudes of shorter periods (Yeats calls them gyres within gyres), which also can be measured by lunar phases: Homeric, Phidian, Doric, Ionic, etc. These smaller, "horizontal gyres" measure the continual "recurrence" of historical phenomena (styles of art, patterns of thought, preferences in literature) that makes the cyclic nature of civilization even more pronounced.

Yeats sees two basic characteristics of classical civilization: honoring the heroic and exulting in "muscular flesh" (*VA* 184, 191). These primary at-tributes take on different hues in each specific period. The relationship among these periods is far more complex than the sort of binary bludgeon-ing that Johnsen's envisions. These periods are generated by contrary rather than oppositional action. For instance, in early Greece, intellectual anarchy gave rise to a complete religious system. An extreme desire for civil order en-gendered independent civil life and thought. Emphasis on collective identity materialized in intellectual solitude (181).

This pattern—an endless flow of contrary reactions—registers both the inherent tensions and the vital energy of primary and antithetical tinctures in various proportions. On rare occasions (phase 15), the two are in balance, and a culture enjoys an abbreviated period of wholeness, a time when intellect and body work in harmony. But such stages are short-lived as the Great Wheel moves on until classical civilization reaches its final days of decay, characterized by a "loss of control" (intellectual bankruptcy) and a "sinking in upon the moral being" (glorification of physical and spiritual force) (180).[2]

While the Christian age refutes the former world and unwinds "the thread another age had wound" (183), it also echoes aspects of the earlier period. As Yeats traces the horizontal gyres, he recognizes the resemblance between the early Byzantium of St. Sophia and the Doric and Ionic period of Greece. Arthurian tales are likened to Homeric songs, the age of Thomas Aquinas to the age of Constantine, Renaissance Europe to the culture of Phidias. These parallels involve true contraries (a period in phase 8, dominated by the primary tincture—a period in phase 22, dominated by the antithetical tincture). But the contraries manifest similar rather than opposite features.

These similarities are perhaps the most paradoxical result of the Great Wheel. Yeats himself speaks of "warring opposites," but the working of contraries results in "recurrence"—the cyclic, phasal repetition of reactions that produces similarities among the millennia. As he ponders the ruin of his own age, Yeats recognizes a familiar story from the classical world.

> In practical life one expects the same technical inspiration, the doing of this or that not because one would, or should, but because one can, consequent licence, and with those "out of phase" anarchic violence with no sanction in general principles. (212; deleted in the second edition)

As in former times, there will be a loss of control, an adoration of spiritual and physical force, a disintegration of the moral being, as the new revelation approaches.

As the present gyre comes full circle, the Leda myth is again enacted: "we have a soil so exhausted . . . nothing is now possible but some movement from above preceded by some violent annunciation" (*VP* 828). In a word, the actions of Zeus stand for the decay of civilizations. Zeus does what he can, not what he should. He takes advantage of his physical power. He bows to no measure of rationality, morality, or mercy. His own will and appetite are law, "divine" in the sense of absolute. He is the very emblem of civilizations disintegrating into arenas where there are only brutes and victims. In this sense, Johnsen is correct in reading this particular "violent annunciation" as the impetus for historical change. An age of power will shape and foster the brute. But he erroneously concludes that the workings of contraries within and between civilizations are governed by that same type of violence so that one dominant element is overthrown by its "monstrous double" (Johnsen's term [87]) in an endless nightmare of brutality and destruction.

The energy of the great tinctures does not perpetuate such cruel and rigid symmetry. On the contrary, it protects against it. The more tyrannical the brute, the more certain his demise because its contrary cannot tolerate oppression for long. Contrary to Johnsen's assertion, violence is not subdued by violence but by its complement (reason, intellect, or faith, depending on the civilization). The so-called iron law of antithesis ensures the free play of contraries, as objective and subjective, solar and lunar, masculine and feminine, are allowed the freedom to encounter and confront each other. If this energy were eliminated, if there were no contrary of power, that very symmetry Johnsen condemns would be assured.

The rape metaphor is therefore an appropriate one to capture the chaos, violence, and terror of a decaying civilization. The next question is more crucial. Given the need to encapsulate brutality within a single image, why does Yeats depict *sexual* violence? There is ample evidence that his decision to read the Leda myth as a rape is deliberate and selective. As Ian Fletcher and Giorgio Melchiori have noted, the Leda myth is not monolithic, with one orthodox version emerging in various expressions. Homer's version differs from Euripides', Euripides' from Hesiod's, Hesiod's from Pindar's. Many of Yeats's contemporaries depicted Leda as a willing sexual partner, even a seductress. The fluidity of the Greek myth reveals the gamut of choices Yeats had in creating his own version.

Yeats's choice of rape takes us into the heart of his theosophy. Rape is an image that Yeats *could not* select haphazardly or frivolously. His exploration and discoveries in the Automatic Script revolve around the mystical power of sexual relations. Yeats does nothing less than venerate this image—the sexual union of male and female. He uses it as a sign of the convergence of spiritual and temporal realms. He sees it as a symbol (and promise) of ultimate wholeness. Consider, then, what it means for Yeats to employ the rape image—the antithesis of what sexual union should signify, the ultimate lie, the ultimate evil. What can he say only through the rape image?

One of the most persuasive answers to this question is Helen Sword's reading of "Leda" as "a fable of divine inspiration" (305). Because sexual union has traditionally functioned as a metaphor for religious inspiration, she argues, rape may be used to approximate the violent confrontation between the "inspiring Other" and the receptive poet. To assert this analogy between rape and inspiration, Sword implies that the divine has no affinity with human existence and hence the touch of the god (or the inspiration of the muse) marks a violent intrusion.[3] She also assumes that the obvious analogy for such absolute otherness is violence between equally exclusive domains: the masculine and the feminine. Boundaries are therefore fixed and absolute between human and divine and between male and female.

Sword's "fable" framework likens Leda's passive, sexual victimization to the muse's possession of the poet's imagination. But if Yeats were a female poet, she contends, Zeus would not only symbolize poetic inspiration but also take on more literal attributes of a male rapist in a literary world, i.e., the patriarchal dominance and critical influence that constrain female writers. Leda would therefore signify a double subjugation—of women and of women poets. Sword continues:

> Women writers confronting the Leda myth, then, might reasonably be expected to identify, at least in imagination, with Leda and her plight; that is, one can hardly conceive of a woman writing about the myth solely from Zeus's point of view, except perhaps with heavy irony. (306)

Whether she expects that one can hardly conceive of a man writing about the myth solely from Leda's point of view (except perhaps with heavy irony) is unclear. Yet in light of Yeats's sex, Sword suspects his use of the rape metaphor; she presupposes that his empathy with Leda is limited. While he seeks to "gain some form of access" to the feminine traits he admires—sensitivity, receptivity, and intuition—he is unwilling to place himself "fully in the imagined role of the female" (306). The reason? He fears Leda's state of powerlessness, and thus his attitude toward the feminine is ambiguous, at best. Yeats fully identifies with neither Zeus nor Leda but rather stands apart, empathetic but detached (306).

Through the course of her argument, Sword introduces essentialist parameters on several levels. First, she hypothesizes a necessary violence between two sets of exclusionary opposites, human and divine, and male and female. In addition, she seems to adopt this exclusionary motif when describing the "female experience"—an aesthetic construct that feminists often jealously guard and aggressively defend. Terms such as "sexual inversion" (Gilbert and Gubar 336), "cross-gendered composition" (Cullingford, *Gender and History* 203), and Sword's own "emotional cross-dressing" (306) attempt to describe the act of a male poet appropriating a woman's identity—crossing over into a territory that by rights is not his. Underlying such labels is an implied, sometimes explicit, essentialism that assumes a male can only appropriate gender roles and disguises, never authentically enact the female's experience.

Sword's reasoning—women writers would intend x, y, and z when using a rape metaphor, but men can only mean a and b—ultimately limits her vision of the poem. What Sword has done is read "Leda" according to a prior set of assumptions about gender roles and attitudes, finding Yeats unable to empathize fully with Leda because, simply put, he is a male. This position directly collides with Yeats's theory of the mask, by which he claims not only the ability but also the necessity to articulate the female within himself. There is no reason to demand that Sword operate out of an aesthetic theory identical to Yeats's. But neither can Sword twist Yeats's principles to suit her interpretation, which she does in two critical ways. First, as she gropes for a rationale to explain Yeats's "visionary" sensitivity to and interest in the feminine, Sword settles on a metaphoric vision of his muse, arguing that Yeats "characterizes the inspiring Other as male and thus explicitly feminizes the inspired poet" (305–6). The difficulty is that the rape analogy does not coincide with Yeats's concept either of the aesthetic process or of mystical revelation. If Yeats has any muse at all, it is his daimon. The feminine daimon eludes him in the shadows of his own psyche but wars with him in the aesthetic process, vying for control over individual verse by throwing up images from his subconscious. His encounter with the daimon cannot be typified in terms of rape. Note again his account in *Per Amica Silentia Lunae:* "Everything fills me with affection, I have no longer any fears or any needs; I do not even remember that this happy mood must come to an end . . . I am in the place where the Daimon is" (*Myth* 365). Nor does the aesthetic process entail "a sudden blow" of inspiration from the outside. The daimon is within; the images are from Yeats's own spiritual memory. Although he seems to have been enveloped in a kind of inspired rapture when drafting the Crazy Jane poems (achieving "the greatest mental excitement I am capable of"), such experiences are not typical of Yeats's writing process, as Sword herself notes. There are no flashes of inspiration but rather painstaking labor and endless revision, as the drafts of "Leda" illustrate.[4] Even the inspiration of spirit guides does not lend itself to the rape comparison. While Sword characterizes Georgie Yeats's role in the automatic writing sessions as that of "a fertile but uncomprehending vessel for the voices from beyond" (308), the Script reveals her active agency and dominating influence, notwithstanding Yeats's fictionalization in "The Gift of Harun Al-Raschid" where, it should be noted, his wife is described as passive but not brutalized.

The second way in which Sword twists Yeats's principles involves her equation of Yeats with his narrator, as if there were no mask at work. The same problem with other poems has already been noted; "A Man Young and Old" and "Michael Robartes and the Dancer" have served as examples. But even the narrator in "Leda," who seems to be almost completely effaced as a gendered presence, is as much a mask as Cuchulain or Sheba. Thus the sins of the narrator are not the sins of the poet. While I would agree that the narrative gaze is indifferent and insensitive to Leda's plight (i.e., Sword's detached observer), it will take a different level of analysis to determine Yeats's position.

Once the narrator's perspective is separated from the poet's, what Yeats is saying through the rape image will become clearer. Who is this narrator, then, and what is his attitude toward the scene? The masculine referent is deliberate, for his inability to understand or relate to Leda reveals a mind that is blind to her experience, even closed off from it in a way that is gender-specific, as I will argue. He beholds the drama either literally (at the same moment in historical time) or imaginatively (standing outside of time). He is not a poet, as Sword contends, but a seer, an important point in light of the poem's context in *A Vision*. The narrator can see beyond appearances. He recognizes the beast as a god and the scene as an "annunciation." He also foresees the consequences of this event: "The broken wall, the burning roof and tower/and Agamemnon dead" (*VA* 179).

The role of seer is not a comfortable one. The narrator is stunned by the violence he witnesses. The octet is saturated with images like "blow," "staggering," "caught," "helpless," "terrified," and "mastered." The cruelty of the scene speaks not only to Zeus' physical power but also to the exercise of absolute self-will. Indeed, the sense of duration in the octet—of time being suspended on the brink of a shattering event—reveals how the beast controls the situation.

Yet the narrator's attention moves from the perpetrator to the victim. He registers the physical violence, the perverted design of the swan, but also Leda's confusion as she faces a brute she can neither identify nor understand, her ignorance of what it is or why it violates her. Paralyzed with terror, she can neither deflect the attack nor score a wound of her own in the deceptively soft bank of feathers. It is a moment of intense emotional, even ontological confusion. Zeus' body is animal ("feathered") yet divine ("glory"). A "brute blood of the air" has no business coupling with a woman. Yet it will enter her. In one terrorizing moment, a complex chain of contraries converges: divine and human, human and beast, violence and union, isolation and penetration.

In the face of such horror, the narrator's response reveals as much about him as about the event itself. He asks no questions regarding the nature or purpose of the attack. As seer, he finds such things self-evident. But what confounds him is Leda herself. How can her "terrified vague fingers" push the swan away? the narrator wonders. Certainly she must "feel the strange heart beating where it lies." Does she experience his knowledge as well as his power in this moment of coupling? Note the progression of verbs the narrator attributes to Leda: first "push from," then "feel," and finally "put on." His expectations escalate even as the violence intensifies. Is this only a moment of violence, or is it a moment of illumination for the woman? In passively viewing the attack, in gazing relentlessly upon the brutalized victim, in wanting to exploit her experience, the narrator commits an intrusive act of violence of his own, demanding to share whatever Leda understands.

Now the seer's own violence engenders questions in the reader. Why does he expect a moment of illumination for Leda, wondering if she put on

Zeus' knowledge along with his power, as if she somehow shared his orgasmic shudder, as if she had an apotheosis of her own? The answer points to the narrator's own limited vision that cannot distinguish between lovemaking and rape. It is the woman's heart that determines the distinction, but the seer remains on the outside of Leda's experience, objective and detached. He sees what happens *to* her, not *within* her. The truth can be deciphered only subjectively. His very objectivity pulls a veil across the woman's experience. The narrator *knows* that she is raped but does not comprehend what that means and, worse, refuses to become involved.

At the moment of ejaculation, the narrator turns his gaze away from the event to its consequences. He looks into the future that involves Zeus, Leda, and all of Western civilization. It is the turning point in the sonnet, in civilization, in the narrator's gaze. Yet his is a partial vision, containing only the destruction of the old order, not the forecast of the new. There is no "revelation" in Yeats's sense of the term: "the irrational cry, revelation—the scream of Juno's peacock" (180). And why is his vision flawed? Because the seer evades the real drama—Leda's inner experience. He is "caught up" in his own hypocrisy because he knows that if there is an answer, it resides only in Leda. The sextet literally breaks apart as the narrator turns back to Leda, seeking the answer that his limited vision alone cannot provide. But it is too late. Zeus has already released his victim, and the narrator is left with his own questions—as much in the dark as before.

The sins of the narrator are clear. Literally, he sees only partway into the future. Figuratively, he cannot see into the feminine experience. This failure is a result of choice—to disengage himself and remain detached and objective. He also contributes to the violation of Leda, initially by attempting to appropriate her understanding for his own without thought of her needs, then by condemning her to silence. Because the female voice is silenced, there can be no complete vision of the past, present, or future and no ultimate insight into the truth of the event. That is, the narrator's gender blindness and insensitivity distort his vision; this distortion in turn leads to a failure of prophetic wisdom and of creative imagination.

Here we find the gist of the poem—why Yeats depicts rape and what he means in doing so. The seer needs Leda's perspective; he needs to be in touch with the feminine principle, in order to achieve complete understanding of the past, present, and future. And here is the similarity between the narrator and the poet. Yeats, too, is a seer, particularly in the "Dove or Swan" chapter of *A Vision*. He seeks to read the present in order to foresee the future. When he looks at past millennia and contemporary events, he sees exactly what this narrator sees: brutal violence and powerless victims.

In this sense, "Leda" is a frame story. Yeats is describing the upheaval and decay of his time, writing about a seer who is witnessing the same kind of brutal chaos. But at this point the similarity ends, for there is a difference in *how* they see. The narrator will not access the feminine because he is too objective, too solar. He fails in gender consciousness. Or put another way, he is a product of his own time. His stubborn, objective stance mirrors the objectivity and imbalance of the scene, "being born from it and moving within it" (215).

Yeats is not so limited because he transcends his own time, with its materialistic "murderousness"—an age when men "own nothing but their blind stupefied hearts" (*Myth* 324). Yeats escapes from such a "self made prison" by being open to the feminine (*AS III* 194). Or more precisely, he embraces the feminine, both as a real, eminent feature of temporal reality and as the fabric of his own bisexual psyche. That is, Yeats's argument in "Leda" goes well beyond an historical application (past and present civilizations in their death throes), even beyond gender dynamics (relations between men and women). Ultimately, Yeats is describing the psychodrama between daimon and human host not in the aesthetic act, as Sword believes, but within the average man in a post-Lockean world. The violation of Leda, interpreted as the repression of the daimon in the present age, can take on two forms: first, in an overt, self-serving brute like Zeus; second, in a passive, curious voyeur like the narrator. What is worse, the license of the "brute blood of the air," or the detachment of the "indifferent beak"? Both result in rigid symmetry, the effacement of a contrary, and the self-mutilation of the ego. Any man who represses his female daimon, any woman who denies her male daimon, are arrogant in their blind isolation. For the daimon will rise up out of the darkness: "If man seeks to live wholly in the light, the *Daimon* will seek to quench that light in what is to man wholly darkness, and there is conflict" (*VA* 28). In the poem, the consequences are apparent: "The broken wall, the burning roof and tower/And Agamemnon dead."

Thus "Leda" is not a frame within a frame so much as a gyre within a gyre. It expresses the "recurrence" of similar elements springing from two contraries: the fictional seer, who is limited by his inability or his refusal to enter into the woman's experience and thus represses the daimonic, and Yeats, who insisted on joining male and female "for knowledge and power" (M. Harper 41).

While my re-reading of "Leda" circumvents both patriarchal and feminist interpretations, it reveals the homology between the poem and Yeats's vision of gender as developed during the automatic writing experiment. The process of producing the Automatic Script as well as the content of the dialogues provides incontrovertible evidence of Yeats's association of the mystical life with the feminine. Even as a young man, he had envisioned women as enjoying a distinctive power: "subtle, complex, full of mysterious life" (*Collected VI* 199). Certainly his wife's role as interpreter further convinced him of women's special sensitivity to the supernatural. If Yeats himself was to discover such access, to press against divinity, as it were, he must first open himself up to the role and power of the feminine, both in the person of his wife and in the presence of his daimon. Woman is far more than a sexual partner. She is a seat of wisdom. She is the pathway to freedom, away from the prison of what Virginia Woolf called "unmitigated masculinity" and what Yeats ruefully referred to as the "timid" and "harsh" sun (qtd. in Bradford, *Yeats at Work*. abr. ed. 7).

In "Leda and the Swan," Yeats creates a speaker who has cut himself off from the feminine (and by extension, the daimonic) with dire consequences. By doing so, Yeats underscores the importance of wholeness, of complete vision, that comes only when masculine and feminine are open to each other and free to function as complements. He also demonstrates the consequences when objectivity and masculinity are unleashed and unrestrained and gender relations are reduced (in Jung's words) to "deadly hostility" (*Psychological Reflection* 94). Rape is exactly that—raw brutality. In "Leda," it is neither excused nor glorified but simply acknowledged as part of reality, both within and outside the human psyche. Yeats is no idealist. His hope of two halves forming a whole is visionary, but his analysis of historical civilizations is not, as the final paragraph of "Dove or Swan" makes clear:

> Though [the thought that controls the new age] cannot interrupt the intellectual stream—being born from it and moving within it—it may grow a fanaticism and a terror, and at its first outsetting oppress the ignorant—even the innocent—as Christianity oppressed the wise, seeing that the day is far off when the two halves of man can define each its own unity in the other as in a mirror, Sun in Moon, Moon in Sun, and so escape out of the Wheel. (*VA* 215)[5]

In this life there is only "a difficult peace/'Twixt oil and water, candles and dark night . . . a brief forgiveness between opposites," as the young Cuchulain observed (*VPL* 478). But Unity of Being is the end point of temporal existence—Yeats never loses sight of this expectation.

This brings us back to Yeats's description of the poem as a "violent annunciation." In his correspondence, Yeats referred to "Leda" as an example of classic "enunciation," a term that Melchiori (76) and Sword (305) pass off as one of Yeats's typical misspellings. But "annunciation" and "enunciation" are synonyms; both mean a "pronouncement," a "verbal expression."[6] Indeed, there is a pronouncement in "Leda"; it occurs through the image that dominates the poem. The rape of Leda marks a world turned upside down, bent on its own destruction. Zeus's actions are onerous, out of control, signifying what can be done but not what should be done. Equally destructive are the narrator's transgressions—his refusal to integrate his perspective with the feminine experience and his determined effort to silence her. If Yeats were like his narrator, he would not have expressed his daimon through his double-voiced verse. Or put another way, if he silenced the feminine in his masks, he would be as guilty and blind as his narrator. But the daimon has driven the poet from his "self-made prison." Yeats understands that he will achieve completion only with the feminine.

Reading "Leda and the Swan" against the backdrop of Yeats's gendered daimonology engages the reader on a new level of understanding. When Yeats writes out of the "universal feminine in soul" in poems like "A Woman Young and Old" and "Crazy Jane," he makes significant claims about gender, about mystical reality, about the human psyche. In the case of "Leda," when the feminine is silenced, Yeats makes claims about wisdom, about complementarity, and about wholeness—all lacking because of the "unmitigated masculinity" of the narrator. We might think of "Leda" and of Yeats's double-voiced verse as two avenues to the same destination, avenues that reveal Yeats's adamant commitment to his vision of gender. Truly, Yeats is "like a country drunkard who has thrown a wisp into his own thatch" (*Myth* 365). He has staked his prize on the feminine.

CONCLUSION

CROSSING THE GENDER DIVIDE IN LITERARY THEORY

What does it mean when a woman writes in the voice of a man? When a man writes in the voice of a woman? This study has examined the purpose and rationale of one poet. In my introduction, I conceded the idiosyncrasy of W. B. Yeats's view of gender, based as it is on an uncommon vision of mystical reality. But rather than minimizing his doubled-voiced verse as an isolated case, I am promoting Yeats as an example of great writers—men and women—who have complex motives, worldviews, and purposes in articulating gendered voices. Indeed, Yeats's case is unique insofar as we have preserved the very personal, exploratory documents that reveal the gamut of his concerns, the process and partnership of his dialogues, the shaping and concretization of his conclusions. In many other cases, scholars have only the finished text, which means we have to work backward to reconstruct a writer's vision of gender that underlies his or her art. In Yeats's case, the rationale is provided for us, if we have the patience to mine it.

Yeats's gendered theory of the mask is of course only one way to explain what most scholars refer to as cross-gendered verse. In fact, I would place Yeats's aesthetic on the innovative or radical end of a continuum in literary theory that addresses this genre. A benchmark on the other end of this continuum is the collection of essays edited by Thaïs E. Morgan: *Men Writing the Feminine: Literature, Theory, and the Question of Genders*. Each contrib-

utor deals with a separate author; each appeals to a different theory of gender to arrive at an interpretation of what is occurring when a man writes in
the voice of a woman. The act itself receives a wide variety of labels: Morgan calls it an "imagined perspective" (1) and "female impersonation"
(193); Deborah Rubin labels it "ventriloquistic illusion" (14); Peter F. Murphy refers to it as "feminine discourse" (83); Béatrice Durand equates cross-
gendered verse with the sociological term "cross-dressing" but regards this
as an act of deception, when a man assumes "the false identity of a woman"
(90). Christopher Benfey speaks of "bisexual poetry," but he sees this as am-
biguously gender-marked text rather than an explicitly gendered act (125,
128). The common thread here is an assumption of fictionalization laced
with the suspicion of duplicity. Cross-gendered verse is a rhetorical sleight of
hand belying the truth of the writer's gender identity.

In examining why men choose to write in a woman's voice, contributors
arrive at various explanations. According to Morgan, frequently it is to
demonstrate masculine superiority, sometimes to critique masculinity, often
to mock and expulse "the feminine in men by men" (193). It can displace
male distress into the female experience (Wolfson 36) or evoke the female
essence in order to construct a feminized reality around the "female shell"
(Siegel 65). That is, attempts to exercise gender outside the conventional
bipolar configuration of male/female are interpreted solely as a political act,
a deployment of power to solidify existing inequalities between men and
women.

The final judgment as to the success of such attempts is predominately
negative. Morgan sees it as an exercise in "narcissism" and "voyeurism" (7).
Benfey discerns "a probing of repressed and evaded aspects of the poet's
own gender identity" (123). No matter who the author in question may
be—Herbert, Wordsworth, Lawrence, Verlaine, Hawke, Jarrell, Berryman,
Diderot, Faulkner, or men in general—these analyses are laced with distrust
of the writers' purposes and motives, and tentative in their uncertainty about
such unconventional and finally unwelcome exercises of gender.

The most serious limitation in these approaches is the tone of skepticism
that unifies the collection as a whole. The underlying rationale of the essays
works to interrogate each cross-gendered text: why is this writer trying to
speak like a woman? What is in it for him? What will women lose because
of it? But no one defends the writers' ability or authority to do so or appears convinced that cross-gendering both enriches the text and enlarges
our understanding of gender itself. The voice of a man speaking as a woman
is pronounced "fictional," but not so the idea of an "authentic" female
voice or a "purely female" voice, which is equally fictional. Contributors label specific behaviors, emotions, and attitudes as "masculine" or "feminine" according to traditional and tired stereotypes—an indication that the
potential of these selections to revolutionize assumptions about gender has

failed. The resulting reading strategies reflect the critics' preexisting theories about gender; they are not a fresh look at gender in action.

It is not difficult to project the limitations of this type of theory in the case of Yeats. On the one hand, Yeats's daimonology would be interpreted on a purely psychological level, and he would be judged as repressed and insecure. On the other, his feminine masks would be seen as an imitation of the feminine voice to display and perpetuate male dominance. But the rich resonance and radical content of Yeats's mask theory—as an aesthetic, mystical, and gendered act—would be lost.

If the Morgan collection, with its application of bipolar gender theory, is at the far end from Yeats's position, then perhaps a benchmark at midpoint on this continuum is *The Routledge Anthology of Cross-Gendered Verse,* edited by Alan Michael Parker and Mark Willhardt. In their conclusion, Parker and Willhardt argue that narrative theory must be enlarged to accommodate this uncharted but persistent genre of poetry that emerged with Chaucer and the birth of modern English. (Actually, it can be found in Anglo-Saxon verse in "The Wife's Lament.") The editors argue that cross-gendered poems should be understood as gendered acts, or gender in performance, and thus differ fundamentally from the dramatic monologue (196). Building on Kate Hamburger's concept of "the feint," Robert Langbaum's "dramatic lyric," and Ralph Rader's expansion of the dramatic lyric to include the reader, Parker and Willhardt ultimately see this genre as a cross between the dramatic lyric and the mask lyric (196–98). That is, the dramatic "I" of each poem expresses part of the poet's own subjectivity but also differs from the poet. The challenge for readers is to recognize "the ability of one gendered subjectivity to act upon and shape another conscientiously" (199). The empathy that makes possible this "third term"—a speaker who is neither purely male nor purely female—shatters assumptions of biological essentialism on the one hand, and subverts literary conventions on the other. What Parker and Willhardt affirm in their closing analysis is the authority of any poet to cross (and break) gender boundaries. He or she may do so for a variety of reasons, but the final results are very often revolutionary, shattering traditional parameters of race, class, language, and sexuality (207).

The value of this collection, aside from alerting scholars to the extent of such verse, is to examine and reflect upon the gendered, aesthetic act itself, then reshape reading strategies to accommodate these unconventional voices. Yet this approach, with its openness to the "third term" of gender expression, falls only midpoint on the continuum—it still is not radical enough for Yeats. The term "cross-gendered" itself proves problematic, since it is appropriate only if the mind is defined as single-sexed. Yeats does not write "cross-gendered" verse, since he is not crossing any gender boundaries at all, given what he believes to be his bisexual nature. The term "double-voiced" is the more accurate description of these poems, referring to the potential in Yeats's masks to articulate either the universal masculine or the universal feminine.

This brings us to Yeats's truly innovative and revolutionary province on this continuum of gender theory. For Yeats, gender cuts to the bone of life. It comprises the "great movement" of the spheres that shapes history and civilizations as well as relations between men and women, human host and daimon. The warring attraction between those great complements—"universal masculine & feminine in soul"—evokes the paradoxical tensions and creative energies of temporal existence. But finally, Yeats does not see masculine and feminine as separate, static subjectivities. Masculine and feminine are complementary actions performed in relation to each other, inseparable, fluid, adamant in their bond. Because of the dynamic quality of these contraries, the bisexual self is not trapped in a monolithic experience, a single-sexed mind, a static state of being. The self is "a constantly renewed choice," a choice exercised culturally, spiritually, rhetorically, that works toward freedom and completion. These are heady purposes for any poet's lifework, let alone for a single lyric. But freedom and completion are possible when men and women are open to their bisexual natures.

Ultimately, the Automatic Script provides in direct, literal, and deliberate terms the *apologia* for Yeats's double-voiced verse. It forces readers to face the spiritual, ontological, and gender components of the mask and, by extension, to enlarge, question, or validate their own notions of the human psyche. The self we call "Yeats" is a terrain that cannot be understood or articulated apart from the "woman in me." His bisexuality gives him the authority to write as a woman, a radical notion that transcends literary theory itself and spills over into fundamental issues of philosophy, metaphysics, psychology, and sociology. In re-reading Yeats's mature verse according to this notion, we enter into a true dialectical process, with Yeats's gendered daimonology changing how we interpret texts, and those texts challenging critical tenets. A fruitful interchange between theory, text, and the act of reading can generate a broader, deeper, and more inclusive vision of gender, freeing scholars from the prison of essentialism and sexism, in any guise.

ΠOTES

INTRODUCTION

1. The term "double-voiced" may have evolved from ideas generated by New Critics who attempted to define the duality of tone or theme in the poetry of Alfred Tennyson. Terms such as "double-character" and "double awareness" preceded Elton Edward Smith's idea of "two-voiced"—all attempts to characterize the "continued strain of opposites" that typifies Tennyson's work (13). Feminists, such as Uma Narayan, Rachel Hare-Mustin, and Jeanne Marecek, use the term "double vision" to refer to women who function in both a male-dominated culture and a female subculture. I am using "double-voiced" to signify the potential in Yeats's masks to articulate either the universal masculine or the universal feminine. Each masculine mask signifies the voice of the male on an archetypal (i.e., universal) level, and not the personal experience (or sexual identity) of the poet himself. Because the daimon is "part of me," the feminine mask or voice of the female daimon is neither an appropriated voice nor a textual/psychological sleight of hand but a window into the perpetual, passionate engagement of male poet and female daimon within a single psyche.

2. Some scholars have noted the importance of gender in Yeats's aesthetic: James Olney ("Sex and the Dead") (who accents the connection in Yeats's mind between sex and the dead), Patrick Keane (who speaks of Yeats's "genital concentering"), and Samuel Hynes (who believes Yeats's aesthetic creations are like acts of sexual love to the muse).

3. There is no evidence of influence. James Olney notes that despite their common roots in Platonic and alchemical lore, neither Yeats nor Jung was aware of the other's work (*Rhizome* 4). In the Automatic Script, Yeats makes no mention of Jung, although he refers to Freud several times.

4. Voice is an especially thorny issue for feminist critics. While discussion has moved from the gynocritical position of the 1970s (advocating an "authentic," sex-specific feminine voice), current dialogue that centers around strategic constructivism (Butler) or strategic essentialism (Fuss) often has two yardsticks for textual analysis—one for advising and measuring the feminine voice generated by female writers, and another for the feminine voice generated by male writers. Indeed, as feminists move further away from the female/sex/biology paradigm to the feminine/gender/constructivism paradigm, it is difficult to define "woman" or "feminine voice" even when speaking of a female writer. Harder still is coming to terms with a male writer like Yeats who not only writes within a feminine mask but also claims it is "the woman in me" that allows him to do so.

5. There are many sources from a variety of disciplines (feminist theory, anthropology, psychology) that address the postmodern concept of multiple selves. I select Owens because he is one of the few theorists who directly apply Hillman's work to the act of writing and of masking.

6. My intent is not to minimize the spiritual dimensions of Yeats's worldview or the ontological dimensions of the daimon. I am suggesting that readers who do not share Yeats's occult orientation can still recognize how the mask functions in terms more familiar to a poststructuralist perspective.

CHAPTER 1: GENDER, THE MASK, AND COMPLEMENTARITY

1. Yeats's theory of the mask does not lend itself to contemporary literary or gender theory, as subsequent discussion makes clear. But I have found constructivist approaches to gender extremely helpful in my own understanding of the mask as a gendered action and of Yeats's strategic use of masculine and feminine voices. I note Alice A. Jardine and Toril Moi, who refer to gender as an unstable process, a fluid act or a behavioral strategy, and Judith Butler, who defines gender as a "performative act." Sandra Lipsitz Bem asserts that gendered personalities are constructed from traits defined as "masculine" or "feminine" from androcentric and gender-polarized value systems. Other approaches argue against gender as repetitious or strategic behavior, emphasizing instead gender as "mental representation" of experience (Holland and Skinner). Pertinent, too, is current debate on the connection between gender and language. Nancy Fraser's work emphasizes how language has been used to oppress women and solidify male power. But Teresa Ebert and Ann Rosalind Jones argue differently: literary history reveals that women have used language to subvert existing power structures. Terry Myers Zawacki contends that if the gendered self is constructed, then language functions as a means of creating rather than expressing that self. Heather Brodie Graves warns against valorizing a language style asso-

ciated with either men or women; Deborah Cameron and Toril Moi reject the
notion of gender-specific language traits but acknowledge the importance of
context (how language is judged or used) in gender relations.

It is tempting to push apparent correspondences between Yeats's theory of
the mask and many of these constructivist approaches. Yeats's vision of universal
masculine and feminine as archetypes suggests he is using gender as a mental
representation. His description of self and daimon in relational opposition creates a fluid dynamic, making the mask itself a "performative act." Yet I resist trying to accommodate Yeats to feminist or poststructuralist theory because the
"fit" is finally artificial and seems to me to serve agendas foreign to Yeats's own.
But there are two points that deserve highlighting.

First, Yeats's conception of gender is especially innovative in light of the cultural milieu at the turn of the century. Studies by Richard Dellamora, Eve
Kosofky Sedgwick, and Sandra Harding describe the late nineteenth century
(those years in which the young Yeats was experiencing the "continual discovery
of difference" between men and women) as a period when middle-class English
society was stabilizing, even entrenching, socially acceptable ways of being male
and female. While Yeats believed gendered behavior consistent and substantive,
he also denied that such traits were always sex-specific. More importantly, he often described masculine and feminine in terms of general, monolithic traits, but
he enacted them as dynamic actions.

Second, one of the limitations of current theory is an inequality in dealing
with "double-voiced" writers, depending upon whether they are male or female.
Feminists tend to laud female writers as subversive, their vision of gender as dynamic and fluid, their choice to position themselves in their texts as courageous,
their revisioning of themselves and womankind as revolutionary. But male writers are described in a different idiom. Yeats serves as a case in point. He is called
a "weak poet," his sense of his own gender identity "inherently unstable" and
tentative, and thus his apparent motivation for speaking as a woman and the
qualities he attributes to the feminine are intrinsically suspect (Cullingford,
"Yeats: The Anxiety of Masculinity" 46, 65).

2. Yeats provides a history of his early aesthetic development in three
sources from his *Autobiography:* "Reveries" written in 1914, and two excerpts
from his 1909 journal, "Estrangement" and "The Death of Synge."

In his *Autobiography,* Yeats confesses that his earliest poetic efforts sprang
from his desire to please his father, John Butler Yeats, who admired Romantic
poetry because "he felt some actual man behind its elaboration of beauty, and he
was always looking for the lineaments of some desirable, familiar life" (*AU* 42).
Responding to his father's taste in dramatic verse, Yeats began to imitate the poetry of Shelley and Spenser but soon tired of highly symbolic and idealized language. The younger Yeats found he was powerfully moved by verse that reflected
the "actual thoughts of a man at a passionate moment of life." He told his father: "We should write out our own thoughts in as nearly as possible the language we thought them in" (68). Yeats began writing in a natural, honest style
"out of my emotions exactly as they came to me in life, not changing them to

make them more beautiful" (68–69). But he quickly found such a style too restrictive, binding him to an isolated, one-dimensional voice.

By 1909 Yeats had entered his "middle" period, reflecting antiromantic influences (such as Nietzsche) and opting for an aesthetic presence far different from sincere emotions. He sought a "style, personality—deliberately adopted and therefore a mask" (311). Here the notion of mask resembles a sort of Wildean escape from the individual ego. Yeats compares the mask to a theatrical role; the poet needs discipline to project into a "second self" and achieves interior discipline only when he assumes this second self. The artist transcends passivity and enters into "active virtue," becoming engaged with life by commanding and enacting the second self in a deliberate, "theatrical, consciously dramatic" act. What Yeats means by "the wearing of a mask" (317) is not a case of one mask fitting each artist; rather, the artist must strive to "play with all masks" (318) yet not dissipate passion through the creation of "innumerable personalities" (339). Yeats wrote, "All happiness depends on the energy to assume the mask of some other self . . . something which has no memory and is created in a moment and perpetually renewed" (340). But by 1915 he had reconceptualized this second self as an "image," an opposite of the daily self. In "Ego Dominus Tuus," his character Ille describes the image as

> . . . the mysterious one who yet
> Shall walk the wet sands by the edge of the stream
> And look most like me, being indeed my double,
> And prove of all imaginable things
> The most unlike, being my anti-self. (*Myth* 324)

3. Yeats is working from Blake's sense of "lineament" or "ratio," synonymous with individual identity. In his discussions of Blake, Yeats equates lineaments with the idea of "boundary," which both defines and limits (see *E & I* 120).

4. I am depending upon Edward O'Shea and Brian Arkins, but James Olney suggests three alternate sources: Hesiod (who defined daimons as guardian spirits of the dead who watch over mortal men), Heraclitus (who described the daimon as a guardian spirit who dwells in the psyche), and Empedocles (who saw the daimon as supernatural and by nature part of the eternal realm) ("Sex and the Dead" 211–15).

5. While I believe that gender-inclusive language is important, since women also host daimons and their relationship with their male daimons is equally sexual, there are occasions in this discussion when the term "man" or sex-specific terminology is more appropriate, especially when describing the action of the mask in Yeats's poetry and addressing his relationship with his female daimon.

6. In the 1890s, Yeats had a far different understanding of the subconscious. Already he believed that "we are never a unity, a personality to ourselves" (*AU* 340). His argument is based then, as later, on the idea of the subconscious. But initially he thought that each person is dogged by past blunders and sins

against him/herself and others—Yeats calls this the spiritual identity—so that acts from previous years bury themselves like "a thought that remains unknown" (340). This burden becomes an unconscious presence "a little below 'the threshold of consciousness'" (340). Yeats's conception of the subconscious as a moral plane anticipates his later use of the subconscious as a link to the Collective Memory.

7. It is interesting that Yeats does not enlarge upon this gender analogy when in 1924 (after he had redefined the daimon as female) he added to *PASL* several editorial comments in footnotes. Perhaps Yeats chose to leave the full discussion of the daimon to his *Vision* text and therefore only very selectively added commentary to *PASL*. Since it is not beyond Yeats to completely overhaul previous essays (e.g., his revisions in 1934 of the original *Vision* text), we can conclude that *PASL* adequately represented Yeats's aesthetic theory in 1917 despite the evolution of the poet's own thinking.

8. Current feminist and literary discussion often use the terms "antinomial," "dualistic," "oppositional," and "dichotomous" interchangeably. But some are more accurate than others when applied to Yeats's worldview.

A. Antinomy is the contradiction between two conclusions or moral principles that begin from identical premises and follow valid steps of inference (Reese). With antinomies there is no meeting ground or dialectic possible. Since Yeats's oppositional thinking requires dialectic synthesis, using the term "antinomy" is not appropriate.

B. Dichotomy is the logical division that separates genus into two species because of the presence of an attribute in one and the absence of that attribute in the other. Species thus exclude one another. In relation to gender, Yeats's conception of "universal masculine & feminine" as discrete and substantive entities may suggest that they work as dichotomies, but he insists that masculine and feminine may coexist within the same psyche. Like "antinomy," the term "dichotomy" is not applicable here.

C. Bipolarity, also called symmetrical opposition, refers to negation: element or principle "A" is "non B." Example: being and nonbeing in Parmenides. Asymmetrical opposition distinguishes between "A" and "B" (A is not B, but their relationship is more complex than simple negation). The polarity found in Yeats's oppositional configuration of masculine and feminine is asymmetrical.

D. Duality is the mental act of separating genus into two exclusive categories or principles with no intermediary states between them (Baldwin). Examples:

1. philosophical duality between body and soul (as in Plato)
2. theological duality between good and evil
3. soteriological duality between God and nature
4. social/historical duality between sacred and profane, or between faith and knowledge.

As Rodney Needham observes, duality in an anthropological sense generally is formulated in symbolic classifications controlled by "the overriding importance of context," both religious and cultural (xxv). I believe that of all of these terms, duality can most accurately be used with Yeats's world for the following reasons:

1. Each member of his oppositional pairs does not necessarily signify a mutually exclusive sphere (xxvii).
2. Polarity is at root an analogy, and oppositional pairs are part of a series of analogies that are relational.
3. Oppositional pairs describe patterns of action as much as patterns of thought, which in their simplest forms can be called "recurrent antithesis" (xxix). Yeats himself uses the word "antithesis," which seems to justify Bloom's use of "antithetical theory." But I would argue that Oppel's suggestion of "dialectical theory" (28) is more apt, since the action of antithesis between man and daimon is never an end in itself, but results in a third stage, the mask.

In Yeats's thinking, conflict arises from opposition between dualities, but he categorizes different types of conflicts: oppositions, contrasts, and discords. See Note 11 below.

E. Relative opposition involves elements labeled as opposites that relate and correlate. This term originates with Aristotle and corresponds to Blake's notion of "contraries." Contrary opposition involves elements that are mutually exclusive (i.e., black and white, sickness and health) (Baldwin). Blake refers to this occurrence as "negation."

9. Frances Nesbitt Oppel argues that Yeats's oppositional view registers a myriad of influences: "genetic" factors (Yeats's relation with his father and other experiences of personalities within his own family), theosophical factors (Hermetic, Platonic, and Rosicrucian works), and literary factors (Shelley, Blake, and Nietzsche are the most notable) (28). Donoghue, Bloom, and Hassett tend to reduce these to a single, dominant factor.

10. There are also fundamental points of departure between Yeats and Nietzsche that must be noted. Oppel points out that Yeats's notion of "mastery" was alchemical in nature compared to Nietzsche's, since Nietzsche denied the existence of the supernatural and Yeats revered and pursued the spiritual at all turns. Yeats is not interested in a raw show of will but in artistically transmuting himself and experience.

The second point of departure, more critical to this discussion of the mask, is the gulf between Nietzsche's and Yeats's treatments of the feminine. Nietzsche speaks of the "abysmal antagonism" and "eternally hostile tension" between men and women as a "danger and diversion" to men (*Beyond Good and Evil* 166 and *Zarathustra* 80). Nietzsche separates women from the human species altogether: "As yet woman is not capable of friendship. Women are still cats and birds. Or at the best, cows" (*Zarathustra* 72). In sexual relations, Nietzsche literalizes his adversarial rhetoric, advocating a static, asymmetrical relation between true, "severe" men and women (who naturally have an "instinct for a *sec-*

ondary role"); in such a relation, the male would treat the female as a possession for her own good to prevent her from degenerating by losing her fear of men (*Beyond Good and Evil* 89, 167–68).

11. This is an interpretive decision on my part, since I am trying to find the closest approximation to Yeats's intent and application of what some so casually refer to as his "opposites." Yeats himself distinguished "contrary" from "discord," "correspondence," and "opposition." The term "contrary" evolved for Yeats, first functioning as a synonym for "contrast" (*AS I* 406). Gradually, he understood "contraries" as specific pairs that are not obvious opposites. For instance, instinct is the contrary to pure energy, emotion to spirit, ego to mask (*AS II* 290–91). Discord is the "enforced realization of a contrary" (226) or the "enforced understanding of the unlikeness of *Will* and *Mask* or of *Creative Mind* and *Body of Fate*" (*VA* 24). On the Great Wheel, discord will develop into opposition (in phase 15) or into identity (in phase 1). Correspondences function in pairs: emotional/creative, instinctive/mathematical (*AS II* 261). "Opposition" can be emotional (between Will and Mask) or intellectual (between Creative Mind and Body of Fate), but it always brings attractions with it: "For the *Will* has a natural desire for the *Mask* and the *Creative Mind* a natural perception of the *Body of Fate*" (*VA* 24–25).

12. By 24 November 1917, only weeks after beginning the experiment, W. B. and Georgie Yeats had defined the twenty-eight Phases of the moon. Within another month, they had translated the phases not only in terms of primary/antithetical or solar/lunar proportions but also in terms of the Four Faculties. The Yeatses amended their understanding of the Four Faculties in subsequent dialogues, i.e., Body of Fate was originally conceived as Persona of Fate, Creative Mind as Creative Genius, Will as Ego (*AS I* 242).

13. I am using the term "mask," as critics generally do, to refer to an aesthetic device, or more accurately, the textual construct and dramatic enactment that I have described throughout this chapter. This type of mask differs from "Mask" as a Faculty, which Yeats defines as an attribute of the subjective or antithetical tincture that allows the dramatization of the self (*VA* 14, 18–19). My primary concern in this discussion is the interaction of the Four Faculties, but each single Faculty exhibits complicated properties. For instance, depending on which Phase of the Wheel is being considered, the Faculty of the mask can either reveal or conceal a being (19). If it dominates the other three Faculties during a particular phase, it produces a sensuous personality (15).

CHAPTER 2: THE SEXUAL DAIMON

1. The title Automatic Script (*AS I, II,* and *III*) refers to the collaborative text drafted from October 1917 to March 1920, the sleep notebooks maintained from March 1920 to July 1923, the vision notebooks generated from November 1917 to February 1918, and the Card File (used to organize information as Yeats prepared to draft *A Vision*).

2. Kathleen Raine quotes from Arland Ussher, who believed that the tone in *A Vision B* is shaped by the influence of Eastern thought. Ussher remains skeptical: "He [Yeats] wrote much about Escape, but one feels this was just another Mask—the Eastern one. World-Renunciation is simply the last Mask of all—'the last kiss is given to the Void' . . . just as Wilde's Christianity was his last pose" (Raine, *Tarot* 25). While this possibility cannot be discounted, I find Virginia Moore's interpretation of this shift into abstraction more applicable. Moore argues that in *A Vision B*, Yeats seems to redefine the daimon, moving away from the notion of a separate spirit to a sense of the daimon as a spiritualized, higher self, the human agent transformed into a "ghostly self." That is, instead of depicting himself and his wife being manipulated by spirit guides during the Automatic Script sessions, the poet implies that the experiments were the product of his higher self interacting with his wife's: "Because of their mutual Golden Dawn training, or something else, they had found a way to bring to the surface, mediumistically, subconscious mutual knowledge" (370).

3. Yeats's treatment of Shiftings in *A Vision A* is especially significant, for it actually *adds* a sexual emphasis that is diffused in the Automatic Script. In the Script, Yeats sees a twofold purpose to this purgation process: the soul meets former lovers, and the soul is purified of ancillary elements within itself. In terms of the latter, he sees the soul as achieving its individuality by becoming free of divisible nature (*AS I* 495), then being taken from the Celestial Body (497, 503), thereby becoming complete as spirit and ghost (*AS I* 497; *AS III* 245). Because Initiatory and Critical Moments take precedence in the Script over posttemporal states as occasions when men and women shape each others' destinies, Yeats chose to emphasize the sexual dimension of Shiftings once he eliminated his "Moments" from the *Vision* text. In the years following the automatic writing sessions, Yeats clearly came to appreciate the gender dynamics to this purification process, a fact evident not only in the first edition of *A Vision* but also in *The Only Jealousy of Emer*.

4. The plot itself goes back to the year when the caliph executed his Vizir Jaffer. That same year, the caliph takes a new "bride with spring," and expresses his concern that ben Luka is brideless even in days when the jasmine blooms. The caliph "seemed for a while to have grown young again," having found a slender bride. He wishes the same for ben Luka, whose initial response is one of refusal. Ben Luka objects that he is too old, implying that his "fall into years" precludes marrying a young bride because his personal life cycle is out of kilter with the larger sweep of time and custom. The caliph objects that neither ben Luka nor he himself is as old as men who "live by habit" without reflection, self-awareness, or knowledge of higher truths.

> The key to the Caliph's youth is that
> . . . Every day
> I ride with falcon to the water's edge
> Or carry the ringed mail upon my back,
> Or court a woman; neither enemy,

Gamebird, nor woman does the same thing twice;
And so a hunter carries in the eye
A mimicry of youth. (*VA* 123)

The caliph is young because he is a hunter, a soldier, and a lover for whom everything under the sun is new. Nothing is predictable, nothing is done by habit, all things change from one moment to the next while the soul is "nearer to the surface of the body" (123). That is, he retains his sense of vitality and endless youth by immersing himself in a life of perpetual and rapid change. He advises ben Luka to follow his example.

Whether Yeats attempts to follow merely the original fable here or whether he blends in the history of his own courtship is not clear. Considering that *A Vision A* is dedicated to Moina Bergson Mathers ("Vestigia"), the caliph may be modeled on her husband, MacGregor Mathers, once a key figure in the Golden Dawn Society but later ousted, in part because of Yeats's opposition to his leadership. Clearly, the caliph is at once master, ally, and antagonist. Against the caliph's belief that love comes and goes with the seasons, ben Luka pits his "Byzantine faith" that dictates he have one and only one bride. He can never be false with her; he would have no defense or remedy if she proved false to him. Losing his one love means a defeat of the heart. (Surely Yeats has his "spiritual marriage" to Maud Gonne in mind.) For ben Luka, as for Yeats, love "separates and individualises and quiets" (*Collected VIII* 98). But for the caliph, love is the passionate bodily drive shared by all creatures, "the peacock and his mate,/The wild stag and the doe" (*VA* 124). There are as many women as springtimes, as nature shows.

5. Yeats cites this date in the second edition of *A Vision* (8), although in a letter to Lady Gregory dated 29 October, he traces the origin of the script to "two days ago" or 27 October (*Letters* 633). The authenticity of W. B. and Georgie Yeats's automatic faculty is not at issue here. There is no question that W. B. Yeats believed such activity possible and pursued occult experiments to prove to himself the existence of the spiritual realm (*AS I* 2). But Yeats himself could not determine whether individual manifestations of the automatic faculty were the result of an overactive imagination or of the subconscious. At the time of their marriage, both W. B. and Georgie Yeats were well-versed in the process of automatic writing. But few critics will hazard a judgment as to whether spirits were actually involved in the script sessions between the Yeatses. Even in his general introduction to the Automatic Script material, George Mills Harper sidesteps the issue by quoting Richard Ellmann, who notes that initially Georgie began "to fake a sentence or two" about W. B.'s decision not to marry Iseult Gonne, but later she discovered her "ability to suspend her conscious faculties" and to allow her hand to be controlled by a more powerful hand (*AS I* 10; Ellmann, *Identity* 225). I believe the subsequent discussion will clearly establish Georgie Yeats's active role without having to establish or refute the authenticity of the experiments. Finally, I agree with Virginia Moore: "I can only eliminate certain theories, reassert the proved integrity of the two people involved, note

that the hypothesis of spirit control is neither proved nor disproved, and, for the rest, shunt aside the question of origin and discuss the system as a thing in itself" (261).

6. As medium, Georgie Yeats was willing to admit mistakes. During a particularly difficult dialogue in which the twenty-eight lunar Phases were first identified, W. B. queries: "You have contradicted yourself?" "Yes I have," is the answer, "not very easy tonight" (*AS I* 213). On another occasion, her reply is even more to the point: "Yes medium wrong" (464). Sometimes she would caution her husband: "It is so big a subject [the crossing of primary and antithetic gyres]—you must go at it slowly" (*AS II* 143). As interpreter, Georgie Yeats refused to "make a discursive statement" (17) and never explained a fact on the same day she introduced it (271), presumably to give herself time to consider the new revelation and its ramifications. Often she would stall for time before formulating a response: "stop now 10 mins" (*AS I* 287), or simply admit her ignorance: "I will try & work it out/yes I will return later" (77). And again: "I will describe tomorrow or later on/I must think a coherent answer" (84; also 96 and 113).

Often the medium did not approve of her husband's questions. The warnings could be advisory: "I told you personal script was inadvisable" (*AS II* 380); sometimes confrontational: "No I do not like this" (*AS I* 386); other times a flat refusal: "I said leave this subject" (*AS II* 351). Once, she responded (no recorded question): "No a damnable thing a damnable method" (*AS I* 81). In fairness, the poet didn't always approve of the answers he received, but the spirits had the final say: "as flippant an answer as the question" (289).

7. On this occasion, there is no recorded answer. But Yeats will subsequently ask the question several more times. On 3 April 1919, the spirits informed him that he had "clung artfully to a delusion" in his relationship with Gonne (*AS II* 228). This delusion was his own creation, manifested "by the poetry which was written before that date as a relief to my feelings" (229). Again on 26 August 1919, the spirits informed him that his "crazy passion" for Gonne could be explained by their respective lunar Phases. Yeats (currently at phase 17) was attracted to Gonne's image (currently phase 16) because it came from his previous Phase: "Your passion for 16 was the reaction from your 16" (390). The spirits also offered Yeats advice about Iseult Gonne. In addition to thoroughly analyzing her phase and personality (calling her "obstinate as a mule") (*AS I* 82), they insisted: "you need not have any of the old fear about her and need not doubt that you should have done otherwise—she will assert herself" (159).

CHAPTER 3: THE FEMININE AND THE HEROIC

1. In the Noh tradition the actors do not signify personalities, the unique attributes of the actor or of the role, but *character*, the portrayal of essential and universal emotions of the human spirit. To enact an emotion that transcends any individual self or specific event, the actor wears a mask. Yeats used masks in his Noh plays as "images of those profound emotions that exist only in solitude and

silence" (*VPL* 416). That is, masks reveal the "deeps of the mind" by veiling the face (*Yeats on Yeats* 224). The second important feature pertinent to our discussion is that for the Noh's successful enactment of universal emotion, the importance of action must be minimized—both the action of conflict and of character development. Thus, the emotion being dramatized must transcend any individual actor, role, or specific event. Here Yeats's motives in adopting the Noh become clear: the Noh promised a tradition and vehicle whereby he could elevate his hero from the predominately personal or mythical (both time-bound dimensions) to the archetypal. Cuchulain thus moves from a fearless man of action to a solar type. On stage, his fate is determined not so much by his personality (hot-headed bravado mixed with selfless courage) as by the universal emotions that animate him and that remain unchanged over the course of his life.

2. Harold Bloom disagrees, insisting that the character of Aoife has only a tenuous connection to Maud Gonne. But he admits the validity of S. B. Bushrui's study that demonstrates growing negative dimensions to the Aoife mask with successive revisions after 1903, the year of Gonne's wedding (Bloom, *Yeats* 152).

3. Given Yeats's lifelong fictionalization of Maud Gonne and their relationship, there is some truth behind the farce. Gonne understood that her choice to forsake normal family ties to pursue the Irish cause was a difficult one. Rather than lobby for the abolition of traditional roles for women, she personally renounced their benefits for the liberation of Ireland.

> I am not unhappy only supremely indifferent to all that is not my work or my friends. One cannot go through what I went through & have any personal human life left, what is quite natural & right for me is not natural or right for one who has still his natural life to live. (*Gonne-Yeats Letters* 130)

At the same time, she had little patience with men who condemned her active life. In speaking about a member of the St. Patrick's Society who spoke against her in 1897, she wrote to Yeats: "I thought more probably that he was some narrow minded idiot who was scandalized at a woman leading an independent life & perhaps was jealous of me into the bargain" (67).

4. This is a revealing boast, since the hawk is Gonne's personal symbol, beginning in the days of her occult involvement (*Gonne-Yeats Letters* 370).

5. In attempting to distinguish between Fand as Sidhe and Fand as a being in phase 15, the spirits tell Yeats: "the people of fairy the souls of one & fifteen and all other legendary states are but parts of one truth.—The truth is in all but in some more concealed by fable & by dream than in others—that is all I can say" (*AS I* 214).

6. This situation is all-important to Yeats, for it enacts the metaphysical theory expounded in section 12, book 4 of the 1925 edition of *A Vision*. Titled "The Spirits at Fifteen and at One," the section is later identified as "'the most important in the book'" (in a letter dated 26 March 1926) because it expresses

the interaction of sun and moon "'in a study of the relation of man and woman'" (qtd. in Hood 37).

7. Although Eithne Inguba pronounces Bricriu to be evil, he serves a necessary purpose. He is the spirit intervening in the fate of Fand the Beautiful; he will engineer the "marriage" of Fand's craving for love with Cuchulain's refusal, an antithesis that will complete Fand's Dreaming Back experience. She will then know what it is to refuse love and what it is to be refused.

8. Obviously, I am excluding the Blind Man in this generalization. Although the Blind Man is a moving force in the time and place of Cuchulain's death, he is a paid lackey, a murderer hired by Maeve because he is interested in twelve pennies. He may be a sign of the cold, calculated man of business, the indifferent, common, unprincipled, and unfit man of modern times who is blind to the spiritual and heroic dimensions unraveling before his eyes, or just a postscript to the Conchubar mask from *Baile*. But in any case, he is himself caught up in a larger pattern of destiny. For the same reason, I am also excluding the six men who either for revenge or from cowardly cruelty delivered the mortal wounds.

9. From the very beginning of the cycle, Yeats had a clear sense of Cuchulain's unchanging character. In his commentary about *Baile*, he notes: "Probably his very strength of character . . . made him quite early in life a deliberate lover, a man of pleasure who can never really surrender himself. He is a little hard, and leaves the people about him a little repelled" (*Letters* 425). Yet in defining personality types according to the phases of the moon, Yeats insisted that each person is more than a type, i.e., characteristics embodied in an incarnated state. At certain critical points in life, a man or woman enters into an "emotional relation" to the past and "in intellectual relation" to the future. He concludes: "It is because of this that he is an individual & not merely a type of his phase" (*AS III* 115).

10. The gold signifies Cuchulain's own solar nature and is a fitting tribute to his nobility. But the veil alludes to Veronica, who approached the bloodied Christ on his journey to Calvary and wiped his face with her veil, as Yeats describes in his poem, "Veronica's Napkin." The veil also suggests a woman's winding, seductive hair that can both entangle a man (as with Medusa) or redeem him (as with Berenice). There is no Veronica to console him, no Medusa to seduce him, no Berenice to save him. Cuchulain is surrounded by the women he once loved in a scene that dramatizes most vividly the identification of sexual love and spiritual hate.

11. In pronouncing Yeats's dialogue "inadequate" in the play, F. A. C. Wilson cites the confrontation between Cuchulain and the Blind Man, comparing it to a similar scene in *The Herne's Egg* wherein Congal meets his own assassin (*Tradition* 193). But the climax of *Death* is the meeting with Aoife, and it is this dialogue that flows naturally and displays none of the understated, anticlimactic verse of the later scene.

12. This scene acts as a corrective to Amy Koritz's judgment about the "misogynistic twist to Yeats's practice of his aesthetic theories" (397). Koritz ar-

gues that in *Hawk* Yeats brings together sexual power and alien presence (both associated with the feminine) in the image of the dance. Thereafter, she contends, Yeats is extremely selective in his use of the dance image, as if he were seeking to "contain" the power of the feminine (397) by not allowing earthly women access to that power. With this scene in *Death*, Yeats allows only mortal Emer the dance, as well as describing her actions in a way that expresses the ultimate spirit and power of the feminine.

CHAPTER 4: THE WISDOM OF THE BODY

1. As F. A. C. Wilson notes, Solomon and Sheba were understood as "perfect lovers" in the literature of the 1890s. Arthur Symon's play, "The Lover of the Queen of Sheba," is for Wilson the single most significant source of the Sheba series (*Iconography* 276).

2. It is tempting and, on the whole, justified to read "On Woman" as thinly veiled autobiography, much along the lines of "Adam's Curse." In 1914 Maud Gonne would not marry Yeats despite her divorce from John MacBride, since the Catholic church did not acknowledge divorce. But the marriage issue was only one impediment between them. As early as 1909, Yeats expressed his concern that Maud Gonne was letting her politics become an obsession, a danger that plagued women more than men. For women conceive of ideas like children, suckling and protecting them "as though a part of their flesh" (*Memoirs* 192). But the child is a monster, stillborn like "some terrible stone doll," and the woman pays a monstrous price by becoming less feminine: "much of their being passes out of life" (192).

Yet I do not wish to reduce the truth of Gonne's career to Yeats's version of it. As Anna MacBride White reminds us: "Most of what is known about her [Gonne's] personal emotions derives from Yeats's writing, coloured and filtered by his intense infatuation and possibly telescoped and rounded by his well-known love of a good story" (*Gonne-Yeats Letters* 15).

3. Here Yeats closely follows Nietzsche's theory of the mask. "Every profound spirit needs a mask," Nietzsche believed (*Beyond Good and Evil* 511). And he would add, every lover needs a mask as well, for the mask commands the heart. Nietzsche disdained the kind of man who wants to be loved as much for his "devilry" as for his "graciousness, patience and spirituality" (107). He is the "lowest of men" because he needs to possess or control his woman so completely that he is jealous of everything, even of her loving "a phantom of him" (107). Such desires are mediocre and effeminate. A true man shows a higher strength that allows him to scorn the "real" self, both his and his lover's. Cultivate a phantom, Nietzsche urges, for the beloved will be captivated.

4. I am treating the poem as it stands alone, not as it functions as an introduction to *Per Amica Silentia Lunae*.

5. The original manuscript version shows more pronoun references that were subsequently deleted; these deletions indicate Yeats's conscious attempt to minimize gender identity.

6. I am using "Ego Dominus Tuus" rather than "The Phases of the Moon" for two reasons. First, "Ego" directly addresses the action of the mask. But more obviously, "The Phases of the Moon" was written in 1919, during the Automatic Script sessions and so does not qualify as a pre-Script poem. Although it is renounced by Yeats as equally abstract as "Ego," this poem is actually full of pertinent material. As Wayne Chapman has noted, the literary references in "Phases" are "more than usually complex" (195). Chapman demonstrates that there is more gendered dialogue here than meets the eye. Citing Milton's *The Doctrine and Discipline of Divorce* and Plato's *Phaedrus,* Chapman finds veiled allusions to the nature of ideal marriage meant for Georgie Yeats alone. The connection is too obscure for the average reader—"The poet could not have expected—nor wished—his public to recognize such slight personal touches" (194).

7. Scholars are imprecise about when these two poems were drafted, but the dates are an important issue in connecting the poems to specific topics in the Script. For this discussion, however, it is enough to note that while "Michael Robartes and the Dancer" and "Solomon and the Witch" were drafted closely together in time, they were published in a particular order of strategic importance.

8. It is difficult to imagine how literary critics could offer such incongruous readings of the same poem. Perhaps it would be simplistic to contend that Unterecker and Cullingford side with the two protagonists along gender lines or suffer from their own case of gender-linked perspectives, but if gender is a factor in the issues and protagonists in "Michael Robartes," it well may be a factor in its interpretation.

9. Curiously, Yeats includes vignettes about what is apparently Robartes' long and stormy history with dancers. In the 1925 edition of *A Vision,* Yeats refers to a brief affair Robartes had with a ballet dancer. "I went from Paris to Rome," Robartes narrates, "and from Rome to Vienna, in pursuit of a ballet dancer, and in Vienna we quarreled" (*VA* xvii). In the 1937 edition, Yeats expands Robartes' story:

> I went to Rome and there fell violently in love with a ballet-dancer who had not an idea in her head. All might have been well had I been content to take what came; had I understood that her coldness and cruelty became in the transfiguration of the body an inhuman majesty; that I adored in body what I hated in will . . . The more I tried to change her character the more did I uncover mutual enmity. (*VB* 37–38)

10. In "Her Triumph," the woman accepts his love at the moment she embraces these masks, seeing him as Perseus and herself as Andromeda. David R. Clark summarizes this process in terms of Yeats's Four Faculties:

> His *Will* sees hers as Andromeda *(Mask).* His *Creative Mind* sees hers as the dragon of resistance to true love *(Body of Fate).* Her *Cre-*

ative Mind sees his as an insistence on unwanted true love *(Body of Fate)*. Her will sees his as an Indomitable Perseus *(Mask)*. *(Songs* 110)

CHAPTER 5: GENDERED VOICES IN MOMENTS OF CRISIS

1. Curtis Bradford argues that "A Woman" was not ready for publication in *The Tower*. He suggests that Yeats had "a great deal of trouble" with the sequence that "was underway for many years" (*Yeats at Work* 127). But A. Norman Jeffares documents that Yeats sold William Edwin Rudge of Fountain Press the rights to sixteen pages of verse in October 1927, which included the "A Woman" sequence (*W.B. Yeats* 288).

2. I use the term "sequence" rather than "series" to acknowledge the complexity of these masks that demand more than simple lyrical expression. As M. L. Rosenthal and Sally M. Gall argue, the sequence as a new genre is a unique facet of modern poetry: "More successfully than individual short lyrics . . . it fulfills the need for encompassment of disparate and often powerfully opposed tonalities and energies" (3). Cautioning against reading the sequence as "a mere thought" or a "biographical shade" (4), Rosenthal and Gall speak about the presence of "passionate preoccupation" or "radiant centers" that reach "a height of responsiveness to all pressures acting on it" rather than conclude an action (11).

3. Phase 1 signifies the solar or masculine principle in absolute form (with no trace of the lunar or feminine), and phase 15 signifies the lunar/feminine principle in absolute form (with no trace of the solar/masculine). Both these phases are incompatible with human existence.

4. W. B. Yeats's Moments of Crisis are identified by year (1896, 1910, 1913, 1917), by women (Olivia Shakespear, Maud Gonne, Mabel Dickinson, and Georgie Yeats) and by type (Initiatory and Critical Moments). Barbara J. Frieling emphasizes the personal element in this discussion from another approach. She argues that the introduction of the topic stems from the birth of Anne Yeats, less than a month old and "firmly expected by her parents to be a son" (283). The subsequent dissection of IMs and CMs helped the Yeatses understand that their daimons desired the birth of their daughter and were designing the birth of their future son (285).

5. For the sake of clarity, I have simplified the material in the following discussion by omitting the added complication of tracing how the Four Faculties align during Moments of Crisis, a process that occurs differently in each of the twenty-eight Phases. I have also minimized discussion of teacher and victim, since Yeats denounces some of this material in a note later penned at the bottom of a page in the Script dated 29 March: "Much of the information in these scripts about IMs & CMs confused and apparently wrong . . . may be caused by confusion of terms some uncertainty about 'victim' etc." As George Mills Harper notes, it is not clear if Yeats's comment applies to that day's script only or to the extended discussion that runs through 5 April (*AS II* 559).

6. Yeats uses the term "suffering" in various ways. On the one hand, he

means "the tyranny of unlikes" (*AS II* 341). The principle of "the unlike" can be applied to opposites (subjective and objective) or to multiple attributes (nerve and flesh, muscle and bone) (341). He also associates suffering with purification, not in a moral sense but rather in terms of self-knowledge. The victim is plagued by self-hatred (220), perhaps caused by a lack of perception (311). Such suffering engenders self-analysis (310). Or the victim may suffer for another person, undergoing a sort of purgation process "for another *not* in place of that other" (340) so that the other may harden subjectively (219).

7. Here Georgie Yeats's personal agenda clearly directs the discussion. She uncharacteristically allows her husband to ask personal questions in defining the difference between pity and affection—pity for his former lovers, affection for her—in order to help him conceive of their marriage in a new way and become convinced of its validity.

8. To encapsulate the Critical Moments, Yeats develops a shorthand scheme of myths. The man's first Critical Moment is summarized by the Glaucus myth, which revolves around the theme of "the bitter grass [desire fades] the plunge into the sea" [Creative Genius liberated] (*AS II* 483). His second Critical Moment is summarized by the myth of Meleager, which Yeats used to symbolize that the brand [lure] does not burn when death is impossible (484). The woman's first Critical Moment is encapsulated by the myth of Berenice, a figure symbolizing desire and sacrifice, who denies herself so that the real man may return (483). The woman's second Critical Moment is signified by the myth of Persephone, unwilling but living (484).

9. "A Man" is usually discounted as the predictable parcel of poetry dedicated to Maud Gonne that shows up in every volume—"a kind of free fantasia on Yeats's own love life" (Unterecker 194), interesting only as autobiographical footnotes. Cullingford comments upon its "heavy autobiographical freight" (*Gender and History* 215). A. Norman Jeffares takes great care to identify the specific women he believes are the subjects of each of the poems in "A Man" series. Maud Gonne is the subject in "First Love," "His Memories," "The Secrets of the Old," and "His Wildness"; Olivia Shakespear in "Mermaid" and "The Empty Cup"; Iseult Gonne in "The Death of the Hare"; and Georgie Yeats in "The Secrets of the Old" (*New Commentary* 325–31).

10. It is even tempting to relate this sequence to what Lawrence Lipking calls the experience of "abandonment"—being forsaken or cast off (xvii). Lipking does not discuss this sequence, but his analysis rings true of this speaker, who "does not internalize his abandonment. Instead, he regards it as strange or unnatural" (xix) and responds with resentment rather than regret. Lipking concludes that "poems about male abandonment tend to sound resentful or puzzled, as if the man could not understand how such an inappropriate fate could have happened to someone like *him*" (xviii).

11. Critics including Jeffares, T. R. Henn, and Wayne Chapman have established that in the later 1920s, Yeats immersed himself in Renaissance poetry, paying special attention to the Metaphysical poets. Their influence is clearly woven into these lines. It is a commonplace notion in Renaissance poetry that the

eye is the portal of the soul. In the daughter's case, sight evokes sexual desire more immediately than any other sense.

Yet Yeats's choice to associate male with auditory sensations and female with visual sensations defies both Platonic and Freudian thinking. Many feminists have pointed to male-authored philosophic positions and male-generated artistic enterprises that privilege the sense of sight over other senses. Evelyn Fox Keller and Christine R. Grontkowski believe "vision" has been used as a metaphor for knowledge since the time of Plato. The allegory of the cave depends upon the light/dark, vision/blindness motif to describe true knowledge versus illusion (208–9). Linda Mulvey cites Freudian theory to explain the use of visual erotica in film. Here the visual image of woman as anatomically defective signifies both the "male other" and the horror of castration. She can be controlled by being objectified through the male gaze (8). While she remains silent and passive, the male can achieve active control through his visual sense (11).

Why does Yeats invert these traditions by associating the Woman with visual sense? Elizabeth Cullingford argues that Yeats "posits the male gaze as its own punishment" and furthermore "criticizes a system of representation that privileges the visual" (*Gender and History* 211). I see this gesture as more positive in nature. On the one hand, Yeats is acknowledging the Woman's own sexual powers, her ability to desire and be aroused by the sight of her lover. On the other, he is demonstrating that the universal feminine is far more dynamic than culture or society pretends. He is not arguing that the feminine is always tied to the visual but that it can operate from the visual just as the masculine can. Finally, I would argue that his decision to align the Man and the Woman with different senses is relational rather than absolute. They operate out of different senses as part of their complementarity; it is the complementarity that is constant; the association of either gender with a particular sense is secondary.

CHAPTER 6: ENACTING THE FEMININE

1. Scholars have worked with this sequence primarily in two ways: on the one hand, they emphasize Jane's eccentric and pronounced appetites, arguing that the sequence indexes Yeats's apparent turning away from occult preoccupation because Jane is "completely physical and anti-intellectual, and viciously anti-clerical" (Ellmann, *Masks* 272). Some contend that after *The Tower* (1928), Yeats felt the need to compensate for its spiritual imbalance: "flesh, too, demanded its due" (Unterecker 201); or that Yeats pitted an "erotic and licentious female figure" against a "celibate clergy" (Cullingford, *Gender and History* 227). Rather than seeing Jane primarily as a advocate of the physical, other critics have noted Jane's balance of soul and body, admiring her attempt to "knit together the natural and the supernatural" (Saddlemyer 153), along with her extravagance of spirit and her wisdom "of a more radical wholeness" (Bloom, *Yeats* 400). Reading the sequence in terms of the daimonic brings these two approaches of opposition and wholeness together.

2. The three original Crazy Jane poems were written within weeks of each

other during the early months of 1929: "Crazy Jane and the Bishop," "Crazy Jane Reproved," and "Crazy Jane Grown Old Looks at the Dancers." The other four poems were gradually added to the sequence—"Crazy Jane on the Day of Judgment" (written October 1930), "Crazy Jane and Jack the Journeyman" (November 1931), "Crazy Jane on God" (July 1931), and "Crazy Jane Talks with the Bishop" (November 1931).

3. References to the daimon are rare during the first year of the automatic writing experiment. But in March 1919, the Yeatses began to seriously explore the concept of the Moments of Crisis, and within two weeks they had defined the daimon as "of opposite sex to ego." From that point on in the Script, the daimon assumes center stage.

4. This is one of the occasions when Yeats deals with his wife's daimon rather than his own. During sexual union between a man and woman, the woman's daimon accesses the man's memory, and the man's daimon accesses the woman's (*AS III* 291).

5. Yeats defines emotion as "the degree of influence the senses have upon the unity of the self" (*AS III* 293).

6. For Yeats, the shell is more than a fine specimen of divine handiwork; it is also an image for the receptacle of the *Anima Mundi:* "I know now that revelation is from the self, but from that age-long memoried self, that shapes the elaborate shell of the mollusc and the child in the womb" (*AU* 182). Because the daimon communicates through the *Anima Mundi,* the shell is a particularly apt image for Jane.

7. These lines are syntactically problematic. On the surface, "yawns" implies that Heaven is bored with such simple demonstrations of power or that Heaven is indifferent to the plight of the helpless sailors. In either of these cases, the lines immediately following the colon would be attributed to Jane's own view. However, because of the additional meaning of "yawns" (male sexual arousal), the lines must be attributed to the sailors.

8. Yeats highlights this same tension in a passage from "Ireland after Parnell": "Is it not certain that the Creator yawns in earthquake and thunder and other popular displays, but toils in rounding the delicate spiral of a shell? (*AU* 167; noted in Ellmann, *Identity* 276). This passage sets one of Heaven's reactions against the other, with the emphasis not so much on the response (yawning versus toiling) but on the occasion (earthquake/thunder as opposed to rounding a delicate shell). To Yeats, both instances display the divine, but the second (the shell) contains more of the divine than the first (the storm). Yeats also privileges the shell as a product of divine art over the less impressive display of violent, destructive power.

9. This reading is based on Yeats's use of the term "yawn" in the Solomon and Sheba poems and in the *The Player Queen.*

10. Yeats is addressing something fundamental, even archetypal, about human experience, laying out issues that lead to what he calls the "question from the Delphic oracle" (qtd. in Finneran 27). The word "Delphi" means "womb"; the oracle originally belonged to the primal Mother under the

guise of sea goddess and moon goddess (Walker 218).

11. The skein image does not simply depict Jane's squandering of herself but also marks a whole series of references in the *Winding Stair* volume, particularly in the poem "A Dialogue of Self and Soul" that precedes the Crazy Jane sequence. Here the body is likened to torn embroidery made by silkworms that spin the silk around the scabbard of the sword or soul. Then there is the image of historical time whirled in pernes and gyres via the "winding ancient stair." Finally, there is the cycle of birth and death signifying the fall of the soul into temporal existence, its liberation at death, and the self's choice to remain in the cycle rather than to return to God as a "lonely ghost," to use Jane's expression (*VP* 511).

Wayne Chapman draws another possible application of the skein image. He notes the parallel to John Donne's "The Relic," which describes a lock of hair buried with two lovers that will lead them to meet after death (178–79). Chapman suggests that the skein image refers, at least in part, to the "Relic" but is adapted to one of Yeats's most valued myths, the story of Berenice. According to the legend, Berenice sacrificed her hair to the gods for the sake of her husband. If it is reasonable to mention Berenice, then the myth of Medusa also comes to mind. Clearly, the image of love-as-skein is ambiguous. It suggests the potential for the lover to be ensnared or trapped, a potential that Jack himself apparently feels.

12. Herein lies a critical difference between Yeats's treatment of Jane and her literary antecedent—the "Crazy Jane" of Romantic literature—a young, abandoned woman driven mad by the loss of her lover (Showalter 11). Within this tradition, Jane devotes her life to commemorating blissful moments from the past (13). Showalter describes her as a cult figure: simple, docile, defenseless, and clinically "mad." Feminine sexuality and irrationality are merged into a "poetic, artistic, and theatrical" image that invites a cautious, protective response from men (10). Lawrence Lipking also advances a view of Yeats's Crazy Jane as a type of victim, one of poetry's "abandoned women." Although she is "forsaken or cast off," Lipking argues, she is also "unrestrained or shameless" (xvii). The tone of Yeats's treatment of Jane does not invite pity or condescension. She is clearly not a victim, neither of her sex nor of her sexual desires.

CHAPTER 7: POWER AND THE MASK

1. In building his case, Johnsen notes Yeats's paragraph about Leda in "Dove or Swan." In the 1925 edition of *A Vision*, Yeats ends the reference with the following statement: "When in my ignorance I try to imagine what older civilisation *she refuted* (emphasis added) I can but see bird and woman blotting out some corner of the Babylonian mathematical starlight" (*VA* 181). In the 1937 edition, Yeats changed the sentence to read: "When in my ignorance I try to imagine what older civilisation *that annunciation rejected* (emphasis added) I can but see bird and woman blotting out some corner of the Babylonian mathematical starlight" (*VB* 268).

According to Johnsen, the 1925 edition treats Leda as an active agent in the drama; she not only rejects but also disproves the values of the passing culture. But in the revision, Leda falls out of the equation altogether. "Refutation" degenerates into "rejection," with Zeus (the annunciator) as the primary agent.

I would concede that the two words may connote different associations that come into play with the closing lines of the poem: "Did she put on his knowledge with his power/Before the indifferent beak let her drop?" "Refute" may mean "to disprove or overthrow by argument" ("knowledge" in that sense) and "reject" may mean "to decline or cast off" ("power" in that sense). But the Oxford unabridged dictionary also defines both terms as synonyms for "refuse," a definition that minimizes Johnsen's point. More significant may be the substitution of "annunciation" for Leda's name, perhaps a minor variant of the revisions in *A Vision B* that tended to degender material in order to abstract more freely.

2. Out of the ashes of the classical world rises the new revelation of the Christian order. Instead of glorifying the athlete, this civilization venerated the ascetic. Miracle replaces reason; thought gives way to theology; the secular intellect is eclipsed by doctrine. As the Christian age comes to a close and Yeats turns to his own culture, he sees the ascetic giving way to the romantic. Philosophy replaces dogma, nature is valued more than miracle. As the veneration of science and economics dominates the human personality, there is a "breaking of soul" (*VA* 206) in an ambitious, greedy, and materialistic age.

3. The fundamental problem with Sword's analysis is her jump from the nature of the divine to the nature of poetic inspiration. While there is no evidence that Yeats associates the aesthetic process with violence, there is a body of texts that support the association of violence with the intrusion of the divine into the human realm (note especially "The Magi," 1914; "The Second Coming," 1920; "Two Songs from a Play," 1927; and "The Mother of God," 1932).

4. Yeats's revision continued with each successive publication of the poem. The 1924 version (published in *The Dial*) differs from the 1925 version in *A Vision* (1925), which in turn is changed in the 1937 edition. The Variorum edition is identical to the *Vision B* version save for the addition of a question mark in line six after the word "thighs."

5. This passage is omitted from the second edition, which again illustrates what Yeats sacrificed in the degendering changes in *A Vision B*.

6. If there is a misuse of terminology, it is in the confusion of "annunciation" with "incarnation." Zeus impregnates Leda, but he does not reveal, express, or announce a message.

WORKS CITED

Adams, Hazard. *The Book of Yeats's Poems.* Tallahassee: Florida State UP, 1990.

Arkins, Brian. *Builders of My Soul: Greek and Roman Themes in Yeats.* Gerrards Cross: Smythe, 1990.

Baldwin, James Mark. *Dictionary of Philosophy and Psychology.* New York: Macmillan, 1911.

Bem, Sandra Lipsitz. "Androgyny and Gender Schema Theory: A Conceptual and Empirical Integration." *Psychology And Gender:* Nebraska Symposium on Motivation 1984. Ed. T. B. Sonderegger. Lincoln: U of Nebraska, 1984. 179–226.

———. "Gender Schema Theory: A Cognitive Account of Sex Typing." *Psychology Review* 88 (1981): 354–64.

———. "Gender Schema Theory and the Romantic Tradition." *Sex and Gender: Review of Personality and Social Psychology.* Vol. 7. Ed. Philip Shaver and Clyde Hendrick. Newbury Park: Sage, 1987. 251–71.

———. *The Lenses of Gender: Transforming the Debate on Sexual Inequality.* New Haven: Yale UP, 1993.

Benfey, Christopher. "The Woman in the Mirror: Randall Jarrell and John Berryman." Morgan 123–38.

Bloom, Harold, ed. *William Butler Yeats.* New York: Chelsea, 1986.

———. *Yeats.* New York: Oxford UP, 1970.

Bornstein, George. *Yeats and Shelley.* Chicago: Chicago UP, 1970.

Bradford, Curtis. *Yeats at Work.* Carbondale: South Illinois UP, 1965.

———. *Yeats at Work*. Abr. ed. New York: Ecco, 1965.

Bushrui, S. B. *Yeats's Verse-Plays: The Revisions: 1900–1910*. Oxford: Clarendon, 1965.

Butler, Judith. *Gender Trouble: Feminism and the Subversion of Identity*. New York: Routledge, 1990.

Cameron, Deborah. *Feminism and Linguistic Theory*. New York: Macmillan, 1985.

Chapman, Wayne. *Yeats and English Renaissance Literature*. New York: St. Martin's, 1991.

Cixous, Helene. "The Laugh of the Medusa." *The Signs Reader: Women, Gender and Scholarship*. Ed. Elizabeth Abel and Emily K. Abel. Chicago: U of Chicago P, 1983.

Clark, David R. *That Black Day: The Manuscripts of "Crazy Jane on the Day of Judgement."* Atlantic Highlands: Humanities, 1980.

———. *Yeats at Songs and Choruses*. Amherst: U of Massachusetts P, 1983.

Clark, Rosalind E. "Yeats's THE ONLY JEALOUSY OF EMER and the Old Irish SERGLIGE CON CULAINN. *Yeats: An Annual of Critical and Textual Studies*. Vol. 8. Ed. Richard J. Finneran and Edward Engelberg, 39–48. Ann Arbor: U of Michigan Press, 1990.

Culler, Jonathan. *Structuralist Poetics: Structuralism, Linguistics, and the Study of Literature*. Ithaca: Cornell UP, 1975.

Cullingford, Elizabeth. *Gender and History in Yeats's Love Poetry*. Cambridge: Cambridge UP, 1993.

———. "Venus or Mrs. Pankhurst: Yeats's Love Poetry and the Culture of Suffrage." *Yeats: An Annual of Critical and Textual Studies*. Vol. 9. Ed. Richard J. Finneran and Mary FitzGerald, 11–29. Ann Arbor: U of Michigan P, 1991.

———. "Yeats and Women: MICHAEL ROBARTES AND THE DANCER." *Yeats Annual*. 4 (1986): 29–52.

———. "Yeats: The Anxiety of Masculinity." *Gender in Irish Writing*. Ed. Toni O'Brien Johnson and David Cairms. Philadelphia: Open UP, 1991.

David, Robert Con and Thaïs E. Morgan. "Two Conversations on Literature, Theory, and the Question of Genders." Morgan 189–200.

Dellamora, Richard. *Masculine Desire: The Sexual Politics of Victorian Aestheticism*. Chapel Hill: U of North Carolina P, 1990.

Donoghue, Denis. *William Butler Yeats*. New York: Viking, 1971.

Durand, Béatrice. "Diderot and the Nun: Portrait of the Artist as a Transvestite." Morgan 89–106.

Ebert, Teresa L. "The 'Difference' of Postmodern Feminism." *College English* 53.8 (Dec. 1991): 886–904.

Ellmann, Richard. *The Identity of Yeats*. New York: Oxford UP, 1964.

———. *Yeats, the Man and the Masks*. New York: Macmillan, 1948.

Finneran, Richard J. *Editing Yeats's Poems: A Reconsideration*. New York: Macmillan, 1990.

Fletcher, Ian. "'Leda and the Swan' as Iconic Poem." *Yeats Annual*. No. 1. Ed.

Richard J. Finneran, 82–113. Atlantic Highlands: Humanities, 1982.

Fraser, Nancy. *Unruly Practices: Power, Discourse, and Gender in Contemporary Social Theory.* Minneapolis: U of Minnesota P, 1989.

Friedman, Barton R. *Adventures in the Deeps of the Mind: The Cuchulain Cycle of W. B. Yeats.* Princeton: Princeton UP, 1977.

Frieling, Barbara J. "'Moments of Crisis' in the *Vision* Papers." *Yeats: An Annual of Critical and Textual Studies.* Vol. 10. Ed. Richard J. Finneran and James W. Flannery, 281–95. Ann Arbor: U of Michigan P, 1992.

Fuss, Diana. *Essentially Speaking.* New York: Routledge, 1989.

Gilbert, Sandra M., and Susan Gubar. *No Man's Land: The Place of the Woman Writer in the Twentieth Century II: Sex Changes.* New Haven: Yale UP, 1989.

Girard, René. *Violence and the Sacred.* Baltimore: Johns Hopkins UP, 1972.

The Gonne-Yeats Letters, 1893–1938: Always Your Friend. Ed. Anna MacBride White and A. Norman Jeffares. London: Hutchinson: 1992.

Graves, Heather Brodie. "Regrinding the Lens of Gender: Problematizing 'Writing as a Woman.'" *Written Communication* 10.2 (Apr. 1993): 139–63.

Hamburger, Kate. *The Logic of Literature.* Bloomington: Indiana UP, 1973.

Harding, Sandra. "Why Has the Sex/Gender System Become Visible Only Now?" Harding and Hintikka, 311–324.

Harding, Sandra, and Merrill Hintikka, eds. *Discovering Reality: Feminist Perspectives on Epistemology, Metaphysics, Methodology, and Philosophy of Science.* Boston: Reidel, 1983.

Hare-Mustin, Rachel and Jeanne Marecek. "Beyond Difference." *Making a Difference: Psychology and the Construction of Gender.* Ed. Rachel Hare-Mustin and Jeanne Marecek. New Haven: Yale UP, 1990. 184–201.

Harper, George Mills. *The Making of Yeats's A VISION: a Story of the Automatic Script.* Vols. 1, 2. Carbondale and Edwardsville: Southern Illinois UP, 1987.

Harper, Margaret Mills. "The Message is the Medium: Identity in the Automatic Script." *Yeats: An Annual of Critical and Textual Studies.* Vol. 9. Ed. Richard J. Finneran and Mary Fitzgerald, 35–54. Ann Arbor: U of Michigan P, 1991.

Hassett, Joseph M. *Yeats and the Poetics of Hate.* New York: St. Martin's, 1986.

Heilbrun, Carolyn G. "Androgyny and the Psychology of Sex Differences." *The Future of Difference.* Ed. Hester Eisenstein and Alice Jardine. New Brunswick: Rutgers UP, 1987. 260–66.

———. *Toward a Recognition of Androgyny.* New York: Knopf, 1973.

Henn, T. R. *The Lonely Tower.* London: Methuen, 1950.

Hillman, James. *The Myth of Analysis: Three Essays in Archetypal Psychology.* Evanston: Northwestern UP, 1972.

———. *Re-visioning Psychology.* New York: Harper, 1975.

Holland, Dorothy, and Debra Skinner. "Prestige and Intimacy: The Cultural Models behind Americans' Talk about Gender Types." *Cultural Models in Language and Thought.* Ed. Dorothy Holland and Naomi Quinn.

Cambridge: Cambridge UP, 1987. 78–111.

Hood, Connie K. "The Remaking of A VISION." *Yeats: An Annual of Critical and Textual Studies.* Vol. 1. Ed. Richard J. Finneran, 33–67. Ithaca: Cornell UP, 1983.

Hynes, Samuel. "All the Wild Witches: The Women in Yeats's Poems." *Sewanee Review* 85.4 (1977): 565–82.

Illich, Ivan. *Gender.* New York: Pantheon, 1982.

Jardine, Alice A. *Gynesis: Configurations of Woman and Modernity.* Ithaca: Cornell UP, 1985.

Jeffares, A. Norman. *A New Commentary on the Poems of W. B. Yeats.* New York: Macmillan, 1984.

———. *W. B. Yeats: A New Biography.* London: Hutchinson, 1988.

Jeffares, A. Norman, and A.S. Knowland. *A Commentary on the Collected Plays of W. B. Yeats.* Stanford: Stanford UP, 1975.

Johnsen, William. "Textual/Sexual Politics in Yeats's 'Leda and the Swan.'" *Yeats and Postmodernism.* Ed. Leonard Orr. Syracuse: Syracuse UP, 1991.

Jones, Ann Rosalind. *The Currency of Eros: Women's Love Lyric in Europe, 1540–1620.* Bloomington: Indiana UP, 1990.

Jung, C. J. *Collected Works.* Ed. Herbert Read, Michael Fordham, and Gerhart Adler. New York: Pantheon, 1953 (1983).

———. *Psychological Reflection.* New York: Harper, 1953.

Keane, Patrick. *Yeats's Interaction with Tradition.* Columbia: U of Missouri P, 1987.

Keller, Evelyn Fox, and Christine R. Grontkowski. "The Mind's Eye." Harding and Hintikka, 207–24.

Komesu, Okifumi. *"At the Hawk's Well* and *Taka No Izumi* in a 'Creative Circle.'" *Yeats Annual* 5. (1987): 103–13.

Koritz, Amy. "Women Dancing: The Structure of Gender in Yeats's Early Plays for Dancers." *Modern Drama* 32 (Sept. 1989): 387–400.

Langbaum, Robert W. *The Mysteries of Identity: A Theme in Modern Literature.* Chicago: U of Chicago P, 1977.

———. *The Poetry of Experience: The Dramatic Monologue in Modern Literary Tradition.* New York: Random House, 1957.

Lipking, Lawrence. *Abandoned Women and Poetic Tradition.* Chicago: U of Chicago P, 1988.

Londraville, Richard. "I Have Longed for Such a Country: The Cuchulain Cycle as Peking Opera." *Yeats: An Annual of Critical and Textual Studies.* Vol. 2. Ed. Richard J. Finneran, 165–208. Ithaca: Cornell UP, 1984.

McDowell, Colin. "'The Completed Symbol': *Daimonic* Existence and the Great Wheel in *A Vision* (1937)." *Yeats Annual* 6 (1988): 193–208.

———. "The Six Discarnate States of *A Vision* (1937)." *Yeats: An Annual of Critical and Textual Studies.* Vol. 4. Ed. Richard J. Finneran, 87–98. Ann Arbor: UMI Research Press, 1986.

Melchiori, Giorgio. *The Whole Mystery of Art: Pattern into Poetry in the Work of W. B. Yeats.* London: Routledge, 1960.

Moi, Toril. *Sexual/Textual Politics: Feminist Literary Theory.* New York: Methuen, 1985.

Moore, Virginia. *The Unicorn: William Butler Yeats' Search for Reality.* New York: Macmillan, 1954.

Morgan, Thaïs E., ed. *Men Writing the Feminine: Literature, Theory, and the Question of Genders.* Albany: SUNY, 1994.

Mulvey, Linda. "Visual Pleasures and Narrative Cinema." *Screen* 16.3 (Autumn 1974): 6–18.

Murphy, Peter F. "'To Write What Cannot Be Written': The Woman Writer and Male Authority in John Hawkes's *Virginie: Her Two Lives.*" Morgan 77–88.

Nahm, Milton. *Selections from Early Greek Philosophy.* New York: Appleton, 1964.

Narayan, Uma. "The Project of Feminist Epistemology: Perspectives from a Non-western Feminist." *Gender/Body/Knowledge: Feminist Reconstructions of Being and Knowing.* Ed. Alison M. Jaggar and Susan R. Bordo. New Brunswick: Rutgers UP, 1989. 256–72.

Needham, Rodney, ed. *Right and Left: Essays on Dual Symbolic Classification.* Chicago: U of Chicago P, 1973.

Nietzsche, Friedrich. *Beyond Good and Evil.* New York: Random, 1966.

———. *Thus Spake Zarathustra.* New York: Modern Library, 1905.

Olney, James. "The Esoteric Flower." *Yeats and the Occult.* Ed. George Mills Harper. Toronto: Macmillan of Canada, 1975. 27–54.

———. *The Rhizome and the Flower: The Perennial Philosophy—Yeats and Jung.* Berkeley: U of California P, 1980.

———. "Sex and the Dead: *Daimones* of Yeats and Jung." *Critical Essays on W. B. Yeats.* Ed. Richard J. Finneran. Boston: Hall, 1986. 207–24.

———. "W. B. Yeats's Daimonic Memory." *The Sewanee Review* 85 (1977): 583–603.

Oppel, Frances Nesbitt. *Mask and Tragedy: Yeats and Nietzsche, 1902–1910.* Charlottesville: UP of Virginia, 1987.

O'Shea, Edward. *A Descriptive Catalog of W. B. Yeats's Library.* London: Garland, 1984.

Owens, Derek. "Composition as the Voicing of Multiple Fictions." *Into the Field: Sites of Composition Studies.* Ed. Anne Ruggles Gere. New York: MLA, 1993. 159–75.

Parker, Alan Michael, and Mark Willhardt. *The Routledge Anthology of Cross-Gendered Verse.* New York: Routledge, 1996.

Plato. *Symposium.* Trans. Walter Hamilton. New York: Viking, 1951.

———. *Timaeus.* London: Heinemann, 1926.

Plutarch. *Morals.* Vol. 2. Boston: Little, 1871.

Porphyry. *On the Cave of the Nymphs.* Trans. Robert Lamberton. New York: Station Hill, 1983.

Pratt, Annis V. "Spinning Among Fields: Jung, Frey, Levi-Strauss and Feminist Archetypal Theory." *Feminist Archetypal Theory: Interdisciplinary Re-Visions of Jungian Thought*. Ed. Estella Lauter and Carol Schreier Rupprecht. Knoxville: U of Tennessee P, 1985.

Rader, Ralph. "Notes on Some Structural Varieties and Variations in Dramatic 'I' Poems and Their Theoretical Implications." *Victorian Poetry* 22: 103–20.

Raine, Kathleen. *Yeats the Initiate*. Mountrath: Dolmen, 1986.

———. *Yeats, the Tarot and the Golden Dawn*. Dublin: Dolmen, 1972.

Reese, William L. *Dictionary of Philosophy and Religion: Eastern and Western Thought*. Atlantic Highlands, NJ: Humanities, 1980.

Ritvo, Rosemary Puglia. "A VISION B: The Plotinian Metaphysical Basis." *Review of English Studies: A Quarterly Journal of English Literature and the English Language*. 26 (1975): 34–46.

Ronald, Kate, and Hephzibah Roskelly. *Further Along: Transforming Dichotomies in Rhetoric and Composition*. Portsmith: Boynton/Cook, 1990.

Rosenthal, M. L., and Sally M. Gall. *The Modern Poetic Sequence: The Genius of Modern Poetry*. Oxford: Oxford UP, 1983.

Rubin, Deborah. "The Mourner in the Flesh: George Herbert's Commemoration of Magdalen Herbert in *Memoriae Matris Sacrum*." Morgan 13–28.

Saddlemyer, Ann. "Poetry of Possession: Yeats and Crazy Jane." *Yeats: An Annual of Critical and Textual Studies*. Vol. 9. Ed. Richard J. Finneran and Mary FitzGerald, 136–58. Ann Arbor: U of Michigan P, 1991.

Said, Edward. *Orientalism*. New York: Random, 1978.

Sedgwick, Eve Kosofsky. "The Beast in the Closet: James and the Writing of Homosexual Panic." *Sex, Politics, and Science in the Nineteenth-Century Novel*. Ed. Ruth Bernard Yeazell. Baltimore: Johns Hopkins UP, 1986. 148–86.

Showalter, Elaine. *The Female Malady: Women, Madness, and English Culture, 1830–1980*. New York: Pantheon, 1985.

Siegel, Carol. "Border Disturbances: D. H. Lawrence's Fiction and the Feminism of *Wuthering Heights*." Morgan 59–76.

Skene, Reg. *The Cuchulain Plays of W. B. Yeats: A Study*. New York: Columbia UP, 1974.

Smith, Elton Edward. *The Two Voices*. Lincoln: U of Nebraska P, 1964.

Sword, Helen. "Leda and the Modernists." *PMLA* 107.2 (1992): 305–18.

Unterecker, John. *A Reader's Guide to William Butler Yeats*. New York: Farrar, 1959.

Walker, Barbara. *The Woman's Encyclopedia of Myths and Secrets*. San Francisco: Harper, 1983.

Wilson. F. A. C. *W. B. Yeats and Tradition*. New York: Macmillan, 1958.

———. *Yeats's Iconography*. London: Gollancz, 1960.

Wolfson, Susan J. "*Lyrical Ballads* and the Language of (Men) Feeling: Writing Women's Voices." Morgan 29–58.

Woolf, Virginia. *A Room of One's Own*. New York: Harcourt, 1957.

Yeats, William Butler. *Autobiography*. New York: Macmillan, 1965.

———. *The Collected Letters of W. B. Yeats.* Vol. 1. 1865–1895. Ed. John Kelly. Oxford: Clarendon, 1986.

———. *The Collected Works in Verse and Prose of W. B. Yeats.* Vol. 6. Stratford-on-Avon: Shakespeare Head, 1908.

———. *The Collected Works in Verse and Prose of W. B. Yeats.* Vol. 7. Stratford-on-Avon: Shakespeare Head, 1908.

———. *The Collected Works in Verse and Prose of W. B. Yeats.* Vol. 8. Stratford-on-Avon: Shakespeare Head, 1908.

———. *A Critical Edition of Yeats's A VISION.* Ed. George Mills Harper and W. K. Hood. London: Macmillan, 1978.

———. *Essays and Introductions.* New York: Macmillan, 1961.

———. *Letters on Poetry from W. B. Yeats to Dorothy Wellesley.* London: Oxford UP, 1964.

———. *The Letters of W. B. Yeats.* Ed. Allan Wade. London: Hart-Davis, 1954.

———. *Memoirs.* Ed. Denis Donoghue. New York: Macmillan, 1972.

———. *Mythologies.* New York: Macmillan, 1959.

———. *The Variorum Edition of the Plays of W. B. Yeats.* Ed. Russell K. Alspach. London: Macmillan, 1966.

———. *The Variorum Edition of the Poems of W. B. Yeats.* Ed. Peter Allt and Russell K. Alspach. New York: Macmillan, 1961.

———. *A Vision: A Reissue with the Author's Final Revisions.* New York: Macmillan, 1966.

———. *Yeats on Yeats: The Last Introductions and the 'Dublin' Edition.* Ed. Edward Callan. Atlantic Highlands, NJ: Humanities. 1981.

———. *Yeats's VISION Papers Vol. I. The Automatic Script: 5 November 1917–1919 June 1918.* Ed. Steve L. Adams, Barbara J. Frieling, and Sandra L. Sprayberry. Iowa City: U of Iowa P, 1992.

———. *Yeats's VISION Papers Vol. II. The Automatic Script: 5 June 1918–1929 March 1920.* Ed. Steve L. Adams, Barbara J. Frieling, and Sandra L. Sprayberry. Iowa City: U of Iowa P, 1992.

———. *Yeats's VISION Papers Vol. III. Sleep and Dream Notebooks: VISION Notebooks 1 and 2, Card File.* Ed. Robert Anthony Martinich and Margaret Mills Harper. Iowa City: U of Iowa P, 1992.

Zawacki, Terry Myers. "Recomposing as a Woman—An Essay in Different Voices." *College Composition and Communication* 43.1 (Feb. 1992): 32–38.

INDEX

www.ingramcontent.com/pod-product-compliance
Lightning Source LLC
Chambersburg PA
CBHW030250100426
42812CB00002B/384